The Caring Role o
the Primary Schoo

Edited by Kenneth David
Cert Ed, BA

and Tony Charlton
Cert Ed, BEd (Hons), MEd, PhD

MACMILLAN
EDUCATION

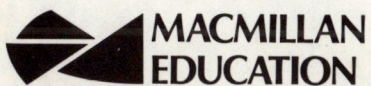

Related titles from Macmillan Education

Resources for Reading: Does Quality Count?
UKRA Conference Proceedings, 1985
Editor, Betty Root

Assessing Reading
UKRA Colloquium on Testing and Assessment Proceedings
Editors, Denis Vincent, A. K. Pugh, and Greg Brooks

Children Becoming Readers
Henry Pearson

Managing for Learning
John Buckley and David Styan

In preparation:

Assessing and Teaching Language: Literacy and Oracy in Schools
Mary Neville

© Kenneth David and Tony Charlton 1987

All rights reserved. No reproduction, copy or transmission
of this publication may be made without written permission.

No paragraph of this publication may be reproduced, copied
or transmitted save with written permission or in accordance
with the provisions of the Copyright Act 1956 (as amended),
or under the terms of any licence permitting limited copying
issued by the Copyright Licensing Agency, 7 Ridgmount Street,
London WC1E 7AE.

Any person who does any unauthorised act in relation to
this publication may be liable to criminal prosecution and
civil claims for damages.

First published 1987

Published by
MACMILLAN EDUCATION LTD
Houndmills, Basingstoke, Hampshire RG21 2XS
and London
Companies and representatives
throughout the world

Typeset by Acorn Bookwork
Salisbury, Wiltshire
Printed in Hong Kong

ISBN 0-333-44828-6
ISBN 0-333-44829-4 (paperback)

Contents

Preface   v

PART I

1. **Education for Changing Lives**   3
   Kenneth David BA
   Tony Charlton BEd (Hons), MEd, PhD

PART II

2. **The Processes of Learning**   27
   Diana Hutchcroft OBE, retired head teacher and member of the Bullock Report Committee

3. **A Coordinated Approach**   56
   Kenneth David BA

4. **School Routines and Administration**   72
   Jim Abraham MA, a primary head teacher

5. **Welfare and Liaison**   98
   Frank Coombes OBE, retired senior educational welfare officer
   Bill Horton, acting principal educational welfare officer, Avon

6. **Body and Mind – Sources of help for young schoolchildren**   123
   Anthony Fairburn MB, BS, FRCP, FRCPsych, DCH, DPM, Department of Child and Family Psychiatry, Royal United Hospital, Bath

7. **Counselling in Primary Schools**   152
   Tony Charlton BEd (Hons), MEd, PhD
   Lynne Hoye BA, Adv Dip Ed, F Coll P, former head teacher, trained counsellor, presently lecturer at St Paul and St Mary College of Higher Education, Cheltenham

8   **Teachers, Parents and Other Professionals**   **176**
    David Galloway MA, MSc, PhD, FBPrS, lecturer in education, University College, Cardiff

PART III

9   **Values in Primary Education**   **191**
    Norman Kirby MA, AKC, formerly head of Middle School Education Department, Goldsmith's College, University of London

10 **An Agenda for Discussion and Possible Action**   **205**
    Kenneth David BA
    Tony Charlton BEd (Hons), MEd, PhD

Index   **214**

ACKNOWLEDGEMENTS

The authors and publishers wish to thank the following who have kindly given permission for the use of copyright material: Croner Publications Ltd. for material from *The Head's Legal Guide* by S. B. Howarth, 1984; Hodder & Stoughton Educational for material from *Infant Rating Scale* by Goeff Lindsay, 1981 and *Personal and Social Education in the Curriculum* by R. Pring, 1984; National Association for Pastoral Care in Education for material from their publication.

Every effort has been made to trace all the copyright holders but if any have been inadvertently overlooked the publishers will be pleased to make the necessary arrangement at the first opportunity.

Preface

We feel that the considerable interest and development in secondary schools in recent years in Personal and Social Education, and pastoral care, ought to be matched in the literature of the primary school world, and this book is a contribution to this viewpoint. We hope that others will wish to contribute ideas and opinions in an area which appears to lack appropriate reference points.

Our confused and changed society has forced much reassessment on secondary teachers as to the ways in which they ought to prepare young people for a different adulthood than that which we have known: pastoral care and revised life skills education have loomed much larger in recent years, and traditional education has been viewed more questioningly. Yet since everything done in secondary schools has its roots in the primary schools, we wonder why primary education sometimes appears to be exempt from challenge on its caring role and its personal education approaches. There can be an amiable contentment in primary classrooms at times, an assumption that the teacher's role as an intuitive generalist must inevitably be beyond reproach and distanced from major challenge in the welfare and social aspects of education.

While many primary schools are superb in their sensitivity to welfare, to family life, and to Personal and Social Education, highly professional in their planning of appropriate modern curricula, and fully aware of hidden and other educational agenda, some schools clearly need help and direction at a time of changing priorities.

This book attempts, in particular, to serve primary teachers and students in training, by reviewing many aspects of the development and care of young children up to the beginning of their teens. All the work will be familiar to teachers, some of it will be difficult and challenging, and all the chapters are intended to be a checklist of the demanding and vital role of the primary schools in preparing children for adulthood in the new world of the third millenium.

The purpose of this book

This is inevitably a controversial and confused area of education, and we must try to spell out our intentions as clearly as we can. The purpose of this book is to:

(a) advocate a wider socialising task in primary education, in preparing for children's future lives in a difficult and rapidly changing modern society;
(b) re-examine the effect of pastoral attitudes, of the curriculum, of teaching methods, and of welfare provision, and to sharpen and professionalise what is sometimes only intuitive;
(c) offer some practical and theoretical viewpoints of how the primary school teacher can organise curriculum, teaching strategies, and administration to achieve a wider socialising role for the school;
(d) revise and emphasise information on the health and welfare aspects of primary schools;
(e) emphasise the 'pastoral curriculum', for we see personal and social education as having a practical curriculum content, and requiring a clear coordinating purpose. It can permeate the work of a school.

In attempting such purposes we appreciate that we can be accused of being too ambitious, of a lack of precision, even of arrogance in our view of society and its primary education. We have to admit that these possible faults have preoccupied us too, but this book is meant to encourage debate and evaluation and may lead others to produce clearer definitions of what primary education can do in this socialising role.

We expect this book to interest and stimulate debate among:

(a) lecturers and students in initial teacher training institutions;
(b) teachers attending in-service training courses;
(c) primary teachers, and their colleagues in lower forms of secondary schools;
(d) concerned parents, educational administrators and academics involved with primary education;
(e) professional workers associated with schools.

PART I

The editors explain their viewpoint and suggest the actions they see as necessary in schools in sharpening education for changing lives. They discuss our rapidly changing society, the needs of children and others, family life today, individualism, and the responses of primary schools. They argue that primary schools' potential influence on children's development is considerable, and that there is a greater need to respond more professionally to pupils' personal and social development, with careful planning and curriculum coordination as well as intuition and goodwill.

PART I

Chapter 1
Education for Changing Lives

Kenneth David
Tony Charlton

Most of us, as pupils, parents or teachers become so overawed by the schooling process that only occasionally do we subject it to any rigorous scrutiny. We rarely question the long-term goals of education and whether these are truly reflected in the education schools offer to their pupils. In the absence of such enquiry it is not difficult for schools to become unresponsive to, or even unaware of, their responsibility to reappraise their curricula continually with regard for the effects of a changing society upon children's learning needs. A failure by some primary schools to conduct these appraisals and act upon them has sometimes caused a mismatch between what they offer pupils and what pupils need to learn. This mismatch is concerned with our claim that schools' preoccupation with academic learning has often promoted a benign neglect of children's personal and social learning.

The purpose of this chapter is to review the changes in society, and the educational practices which have given rise to this claim, and consider initiatives required to help schools redress this mismatch where it exists.

Many titles are used in describing the work to which we refer. We hear of:

personal and social education,
social and moral education,
affective education,
life skills teaching,
personal education,
pastoral care,
guidance and care,
welfare and counselling.

While subtle differences sometimes exist between them they generally share two common themes:

1. The knowledge, skills, understanding, attitudes and values which children need to become happy members of, and valued contributors to, society. These may permeate, or be additional to, traditional primary class work.
2. The guidance, welfare, counselling and support which enable children to cope with their personal situations at home, in school, or elsewhere.

Human needs

The planning of aims and objectives in a modern democratic community or institution ought to start by considering the needs of the individuals concerned: in an ideal world the needs of a society could then follow from a consensus of basic needs.

Does life in our late-twentieth century society meet our basic human needs in fact, or does it threaten them, or precipitate a new selfishness? More comfort and apparent pleasure in everyday life, better health measures, and comparative affluence in much of our society have provided for most of our physiological needs and eased many basic human demands. Yet our affluence and cleverness may have increased other fears: the fear of insecurity and of being unable to influence the major events of our lives, the distrust of innovative and constantly changing technology and knowledge, the fear of having to face new competitive and demanding occupations, the confusion of decision making in bewildering new situations, and the fear of never reaching calmness and achieving autonomy as individuals.

Kellmer-Pringle (1980) lists as children's needs: love and security, new experiences, praise and recognition, and responsibility. Maslow's (1954) hierarchy of needs suggests in ascending order: physiological, safety, belongingness and love, esteem, and the relatively uncommon achievement of self-actualisation and maturity. One can reword these needs in simple adult terms:

> good positive health for ourselves and our family;
> job and home security, and privacy at appropriate times;
> having the expectation of giving and receiving affection;
> feeling valued by others in our everyday lives;
> having simple ambitions encouraged, having efficient learning skills encouraged throughout life, and being guided towards appropriate academic and job qualifications;

having the skills of listening and of speaking about our feelings and desires;

and being helped to comprehend some values to underpin our existence.

Is it in fact becoming more difficult to achieve such needs in modern life?

From these suggestions we can attempt to identify basic needs for those we educate, and may conclude that many are not met; so what better preparation and support is needed? Adults need support for living in our complex society, as the increasing demands made on Citizens' Advice Bureaux and similar agencies show, and our share in education for such adulthood starts with primary children. Many skills and attitudes need to be better sustained in schools: an ability to speak one's feelings, to listen purposefully, to comprehend relationships better, to reason with criticism and rejection, to be assertive when necessary, and to have a better sense of societal or civic responsibilities. Our education system still largely regards such needs as secondary to cognitive development.

Our society

We are an increasingly urban and anonymous society, with less sense of community and much that encourages feelings of alienation and loneliness. Rural life can have its problems, but city and town life seem to present a greater challenge to the stability and happiness of the individual. Even apparently attractive suburbia can be a lonely place, without the 'roots' feeling of belonging and being known and accepted, and with the demands of a possibly competitive and materialistic lifestyle, compounded by mortgages, commuting and disparate family lives.

There are so many changes, options and demands in modern family life. The incidence, and possible security, of belonging to a religious faith and membership of church bodies has lessened markedly. We are increasingly obliged to accept that we are a multi-cultural society, with continuous racial and religious tensions. An apparent increase in crime and violence is reported by efficient and influential television communication, and 'media power' must be as influential in many families as traditional education influences. Authority has to be hard earned, for we have created a questioning, and perhaps cynical, population, and this wariness and distrust of authority, together with a clear decline in deference to age and experience, is linked with an increased centralisation of state authority and a lessened feeling of local or individual responsibility. Legislation proliferates in our complicated modern society, and the Children and Young Persons' Act of 1969, amended by the Childrens' Act of 1975, lists a wide variety of reasons by which children may be removed from their families into state care, and illustrates state not family authority.

Add an explosion in communication and knowledge, a depressing change in prospects for regular employment, the reduction in value of apprenticeships and experience in many occupations, the disappearance of unskilled jobs with automation and new technology, and electronic wizardry edging tradition aside, and we can begin to comprehend some of the pressures which bedevil ordinary people and which may make them less independent and more vulnerable in times of personal crisis.

The impersonality and anonymity which increasingly pervade our lives can be a potentially destructive part of contemporary life. Many people live in densely populated conurbations, their children attend large schools, they shop in narrow, packed corridors in supermarkets and hypermarkets, and deal with impersonal bureaucracies usually centralised in distant locations. Megastructures of this type often appear indifferent to individuals and deprive large numbers of people (particularly the elderly and lonely) of valued personal contacts and interactions.

It is remarkably easy now for people to become alienated from, and antagonistic towards, a society which seems remote from and oblivious to them, and from which they feel rejected. With particular reference to young people Bazalgette (1983, p. 152) claims that today they 'face a more hostile environment than faced any of the generation of adults who surround them'.

In the current climate there is also the danger that people will become less accountable to, as well as less compassionate and considerate towards those around them. Selfishness grows easily. Without this accountability and consideration the same people risk becoming egocentric and intolerant of others – feelings which incite aggressive and selfish behaviour. Others may react differently by passively acknowledging (and accepting) their perceived inadequacies and helplessness. The vast number of tranquillisers dispensed daily by doctors, the increased incidence of drug, solvent and child abuse (current estimates of the latter suggest a handful of children in each primary school class), crowd violence in football grounds, violent crimes, delinquency, alcoholism and racial unrest may provide an indication of the large numbers of stressed, anxious and at times perhaps lonely, selfish or violent people.

Anxiety and stress have always existed; we think they now affect people more, and they certainly affect schools and teachers more than in the past. Dunham (1981) referred to the effect of demands made on a teacher of a special class in a primary school, and noted that:

> Strong emotions were expressed by these children and the teacher became the target for 'displaced feelings of hostility, jealousy, disappointment, affection and dependence'. (p. 207)

The observers themselves were exhausted by the high noise levels, the torrent of verbal abuse and the sudden eruptions of violence. These actions cannot be unknown in 'normal' classrooms as well, and the causes frequently lie in family breakdown or society's pressures.

Of all the symptoms of change in our society a changing and disrupted family life is a major modern phenomenon, and is clearly the cause of much anxiety and stress among children. It thus needs to be a primary concern within our schools and our teaching cadres.

Family life

We have read recently of feminist writers, highly critical of family life in the past, accepting again the family as a foundation in which men and women can mature; but that family base which could be a haven in a changing society is itself changing radically as are the moral attitudes formerly associated with it.

The National Marriage Guidance Council in a recent newsletter summarised some evidence of these changes. Of the 396,000 marriages in the UK in 1984, 35 per cent were re-marriages, compared with 20 per cent in 1971 and 15 per cent in 1961. While the steep upward climb of divorces in the 1970s has evened out to 158,600 in 1984, 21 per cent of these divorces involved at least one partner who had been divorced before, compared with 9 per cent in 1971. Pre-marital cohabitation appears to be increasing: 24 per cent of women aged 16–34 at the time of marriage in 1979–82 had cohabited with their husband before marriage where the marriage was the first for both partners; 65 per cent had cohabited where one or both partners had been married before; in 1970–74 the proportions were 8 per cent and 42 per cent. The prevalence of cohabitation is higher among widowed, separated or divorced women than among single women. There were an estimated 900,000 one-parent families in 1981, 90 per cent headed by a woman, two-thirds of these women separated or divorced, 40 per cent of the families on supplementary benefit. One baby in three is conceived outside marriage according to government statistics.

The changes can be listed further: more than half of married women with dependent children are in paid employment, and the number of families living on the borders of poverty would be four times greater without their wages. As it is, there are an estimated 3.7 million children living in families in or near the poverty level. Perhaps it is no wonder that one in four people suffer from some form of mental illness at some time in their life, according to the National Association of Mental Health. Perhaps all this picture is normality for our society, perhaps inevitable; if that is the case, and if education cannot cure ills, perhaps it can reduce the effects of ills?

The break-up of families and the changing nature of families is becoming more marked. Whitfield (1983) points out:

> over the past two decades the major changes in household type have been a doubling of the number of people living alone (now about a quarter of households), a reduction by about one fifth of the number of married households with children (now about two fifths of households) and the steady increase in one parent families (now at any one time about one in eight of families with dependent children). (p. 5)

The effect of such changes in family stability upon men, women and children is still only half understood, though the obvious stresses are easier to identify when one examines the pastoral work of school staff and other agencies of care. Feelings of jealousy and rejection have not disappeared because we are more emancipated and sophisticated.

Young people are more sophisticated at a younger age, perhaps more mature too; perhaps adult behaviour is merging with adolescence now, as used to be common until a century ago before education properly claimed the young. The elderly live longer, though modern houses are seldom geared to accommodate them within families. Expectations of personal fulfilment are constantly encouraged, though the national economy may not further the expectations. The emancipation of women through employment changes, equal opportunity legislation, and the availability of contraception and abortion facilities have freed them as individuals in many ways, but have not lessened anxiety and stress. The modern family is essentially more isolated in nature, and more intensive in the nature of its relationships. New kinds of parental authority have developed, sometimes controversial. The family should be the first refuge for troubled people, and if the family itself is troubled, then individuals more often have to seek help elsewhere. Familiar patterns are changing, and the potential for conflict and confusion does not seem to be lessening.

Robert Frost wrote, 'Home is the place where, when you have to go there, they have to take you in.' Family life in many pupils' homes is less stable, perhaps more cynical and questioning, almost certainly more materialistic, and increasingly a less certain agency for socialising children for their future than it used to be. Yet it still remains the chief unit for affection in society, and remains the place where individuals begin the process of mediating with their demanding society. Increasingly we must make more positive and professional efforts through children's schooling to support family life, and to offer a process whereby the harm from failures and gaps in family life can be lessened.

Family breakdown and schoolchildren

When stress within a family unit brings a breakdown in normal relationships there may be separation, divorce or bitterness, the effects of which must dominate all the emotions of the family group. Schooling for children may be a relief from home tensions, or it may be a distraction difficult to cope with, with mutual incomprehension between child and teacher. Children may sit watching our teaching endeavours with their minds filled with adult matters and pictures of anger, despair, inadequacies and violence in their minds, or they may watch us with the knowing eyes of precosity.

One in every four children born today are likely, before they reach the age of eighteen, to witness their parents' divorce. While children of divorced parents may not necessarily experience behaviour problems The Children's Society (1981) noted with regret that:

(i) the children may be penalised for socially unacceptable behaviour which may be a natural response to an emotionally unbearable situation;
(ii) the children preoccupied by the separation or divorce of their parents appear to be more prone to accidents and illness; and
(iii) conflict about sexual identity and relationships can arise for children affected by the divorce or separation of their parents (includ-

ing the resentment of, or reaction against, a parent's new relationship).

Rutter (1975) noted that the type of home experiences which give rise to divorce, as well as those consequent to the judicial separation, are related to a range of children's emotional and behavioural problems, as well as child abuse.

Children will, of course, vary in the effect that family breakdown has upon them, and their age and personality will affect their resilience. As teachers we have an increasing problem in judging whether objective normality in the classroom is what is needed, or whether personal attention and counselling can bring them towards relevant learning. There are great demands on the sensitivity of teachers nowadays.

The individual

Are adults and children different now from past generations? In their emotions and basic needs they are not, but in their attitudes and habits they clearly are different. There is, despite the considerable increase in state authority, and despite the huge impersonal scale of many modern enterprises, a greater recognition of individualism and the need for personal fulfilment. So we encourage the individual, and yet isolate him. The family is more democratic, and young people are seemingly encouraged to be themselves as unique persons at an early age; yet, like the sombre forces of a Thomas Hardy novel, the pressures to shape and conform the aspiring individualism seem greater each year. There must be stress in this apparent dichotomy, for we are fostering questioning individuals in our education, and abandoning them to modern trends and forces they may not comprehend.

So increasingly the years of a child's compulsory education are years of socialisation for a very flexible and problematic future supporting weakened family structures, and demanding better planning and coordination than in the past. Whitfield (1983) comments:

> Many families might not land in trouble or deepen their wounds in a crisis if their members had been provided in advance with the insights, skills, tools and confidence which are needed for the successful management of close relationships, and their adjuncts, in a social context of high expectation and pluralist values. (p. 19)

Her Majesty's Inspectorate (1979) write, 'The personal and social development of the pupil is one way of describing the central purpose of education . . .', and:

> Most aspects of the life of a school impinge to some extent and in some way on the development of the attitudes and self esteem of the pupils. (p. 206)

Clearly it is time we gave deeper thought to the contribution of the primary school in personal and social education.

Meeting children's educational needs

Zigler (1979) has suggested that the extent to which people's potentials to lead satisfactory lives are developed, will be influenced by the opportunities they have had to acquire those attitudes, values, motives, understanding and skills conducive to a life of effective social participation and self-fulfilment. A wise society, therefore, has to ensure:

> that those opportunities are made available to its members, particularly when young, in order to maximise their potential to lead happy and purposeful lives. (Charlton, 1984, p. 33)

Pring (1984) emphasises that, while the quality of our life is influenced by the society in which we live, 'the type of society which we live in will depend upon the personal qualities developed in young people' (p. 5). Clearly, while society has a responsibility to help educate young people it should also appreciate that the quality of the education which it makes available will have ramifications for society itself – a sobering thought!

As research studies have demonstrated that what children do, and do not, learn in their earlier years has a crucial impact upon their all-round functioning in later years, the period of time which children spend in their primary school represents a critical period in their development which society should use for the benefit both of itself and individuals.

Family life shapes children's development obviously: the question of where else responsibility may lie for children's personal development is one to which we, as a society, have never satisfactorily responded. While, traditionally, academic learning has been the concern of schools and the responsibility for children's personal and social learning has been placed predominantly upon the home, this dichotomy of duties has rarely proved successful. Not all children come from homes where parents are able and willing to oversee competently their children's non-academic learning. Similarly, not all pupils attend schools which have good pastoral care, and Personal and Social Education as a defined and integral element of their curricula. Consequently, whether or not pupils receive adequate education in the personal and social domains will often be determined 'by accident of birth, school attended and the teacher to whom he or she is exposed' (Hopson and Hough, 1976, p. 16), or fortuitous encounters elsewhere.

In an advanced society such as ours it seems iniquitous that a neglect of some children's all-round development in schools and homes should deny many pupils 'an education of the whole person for the type of society that he will meet when, eventually, he leaves school' (David and Cowley, 1980, p. vii). If society knows that not all children will have competent guidance and instruction in their personal and social development at home it seems 'logical, therefore, to concentrate on the school as the major provider for those skills' (Hopson and Hough, 1976, p. 16). Even though such thinking may not be wholly acceptable to Lang (1983, p. 173), who suggested 'a greater involvement of parents in pastoral care on the basis of negotiated partnership' with schools, a consensus of opinion in the published literature indicates that such a notion is both necessary and practicable.

The status quo

For some time now considerable criticism has been levelled at schools, both in the USA and Britain, for not responding earlier to this type of thinking. In the USA Elias and Maher (1983) expressed concern that social and affective education has been regarded as of secondary importance to the teaching of basic academic skills. As an apology for the neglect of non-academic skills they remarked that:

> Any notion that schools are 'learning factories' with the output solely the development of academic skills, can be seen as an unfortunate by-product of our educational age. (p. 339)

In a similar vein, Morse (1974) claimed schools were 'cognition factories' and Charlton (1984) was highly critical of:

> a curriculum imbalance in schools where a preoccupation with traditional academic learning has been to the detriment of pupils' non-academic learning. (p. 34)

We conclude that this practice has often been founded upon the erroneous belief that, while successful academic learning is conditional upon schools providing adequate resources, personal and social learning and guidance either does not require comparable resources or is of insufficient import to warrant it. This reasoning, however, should not disregard the considerable influence which some parents, employers and the media have had in promoting the academic curriculum. Parents, understandably concerned about dwindling employment prospects for their children and the rising number of unemployed, have seen academic success as a means of enhancing career prospects; employers have sought young employees who were literate and numerate in examination terms, and the media have never been slow to capitalise upon what it perceives as 'good' news material about academic and examination success or the lack of it.

The catalysts of change

However, while a traditional academic type of curriculum in primary schools has undoubtedly proved effective in equipping the majority of young children with what are commonly, though erroneously, referred to as the basic skills, there is now a pressing and very apparent need for curricula modifications to reflect the far broader educational goal of preparing pupils, in all aspects of their development (in all basic skills) for life.

In a planned and systematic way primary schools need to assume a more central and supportive role in preparing children for their future working and non-working lives, for family life, in helping them to understand better their own and others' feelings, and to appreciate the benefits derived from organising their lives in a manner accepting of, and considerate towards, other people.

Not all primary schools need these innovations. Some, through considerable insight and initiative, and access to the resources required, already respond well to their pupils' all-round needs. The reasons that others have been unable to follow such example may not necessarily lie solely within the schools. While schools have retained a considerable degree of autonomy, what they do (and do not do) is influenced by government decrees and central (e.g. DES) and local (e.g. LEAs) education authority recommendations and policies. These sources are often the primary catalysts of educational change.

Stagles (1985) noted that:

> at a national level all teachers are working in a general educational climate where there is, for example, pressure for schools to review their pastoral systems, the kinds of support and guidance they offer pupils and the provisions they make for personal and social education. (p. 23)

She also suggested that in some local authorities there is a much greater awareness of these pressures, and a climate more conducive to teachers being alerted to the need for change. A number of examples of healthy LEA responses to these are included in Pring (1984). Clearly, the quality of the advisory and support services (particularly in terms of leadership) which local authorities make available to schools is crucial in promoting an awareness, and in guiding the planning and implementation of good practice in primary schools.

Some of this awareness is facilitated through local inspections and enquiries. The Thomas Report (1985) is one such example. Commissioned by the Inner London Education Authority, its brief was to enquire into primary education with particular reference to the children of working class parents. Part of that brief was to note ways in which pupils' education was affected by factors such as the aspirations and expectations of teachers and parents, and the effects of deprivation, family mobility and stress; then to relate these issues to the curriculum and effective teaching practice. In its conclusion the committee declared that it was impressed by the way in which its teachers were prepared to examine and modify their work in the light of children's home experiences. Such practices suggest a flexibility and awareness within these schools as well able and willing to respond to individuals' all-round needs.

In more recent years central authority publications have increasingly drawn attention to pupils' needs in personal and social areas. A most recent example is included in 'Education Observed 3: Good Teachers', an HMI (1985) paper, where it was noted that appraisal of teachers should 'include recognition of the teacher's role in relation to the aims and expectations of the school as a whole and reflect personal strengths in scholarship, administrative skill and pastoral care' (p. 1). The document also noted that:

> Teaching which is well matched to pupils' abilities and needs will produce desirable results in terms much wider than examination grades and achievements which are matched to the pupils' abilities

across a wide range of performance whilst reflecting challenge and vigour at all levels. It is by these wide measures of pupil performance, including attitudes and personal and social responsibility, that teachers' success should be judged. (HMI, 1985, p. 7)

In an earlier paper entitled 'Training in Schools: The Content of Initial Training' (HMI, 1983), reference was made to the need for teachers to be aware of how moral and social awareness can be fostered within the whole curriculum. Elsewhere the paper highlighted the need to prepare children for adult and working lives.

Unfortunately, central and local education policies have not always been determined in a manner supportive to the promotion of personal and social education. Taylor (1984) remarked that:

It is unfortunate that, for the best of reasons, the HMI, through papers like 'New Teacher', are 'honing' in on the need for training in narrow specialist academic subjects. This is happening at a time when the demand for the teaching of 'life' skills is steadily increasing, as is the recognition by all teachers to the special needs of pupils. (p. 220)

More disturbing was the inability of Maher and Best (1984) to uncover in their survey a single LEA where an adviser had been appointed with a responsibility solely for pastoral care in schools. We can be impressed, however, by the attendance in June 1986 of some 80 LEA advisers at a conference on Personal and Social Education.

Reasonable access to the resources required is, understandably, a prerequisite for innovation to take place. While the current climate of financial constraint is unlikely to help effect change dependent upon considerable funding, primary schools are more likely to be concerned (in the context of this book) about the paucity of suitably trained teachers available to help integrate Personal and Social Education within the curriculum. Opportunities for changes in education philosophy to become translated into pedagogy become practicable only if teachers with appropriate skills are available to help initiate that change.

There is evidence in the published literature which supports the concern we have expressed in the previous paragraph. In the USA Kavale and Hirshoren (1980) and Parker (1980) have commented on the apparent lack of teacher preparation in the social and affective domains. Good and Brophy (1977) pre-empted such comments by suggesting that teachers know more about children's cognitive than they do their affective development.

Similar findings have been reported in this country. A majority of primary (and secondary) school teachers invited to reflect upon their initial teacher training, indicated that they felt ill-prepared to cater for their pupils' pastoral needs (HMI, 1982). In Maher and Best's (1984) survey they discovered that 90 per cent of the teachers consulted expressed the opinion that their training had included very little, if anything at all, that related to children's personal and social education. This discovery was in close accord with an enquiry of ours (Charlton and David, in preparation) where 83 per cent of the primary and secondary schoolteachers sampled (N = 173) expressed dissatisfaction with the instruction they had received in the areas of personal and social development. Nearly 70 per cent admitted that they could not recall a series of lectures which dealt predominantly with this facet of children's development and needs, and the vast majority (91 per cent) confessed a need (though not necessarily a wish) to receive in-service training in this area.

While these findings are somewhat tenuous, they do imply that those responsible for initial and in-service teacher training should scrutinise the provisions they make available to students and teachers to acquire not only the theoretical underpinning, but also the practical skills and understanding, to assist them to promote their pupils' all-round development.

The National Association for Pastoral Care in Education comments as follows (NAPCE, 1986):

> Whatever the merits of existing arrangements for teacher training of all kinds, one evident failing has been the lack of attention commonly devoted to the pastoral dimensions of schools and colleges. However, in response to a number of initiatives, many of them emanating from the Central Government, the provision of teacher training is going through one of its periodic phases of examination. In some ways this phase of examination is unusually wide-ranging in the scope of its attention and has included reviews of initial training (see Circular 3/84 and the CATE exercise), of the provision of in-service training for senior managers in schools (see Circulars 3/83 and 4/83), the TRIST proposals (initially to be mediated through the MSC but subsequently through the DES) and, perhaps most important of all, the new funding arrangements for in-service proposed in the White Paper *Better Schools* (cmnd 9469).
>
> Not since the era of the James Report in 1972 has there been such an opportunity to reshape the character of so many aspects of teacher training. (pp. 33–34)

They comment earlier (pp. 13–14):

> 'New teachers come to school unprepared for this crucial work, and improvements have been wanted for some time' (NAPCE, 1984). Even this may understate the extent of the problem. Many new teachers seem barely aware that they will have a significant pastoral role to play. These conclusions are based upon a number of sources of evidence including the HMI (1982) Report *The New Teacher in School* which made the point that new teachers felt less well prepared to undertake the pastoral aspect of their work than almost any other with some 56% of respondents describing themselves as 'not well prepared to undertake pastoral duties'. Even this view may overestimate the impact of initial training in this area. In a more recent report, Maher and Best (1984) found that of the teachers they surveyed '87% argued that their initial training contained either a negligible amount of work on pastoral care or nothing at all'. Such a situation can be justified only if pastoral care could be considered a peripheral aspect of the work of schools and colleges and an optional aspect of the role of the teacher. NAPCE forcefully rejects this view.

A way forward

If we are convinced that education should function as a vehicle for helping to promote children's all-round development in order to enhance their potential to become competent people in their adult and working (or non-working) lives, and if we are unconvinced that all young members of our society will receive adequate guidance and instruction in the home to complement that which schools traditionally have provided, then society has an obligation to assume a greater responsibility for meeting pupils' personal and social, as well as academic, needs in school. If society and schools do not respond in this way, then who will provide for the less fortunate and most needy; and if schools are not intended to help prepare children for life in the post-school years, then for what are they intended?

It is difficult, therefore, with a regard for the changes now taking place in our society, the nature of the needs which these changes are precipitating, and the unhealthy symptoms often evident which seem a consequence of unmet needs, to remain unconvinced that schools have:

> a societal mission to help children to become competent persons, thus explicating the importance of social and affective areas in the process of schooling. (Elias and Maher, 1983, p. 339)

While primary schools and their teachers are unlikely to need convincing that this mission is necessary, they are likely to require support, and the following factors appear essential:

(i) An obvious requirement is informed and enthusiastic leadership. The confidence and occasional courage of primary head teachers may well be the necessary start to more professional pastoral care and development in primary work. The head teacher's leadership is often supported by an influential and respected LEA adviser's work, and with lay encouragement and understanding from chairmen of governors and others.

(ii) This school leadership is linked with more and continuing guidance from sources external to the school (e.g. DES, LEAs, and related professional associations), indicating what changes need to be made to existing curricula, and how these can be accomplished without adversely affecting the quality of the academic curriculum with which they have achieved much success.

If a genuine concern for children's all-round development is to become fully translated into classroom practices, considerable initiatives will first need to be exercised by teacher training establishments, LEAs, schools and individual teachers in attempts to insert Personal and Social Education as an integral and defined element within the curricula of all primary schools.

The promotion of Personal and Social Education is not intended to rival the academic curriculum or relegate it to secondary importance. Indeed, there is much evidence to show that children's personal and social functioning both affects, and is affected by, their academic performances (Lawrence, 1985; Stott, 1981; Charlton, 1985). These findings suggest that the academic curriculum can benefit from, as well as contribute to, pupils' healthy personal and social development.

(iii) Schools need to recruit teachers suitably trained and skilled in counselling and all aspects of Personal and Social Education. This need has implication for LEAs as well as colleges of higher education and universities. Initial training establishments need to ensure that all teachers receive adequate instruction in this area, for the responsibility for pupils' personal and social development should be a central role of all teachers (David and Cowley, 1980).

While some staff may be required to assume a responsibility for pastoral care and Personal and Social Education in schools, all teachers should be expected to facilitate such learning within a defined element of the curriculum, in addition to integrating it, wherever practicable, within other subject areas. It is, therefore, unacceptable where this learning is offered in initial training courses only as an option; rather it should be a central element in a core course of Professional Studies, and reflected within specialist subject areas.

(iv) Provisions for teachers already qualified are also likely to need extending. LEAs may need to make more of their own courses available. They will also need to liaise with colleges of higher education, universities and professional associations (such as the National Association for Pastoral Care in Education) to provide others. In accord with current trends at least some of these INSET (In-service Education and Training) programmes may work best if groups of primary schools meet together to plan and organise their training needs. Taylor (1984) has commented that:

> Teachers' practice in the classroom is most markedly affected where they themselves recognise the need for training and when it has been possible for them to discuss alternative teacher strategies with colleagues in their own and other schools. (p. 219)

(v) This arrangement for INSET provisions should not negate the need for more protracted and award-bearing courses. Some teachers may require access to this type of course if they hold, or intend to seek, teaching posts in primary schools with a defined responsibility for Personal and Social Education. Others may seek such courses because they wish to broaden and deepen their professional expertise. Schools may benefit in a variety of ways where their members, for whatever reasons, pursue these courses, particularly if they employ a 'pyramid' system where those who are trained return to schools to disseminate their learning to colleagues.

(vi) On a final, pragmatic note, we should realise that as the effect of society's changes impinges more and more on the work of schools, teachers will need increased ancillary and professional referral support. Teachers are not able both to sustain their present work and to improve their pastoral role without proper help – the majority work hard enough as it is. The reallocation of priorities of work can go so far, but increased responsibility as a socialising agency requires greater supportive measures.

Optimism for the future!

While, as mentioned earlier, radical change in education is more often reflected within educational philosophy than pedagogy, those who advocate a greater commitment to Personal and Social Education in schools should derive satisfaction, and optimism for the future, from the changes which are being effected in a related area of education. The unprecedented attention which has been directed towards special education within the last decade (e.g. Warnock, 1978; Education Act, 1981) has served not only to highlight the special educational needs of a sizeable proportion of the school population, but also to clarify the responsibility of schools and individual teachers in meeting those needs. The special educational needs of children are now considered in terms of their all-round development, and in terms commensurate with those educational provisions each child requires first to enlarge his:

> knowledge, experience and imaginative understanding, and thus his awareness of moral values and capacity for enjoyment: and secondly, to enable him to enter the world after formal education is over as an active participant in society and a responsible contributor to it, capable of achieving as much independence as possible. (Warnock, 1978, 1:4)

An acceptance that the vast majority of children with special educational needs are both located within mainstream schools and the responsibility of all teachers, is promoting an awareness within staffrooms that the content and organisation of schools' curricula, as well as the physical structure of the school, and teaching strategies, may need adapting if all individuals' needs are to be fully met.

The impact of change upon an area of education, which in past years has been given scant regard and low status, is likely to be such that it may well emerge as the vanguard of a thrust within schools where the education made available to all pupils becomes more responsive than it often has been in the past to individuals' learning needs. This contention is based upon our observation of good practice in special education in primary schools, where:

(a) educational provisions are needs-oriented;
(b) those provisions make reference to children's all-round development;
(c) all teachers hold a responsibility for identifying children with special needs;

(d) they have responded to DES and LEA guidelines concerned with their curricula content and organisation, and have become involved in in-service training courses made available by LEAs and teacher training colleges/universities.

These achievements have been helped by the vast majority of initial teacher training courses, which now include at least a special education element within their core courses.

These responses are not dissimilar, in type, to those advocated earlier to foster the inclusion of Personal and Social Education within the curriculum. With this pathway forged there are grounds for optimism that a call for schools to assume greater responsibility for children's all-round development can generate a similar route.

Bibliography

BAZALGETTE, J. (1983) 'Taking up the Pupil Role', *Pastoral Care in Education*, 1, 3, 152–158.

CHILDREN'S SOCIETY (1981) *Children and Divorce*, Church of England Children's Society.

CHARLTON, T. (1984) 'A special need in the curriculum: education for life.' *Links*, 10, 1, 30–33.

CHARLTON, T. (1985) 'Locus of Control as a Therapeutic Strategy for Helping Children with Learning and Behaviour Problems.' *Maladjustment and Therapeutic Education*, 3, 1, 26–32.

CHARLTON, T., DAVID, K. (1987) 'Personal and Social Education: Teachers' Perception of Initial Training' *Links* (in press).

DAVID, K., COWLEY, J. (1980) *Pastoral Care in Schools and Colleges* (London: Edward Arnold).

DES (1978) *Special Educational Needs* (The Warnock Report) (London: HMSO).

DES (1983) *Aspects of Secondary Education in England* (London: HMSO).

DUNHAM, J. (1981) 'Disruptive pupils and teacher stress'. *Education Research*, 23, 3.

EDUCATION ACT (1981) *Education Act 1981* (London: HMSO).

ELIAS, M., MAHER, C. (1983) 'Social and Affective Development of Children: a Programmatic Perspective.' *Exceptional Children*, 49, 4, 339–345.

GOOD, T. BROPHY, J. (1977) *Educational Psychology; A Realistic Approach* (New York: Holt, Rinehart and Winston).

HMI (1979) *Aspects of Secondary Education in England* (London: HMSO).

HMI (1982) *The New Teacher in School* (London: HMSO).
HMI (1983) *Teaching in Schools: The Content of Initial Training* (London: HMSO).
HMI (1985) *Education Observed 3. Good Teachers* (London: HMSO).
HOPSON, B., HOUGH, P. (1976) *Life Skills Teaching Programmes Nos 1 and 2*. Leeds Life Skills Associates.
KAVALE, H., HIRSHOREN, A. (1980) 'Public School and University Training Programmes for Behavioral Disordered Children: Are they Compatible?', *Behavior Disorders*, 5, 151–155.
KELLMER-PRINGLE, M. (1980) *The Needs of Children* (London: Hutchinson).
LANG, P. (1983) 'How Pupils See It', *Pastoral Care in Education*, 1, 3, 164–174.
LAWRENCE, D. (1971) 'The effect of counselling on retarded readers', *Educational Research*, 13, 2, 119–124.
LAWRENCE, D. (1985) 'Improving self-esteem and reading', *Educational Research*, 27, 3, 194–200.
LINDSAY, G. (1983) *Problems of Adolescence in the Secondary School* (London: Croom Helm).
MAHER, P., BEST, R. (1984) *Training and Support for Pastoral Care*, NAPCE.
MASLOW, A. H. (1954) *Motivation and Personality* (London: Harper and Row).
MORSE, W. (1974) Personal Communication (Annarbor: University of Michigan).
NAPCE (1984) *Initial Training for the Pastoral Aspects of the Teacher's Role* (London: NAPCE).
NAPCE (1986) *Preparing for Pastoral Care. In-service Training for the Pastoral Aspect of the Teacher's Role* (Oxford: Basil Blackwell).
PARKER, L. (1980) 'Teacher Competencies or Certification Competencies', *Behavior Disorders*, 5, 163–168.
PRING, R. (1984) *Personal and Social Education in the Curriculum* (London: Hodder and Stoughton).
RUTTER, M. (1975) *Troubled Children* (Harmondsworth: Penguin).
TAYLOR, P. (1984) 'Pastoral Care and In-Service Training', *Pastoral Care in Education*, 2, 3, 218–222.
STAGLES, B. (1985) 'What Teachers Like About Active Tutorial Work', *Pastoral Care in Education*, 3, 1, 13–24.
STOTT, P. (1981) 'Behaviour Disturbance and Failure to Learn: A Study of Cause and Effect', *Educational Research*, 23, 3, 163–172.
WHITFIELD, R. (1983) 'Family Structures, Lifestyles and the Care of Children', *Aston Educational Monograph*, No. 9.

PART II

Seven different viewpoints on managing and supporting the caring role of primary schools are given. Learning and knowledge are dealt with, a 'pastoral curriculum' is suggested, and improved recording and monitoring procedures are discussed. Welfare and health are considered in detail, effective counselling is reviewed, and the means of achieving a cooperative approach with parents and others is discussed. Contributors other than the editors were not invited necessarily to complement the editors' views. Their contributions are personal views and reflect their expertise, and their chapters should be seen as a series of separate statements, though we detect a common sympathy throughout.

Chapter 2: The Processes of Learning

Diana Hutchcroft OBE, a retired head teacher and member of the Bullock Report Committee, writes of teachers' influence and teaching styles, on rates of learning, of talk in classrooms, of classroom organisation and the use of time. All this adds up to the classroom as a place where children learn not only academic skills, but social and life skills.

Chapter 3: A Coordinated Approach

Kenneth David reviews the range of topics, knowledge, attitudes and values which may be involved in the socialisation of children, and suggests a checklist approach to desired skills, and to knowledge regarded as basic and essential, in preparing children for a testing future life.

Chapter 4: School Routines and Administration

Jim Abraham MA, a primary head teacher in Cheltenham, who has specialised in curriculum development and educational technology, shows, with examples, how profiling and monitoring of pupils' progress can be combined with computer technology to give a more accurate and helpful view of individual children's development.

Chapter 5: Welfare and Liaison

Frank Coombes OBE, a retired Senior Educational Welfare Officer, and Bill Horton, Acting Principal Education Welfare Officer in Avon, write of welfare work in primary schools, and review from their extensive experience in schools how teachers and other involved professionals must seek better liaison in supporting children and families.

Chapter 6: Body and Mind – Sources of help for young schoolchildren

Dr Anthony Fairburn MB, BS, FRCP, FRCPsych, DCH, DPM, of the Department of Child and Family Psychiatry at the Royal United Hospital, Bath, reviews many aspects of the school health service. He discusses pupils' handicaps, the monitoring of growth, physical well-being and some psychological needs. He argues, with case studies, for better liaison between teachers and those whose job it is to support them when children are malfunctioning or ill.

Chapter 7: Counselling in Primary Schools

Dr Tony Charlton and Lynne Hoye BA, Adv Dip Ed, F Coll P, a former head teacher in Liverpool and a trained counsellor, presently a lecturer in initial teacher training at The College of St Paul and St Mary, discuss basic counselling theories and concepts. They write of individual children's problems and with case studies explore how teachers can contribute to the support of children in primary schools with varied problems.

Chapter 8: Teachers, Parents and Other Professionals

Dr David Galloway MA, MSc, PhD, FBPrS, lecturer in Education at University College, Cardiff, considers that the professed aim of primary schools is to establish close cooperative links with parents, but policy and practice in many schools makes this aim unrealistic. The arguments in favour of closer links with parents are discussed in the light of factors which militate against such links.

The concept of parents as partners is discussed and consideration is given to recent evidence on the beneficial effects of parents listening to their children read. When children's behaviour or progress causes teachers concern the partnership between teachers and other professionals does not always include parents. When the problem is located in the child and/or the child's family, the effect is to 'de-skill' teachers as well as parents. Alternative models, involving a more genuine partnership between teachers, parents and other professionals are considered.

Chapter 2

The Processes of Learning

Diana Hutchcroft

The teacher's influence on children's personal development

It used to be said that, compared with the home and the wider environment, the school had very little influence upon the child's development. While acknowledging the first two powerful factors in a child's life, the teacher's effect upon his development (academically, socially and emotionally) is great. Indeed the processes of learning can affect the whole of a child's life-chances and this is a heavy burden to bear.

In the personal development of children influence lies, of course, not only in what teachers teach, for the hidden curriculum is at least as important. One part of this is classroom organisation which stems from the study of the curriculum, which itself can only be drawn up in the light of one's own educational philosophy. To some extent this will depend upon the ethos of the whole school, though not entirely, for each teacher has a responsibility for the organisation and management of her own classroom. The successful teacher is usually the one with a clear view of her aims and objectives, able to evaluate her successes and failures and so plan her future programme.

Teachers need to be very aware of the messages conveyed to children by their attitudes. Do children feel that they are thought of as responsible human beings, capable of self-discipline and the solving of some of their own problems? Are their contributions to class discussion waited for when a teacher has asked a question? When a reply is received is it valued, even though not the answer the teacher expected or wanted? When children raise a question themselves is this topic treated as important and followed up or is it brushed aside as an irrelevance?

ME MAM'S TEETH

One extremely frosty morning in a reception class it was time to go to the Hall for Assembly. But one small boy who lived in a damp, dilapidated caravan could not wait to tell his news which was, 'When we got up s'morning me Mam's teef was frozen in the glass'. Sensibly his teacher did not dismiss this report of an interesting phenomenon as a hindrance to her timetable. Had she hastened the class away into the Hall she would have emphatically, though unintentionally, pointed out that school routine was of far greater significance than Jack. A message was sent to the Head of the school that something of importance had arisen – and for the following two weeks of freezing weather, the five-year-olds explored many of the possibilities that frost offers for scientific exploration.

Are children given responsibility for much of the organisation, recording and evaluation of their own work? Or is everything teacher dominated, thus indicating that all value-judgements come from without? Self-assessment can be a driving force in learning. Indeed, do children feel that they are responsible human beings capable of self-discipline, self-direction and self-motivation?

The effect of teaching styles on children

A powerful influence is teaching style categorised as, on the one hand, traditional and, on the other, informal. This is an unfortunate polarisation of the conventional didactic method and the informal, progressive method. There is no need for this dichotomy; in the good classroom there is no such divide, there is a continuum. Neville Bennett (1976), did little service to the profession when, after looking at a very small sample of schools, he gave the impression that there was a hard and fast division between the two. Of course, in some cases this is, unfortunately, true; witness those chaotic places where 'progessive' has been misinterpreted as 'permissive', and 'liberty' as 'licence'! See also those classrooms where only one learning mode is used – silent children being regarded as containers into which the omniscient teachers can pour knowledge.

The good teacher selects the place on the continuum, between these methods, which fits the learning and the teaching of the particular item at a particular time and which enables the particular child to work in the best manner. But to do this successfully one needs to know both the practice and theory that underpins it. There are three main ways in which teachers organise their classes during the day; having all the children together, using a group formation or teaching individually.

Whole class tuition

Careful consideration needs to be given to the selection and the variety of this organisation, and the following may be occasions when all the children in the class are taught together.

(a) Giving instructions about organisational matters to the whole group to save repetition.
(b) The early stages of handwriting instruction.
(c) The unlikely event of every child being ready for, and needing the acquisition of, a certain skill when the teacher's purpose is pure instruction.
(d) The introduction and planning of a topic/project/thematic work.
(e) A 'brain-storming session'.
(f) General discussion of the progress of the topic.
(g) The sharing of knowledge at its conclusion.

The limitations of whole class tuition are, however, many:

(a) Discussion usually degenerates into a question and answer session where the teacher asks a display question, the child responds with a short, learnt phrase or a monosyllable, and the teacher either repeats this or possibly rephrases it.
(b) It is a daunting situation for the shy or academically less able child.
(c) It can be a very boring experience for the able.
(d) Few people *really* take part.
(e) It is unsound practice to use whole class groups in which to try to develop children's powers of description, recall, sequencing or reasoning, because the majority of the class then have to remain silent for long periods at a time.
(f) It leads to teacher dominance and the frequent use of monologue.

Individual teaching

Individual teaching is often necessary for the child who has misunderstood a concept or who has missed out on some essential teaching points through illness or absence. There are also times when the teacher will need to hear individual children read in order to diagnose their difficulties and so plan a systematic learning programme. On occasion some pupils respond well to the challenge of working completely alone and producing records of their own solo research. But individual teaching takes up an inordinate amount of the teacher's time, queues build up, and individual contact time can be so brief that there is little opportunity for real challenge in depth.

Furthermore, children are not encouraged to speak, to clarify their ideas in order to express them aloud, or to cooperate with other people, which is an important social skill in their development. Individual work is frequently organised on the workcard system, which often degenerates into mere practice of known skills or a resort to the copying out of great chunks of undigested text from reference books. Compare this with work done by any two children who research together, using two or more books of the right level, discussing what is of importance to them, in their own words, and collating the material from different sources. They rarely copy; they have no need to, they have talked together and, through discussion, understood the text in hand.

Group teaching

First let it be said that many teachers think that the children are working in groups when in plain truth they are seated around tables in a group formation but employed upon individual tasks.

Nevertheless, when children really are working together, this can be the very best of learning situations. For one thing, they learn to listen to one another, and they also learn to put their ideas into words in a secure situation supported by other children. They are free from the fear of ridicule and can overcome shyness. If the teacher plans her time well she can spend time with every group for a period long enough to be of real value. If the groups are skilfully changed and the formations recorded, it can be arranged for social development also. Children can learn to work with different types of people – the able, the reticent, the child with physical handicaps or behavioural problems, and so learn to understand one another.

Children's basic study skills

For all work which children undertake without the teacher's direct assistance they need study skills and, furthermore, these skills must be taught, not in isolation – for this is a sure way for them to be forgotten – but when the need for their use is evident. This demand may have to be engineered, but this warrants no apology for study skills will be wanted for the whole of a child's life in order to read and understand the print of adulthood.

All the following study skills have their place and none is of any avail without comprehension.

Study skills

uses contents tables	assesses reliability in books
uses index	assesses suitability in books
uses dictionary	recognises bias
uses encyclopaedia	indexes and cross references
uses library system	sequences
skims	makes notes
scans	collates information
reads rapidly	uses information read
reads intensively	produces bibliography
defines purpose for reading	constructs flow diagrams
forms questions for reading	

Comprehension skills

literal	or	reads the lines
reorganisation		
inference		reads between the lines
evaluation		reads beyond the lines
creative		

> Comprehension of the printed word should not really be classed as an advanced reading skill, nor should it be seen as the ability to work through comprehension exercises; it begins, or should begin, when a child first listens to a story. (Hutchcroft, 1981, p. 142)

It is an absolute essential for true reading and without it none of the study skills mentioned is of any avail. The *Times Educational Supplement* ran a competition for children in February 1980, entitled 'The Monday Report'. Read what the consumers think of comprehension exercises.

> 'There's one thing I hate and that's doing English'. In virtually every junior-age school, even ones with an interesting and varied curriculum, the children hated English. They were very sensible... Their chief dislike was comprehension exercises. The phrase: 'Just

the same boring thing over and over again' kept recurring about a variety of English schemes. 'My worst English is called "Basic Course in English", it goes on and on'. ' "English for Primary Schools", both boring and nasty', 'I dislike S.R.A. because it's comprehension and we also do comprehension in "Primary English" ', 'The most boring and horrible subject is "Effective Comprehension" '.

Try for yourself this comprehension exercise about 'The Maily Blonke', (Merritt, 1980).

> The maily blonke was tunfled, like the others, with nice spiss crinet covering its fairney cloots. But it seemed almost samded – lennow, sloomy and drumly – unlike the other blonkes, which had not, of course, eaten any fasels. The fasels were probably venenated. It would be sensible to dispose of them in the flosh.
>
> Questions:
> 1. What covered the maily blonke's fairney cloots?
> 2. Why did the maily blonke seem almost samded?
> 3. How was the maily blonke like the others and how was it different?
> 4. Is it wise to dispose of fasels in the flosh if they are venenated?

You probably had no difficulty with the first three questions, but you need some additional information in order to answer the fourth question.

You will be able to locate the answers easily enough without any understanding of the Old English words in which it is written. Children, once they have learned the trick, can churn out correct answers to these so-called 'comprehension exercises' even though some of the questions are not simple literal ones but go somewhat beyond the text. It is very easy to fool ourselves into thinking that children are working meaningfully, whereas in reality we are teaching children not to think but to manipulate the text, which hardly helps either achievement or personal development.

Phonics

Frequent phonic teaching, undertaken before a child can read, may well prove to be a severe handicap, a barrier to text and a deadener of enjoyment. While not denying that a sound knowledge of the phonic structures can greatly help a reader tackle an unfamiliar word and does help (to a very limited degree) to translate the written code, the strategy of 'building up' a word by phonic analysis is far more a hindrance than a help to a young and hesitant beginner. For a start, young children find the synthesising of the individual sounds an extremely difficult task. In addition, our language is, for about 50 per cent of our words, phonetically irregular, and the often used short words which are so necessary to make simple text interesting, are frequently in the category of 'non-phonic' (come, want, when, one, what, who, why, for example).

To add to the argument against the very early introduction of phonic teaching, any reading scheme tied to a rigid phonic approach is bound to be dull and stilted because of the restrictions imposed upon the vocabulary, and therefore guaranteed to teach children that reading is a tedious occupation, so that learning ceases to be a joy.

At the opposite extreme to the children mentioned above, we sometimes find the child who can 'bark out' whole pages of simple text, whose parents firmly believe him to be a competent reader, but who has absolutely no comprehension of what he has read. He is probably a product of mechanistic phonic drill.

Further mechanistic exercises

Many other drills come into the category of teaching children not to think; the rote learning of mathematics tables and computation methods taught with no understanding of concepts, are obvious examples.

One picture comes clearly to mind; it is of a so-called 'remedial' class doing 'dictionary work'. This involved writing out a set of given words, searching for them in a simplified dictionary and copying the printed definition. Two examples will suffice:

telephone . . . an instrument of communication
birthday . . . a natal day of celebration

In every instance the children questioned understood the original words but were defeated by the explanations!

Skills and personal development

In the past teachers have been encouraged to take 'the view that skills are best learned in a linear fashion, with each step an essential precursor to the ensuing one' (Blenkin and Kelly, 1981, p. 121). This theory has led to many a teacher giving children mechanical practices in skills, in isolation from all other activities in the classroom; and for those unfortunate members of the group slow to acquire the knack, has resulted in even further dull repetition. Blenkin and Kelly (1981) suggest that:

> ... the most effective teaching of skills, that teaching which encourages learners to relate their learning to broader principles of an educational nature and supports them in their development, requires a teacher who is constantly developing his own expertise and understanding of the process.
>
> It also requires a learner who is positively encouraged to be active whilst he is learning, to invent and discover as well as practise, and judge his own performance, using the teacher's instruction as a starting point. (p. 125)

Nevertheless, the so-called basic skills must be learnt. The pressures upon teachers from many outside sources to return to drills and rote learning is great, and will in all probability intensify. Of course these sources often lack knowledge, but this does not prevent utterance! Modern research is suggesting more and more that mechanistic and psycho-motor practices are far less efficient methods of learning than those of linking the acquisition of skills to intellectual development in its true educational form. Referring to this latter approach Donaldson (1978) stresses:

> This way of proceeding would not only appear to offer the best hope of mastering word decoding skills. It must have the further general advantage ... of encouraging reflective thought. (p. 106)

The same writer states that:

> ... the process of becoming literate can have marked – but commonly unsuspected – effects on the growth of the mind. (p. 97)

Topic work and study skills

The curriculum of every good primary school provides innumerable opportunities for learning and using study skills, most particularly in topic, thematic or project work.

Planning and evaluation should not be entirely teacher oriented. Children should be totally involved in the whole process from the initial decisions to the final assessments; not only should their involvement include ideas about knowledge to be sought but about skills to be acquired or perfected. 'Begin where the children are' is an oft-stated maxim; but 'where exactly are they and how do I find out?' must be the cry of many a teacher. At the introduction of a topic, possibly to a full class, a 'brain-storming' session will help both teacher and child to recognise how much is already known about the subject. Then the teacher has to plan:

(a) what further knowledge she intends the children to have gained by the end of the project;
(b) more importantly, what new skills the children will have acquired;
(c) what previously learnt skills they will have had the opportunity to practise.

In all of this the children themselves must play a major part, not only thinking about the knowledge they hope to gain but, more importantly, those skills they would hope to be able to use expertly by the end of the project work. This type of commitment gives the work more force and also makes it possible to evaluate effectively how good the learning has been. It is only then that future programming can be truly purposeful.

DARTS – an escape from the drill trap

Directed Activities Related to Text, when closely connected with real topic work in which the children have a lively interest, are extremely useful. Used in isolation they can prove as arid as most other exercises. Using text which is closely allied to the research in hand, the teacher can decide where she feels that detailed attention is necessary and use a number of ploys to draw the children's minds to focus on the exact areas. One can ask children to analyse straight text by:

(a) underlining specified parts of the text relating to a certain aspect. If money is short and reproduction of the text too expensive, books can be put into plastic envelopes, water-soluble felt-tip pens used, then the data so located can be recorded prior to the plastic cover being wiped clean for further use.
(b) segmenting the text, either by the teacher, when the children can be asked to 'sub edit' and supply paragraph headings, or by the children who can be asked to divide the text into information units. (These two ploys help children towards that difficult concept, 'what is a paragraph?').
(c) making diagrammatic representation of what they have read in the form of flow-diagrams, models, webs, continua, hierarchies, tables,

graphs, etc. Transformation of the written word into a more visual form needs true understanding of the message from the author, and the very task itself helps towards this. Furthermore, information is readily remembered when it has been so translated.

Text, of course, may be modified by the teacher for use in:

(a) cloze procedure;
(b) sequencing exercises;
(c) group prediction sessions. For further information refer to Walker (1974), and Lunzer and Gardner (1982).

Differences in progress and development

Good classroom organisation work in groups leaves the teacher space and time to consider the differences between children. There are those who learn through their finger tips, there are many whose preferred learning mode is visual, and yet again those who gain most when the information is in the oral mode. Obviously, there are no watertight compartments and we would suggest that all children need all approaches; but the teacher needs to recognise which is the child's strongest area.

> We learn through experience, but do not learn by merely being exposed to experience in our mind ... to explain, relive it, select from it, evaluate it and gradually absorb it ... until it becomes part of ourselves, lasting for ever. (Schiller, 1984)

Rate of learning

Children develop along very similar lines; the difference between them is the speed at which they advance along these lines. *English from 5 to 16* (HMI, 1984) puts the clock sadly back and ignores research when it ties achievements to chronological age.

Perhaps, above all, children need to see the purpose in any learning before they undertake it. Why learn to spell? Indeed, why read?

Learning can also be hindered by all manner of pressures, handicaps, and circumstances: catarrhal deafness, for example, is often unrecognised.

SARAH

Catarrhal deafness can be a handicap hard to identify. One day during the winter the teacher noticed that Sarah (aged five and a half) seemed a trifle deaf, so she was referred to the audiometrician who, when she visited the school a fortnight later, found no hearing loss whatsoever. Three weeks later Sarah was absent from school suffering from a heavy cold; on her return to school she again seemed not to hear normally. The whole pattern was again repeated, her full hearing was completely restored by the time she was retested. Fortunately Sarah's mother, her doctor and her teacher were now alerted to this recurring problem and, in consequence, Sarah did not suffer.

But how many others with a similar problem are missed? Again, those children who have a high-frequency deafness can be unidentified unless very adequate screening takes place. These children often have apparently inexplicable difficulties with the spelling and the reading of certain letter combinations. It is noteworthy that in Zita's case it was short-term illness that caused her to miss an important teaching point. Teachers always have to make great efforts to help a child regain lost ground when he or she has been absent from school for any length of time. To lag behind the peer group can be cumulatively retarding. Most teachers are very aware of this need for those children who have had long periods of illness, but they need to be equally aware of the exigency of the child who has frequent short-term loss of education, for even the odd half-day absences are damaging.

It is patently obvious that home circumstances influence a child's attitude to school and his ability to cope with the learning on offer. Under-nourishment, deprivation, deep unhappiness, poor status in the peer group, parental estrangement or divorce, a death in the family, and parental pressure all take their toll. Most of these are dealt with in later chapters, but two children whose school situation was the root cause of their educational problems spring to mind.

WAYNE

Unfortunately the situation in which Wayne found himself was not an uncommon one, especially for a boy. He was slow in starting to read and had not firmly mastered the skill when his sister, two years younger than himself, started school. She became a fluent reader in what seemed no time at all, to Wayne's chagrin. His mother compounded matters by making frequent unfavourable comparisons and by enforcing evening sessions of reading aloud to the family. It was the most perfect way to build up such emotional tension that reading became impossible, a nightmare. Wayne took what was for him the only route to sanity; 'If I don't try, I don't fail'. He became the class clown. And the school were faced with a long and uphill struggle.

The very slow child is often obviously at risk of being ostracised by his peers, and the very able child sometimes conceals his difficulties; children at either end of the ability range can be in danger of isolation from the peer group. Teachers need to be aware of this possibility lest the problems of the most academic go undetected.

PETER

Peter, a brilliant boy, whose only failure in school seemed to be a lack of ability in outdoor games, nevertheless was showing signs of stress. He did not suffer fools gladly, and was highly critical of his peers, always commenting on their faults and pointing out their errors – and he was always right. He did not endear himself to his classmates who, as they progressed through the junior years, left Peter more and more alone and friendless. He was unhappy because he did not understand, but luckily for him he had a sympathetic teacher who recognised the signs. His teacher decided to tackle the problem on two fronts. First, he talked to Peter and explained; he knew the boy would be able to appreciate positive criticism of his behaviour, would be able to recognise, to some extent, how his peers felt when constantly corrected. Second, he used Peter's own considerable talent in the writing of stories to give him status. Gradually Peter became a most acceptable member of the class.

Talk in classrooms

To be able to speak clearly, with confidence, and to the point, must be one of the greatest of life skills.

> There are differences between children, of course, both in the age at which they begin to talk and in the stage they have reached on entry to school, but these are relatively insignificant when compared with the amount that all children learn in these early years. All but a very small minority of children reach the age of schooling with a vocabulary of several thousand words, control of the basic grammar of the language of their community, and an ability to deploy these resources in conversation arising from the many and varied situ-

ations that occur in their everyday lives ... Learning one's native language is not simply a matter of learning vocabulary and grammar, but rather of learning to construct shared meanings as part of collaborative activities in which the words and sentences both refer to the shared situation and reflect a particular orientation to it. (Wells, 1985, p. 101)

Wells continues:

> ... any suggestion that working class children *as a whole* are 'disadvantaged', in any absolute or irrevocable sense, because their home experience leads them to use language differently, is certainly not appropriate ... As well as being inaccurate, such sweeping assertions about the inadequacies of homes have the additional disadvantage of distracting teachers from their obligations to examine their own role in helping children to make a success of the transition from home to school. (p. 113)

Children have usually been very free to talk at home, to ask questions, to initiate topics; it must, indeed, be a traumatic experience for them to find themselves in a room where only one person is really allowed these 'privileges'. The day, the talk, the tasks, the questions, are dominated by one adult. Every teacher should develop a style which allows far more latitude to children, taking account of their interests, enthusiasms, and vital curiosity, building on their own previous knowledge, yet still pursuing those curriculum aims that the teacher and the school have in mind.

Language is obviously used for communication, and if children are encouraged to work cooperatively in small group situations where support will come from their peers, there is much opportunity for the sustained and complex use of language. Children feel safe and so can talk more freely, introduce ideas, extend and clarify them with references to previous experience, and also learn to listen and modify their opinions in the light of the arguments offered.

If the composition of the group varies, the children will also learn how to adapt their own speech for differing audiences. They will begin to appreciate metacommunication also; as the group struggles towards the resolution of a problem, for instance, the children will recognise when certain members have not participated, when the group is failing to reach the goal, when 'red herrings' have been introduced, when time is running short, and so on. They will indeed be learning how to communicate.

Yet, important as this function is, language has deeper uses; to solve problems on a high cognitive level, to recall, to classify, to anticipate, to shape meaning for ourselves, to think, to understand something of the world. It is also a gateway to learning.

This is why one must pay serious attention to all modes of language in the classroom, for not only does language cross the whole curriculum but it is an essential ingredient in the development of the full being. Oral language is the form that is surely the most natural, the most used in everyday life and yet frequently the most neglected in our schools. The best way for children to make knowledge their own is to translate it into words. One of the most telling statements in the 'Bullock Report' (1975) is:

> It is a confusion of everyday thought that we tend to regard 'knowledge' as something that exists independently of someone who knows. 'What is known' must in fact be brought to life afresh within every 'knower' by his own efforts. To bring knowledge into being is a formulating process, and language is its ordinary means, whether in speaking or writing or the inner monologue of thought. (DES, 1975, p. 50)

During the primary years it is helpful to encourage the children to translate their own 'inner monologues of thought' into words spoken aloud and often shared by their partners or members of their group.

Oral language is so obviously necessary that great care needs to be paid to the planning of situations best suited to its full development. Talk interchange happens on a wide variety of occasions; the teacher working with the whole class, small groups or individuals; the child working with a partner, in a group, or in whole class discussion; in unscheduled activity in the playground or around the school; in Drama; in communication with other adults they meet in school or outside, and so on. The teacher needs to work out for herself which context is preferable for the particular kind of talk she wishes the children to pay attention to, and, because oral language is not a single 'skill' but an important aspect of learning in most subjects, she has an extremely wide curriculum to choose from. Teachers must take courage; although they must always be in full control they ought to give children plenty of opportunity to work together, far more than is commonly seen in practice. The day should be so planned that talk has time to develop, and the class must fully understand that although talking is welcome, shouting and fooling about are not!

Douglas Barnes (1976) suggests five headings to encourage useful learning strategies when planning group work for secondary school children. They are equally applicable in the primary field. First, he says that it is essential to give children a feeling of competence in their own abilities, to make sure they know that any contributions they make to discussion will be valued and treated with respect. Second, offer the group common ground for their discussion. Herewith some suggestions:

> Construction of models (at any age)
> Invention of games (indoor or outdoor)
> Story telling
> Cooperative ploys linked to reading or writing:
>   composing a poem;
>   planning a plot for a story;
>   collating material from various sources;
>   producing a newspaper, magazine or a record of thematic work
> Conversation about a book read
> Sequencing
> Cloze procedure
> Group prediction
> Solution of problems (scientific or mathematical)
> Cookery
> Discussion of difficult excerpts from literature or poetry
> Drama
> Discussion of shared experiences (in or out of school)
> Discussion of films or film-strips

Third, the attention of the group should be focused in some way. Probably the two main methods to encourage children to bring their minds to bear on the task in hand are, (a), to ask pertinent questions which will point the child's attention in the desired direction and, (b), to encourage the children themselves to ask questions and then follow them up. One's own queries are powerful spurs to learning. Fourth, pay attention to pace; remember always that it is the process rather than the final outcome that is the core of the learning and that too hurried a performance will not give time for any depth of study. On the other hand, take into consideration the fact that, for many people, a deadline for the completion of a project can be helpful. Finally, Barnes suggests that children should be asked to make their findings public. It should be apparent that a child ought to be allowed to use his own speech register whenever he is struggling to come to terms with new experiences or new knowledge; therefore, it is common sense to allow children to speak in their own way during group discussion. This may carry grammatical errors or faulty syntax which can be gently screened out when they are asked to share their findings with a wider audience, the year group, the whole class, the school, parents or even further afield.

The use of this wider audience with whom to share knowledge enables the teacher to challenge the group to bring the records of their research to a far higher standard than if the work were to be buried in an exercise book.

Because of the essential contribution of oral language it is suggested that every teacher should run a tape recorder in her classroom for a whole day, and then analyse both her own and the children's oral contributions throughout that day. It will be evident when she has asked closed-ended questions requiring simple known answers, or where the questions were open ended, challenging the child to think, and, if enough time was left, for a thoughtful answer to be prepared.

Group work should also be recorded and analysed. Though not exhaustive, the following checklist may be of help. Think about:

(a) Cognition – how well do the children
   explain
   reason
   interpret (usually a
      process)
   clarify
   predict
   deduce
   speculate
   anticipate
   recognise sequence
   recognise cause and effect
   sustain the line of enquiry
   appraise
   make judgments
   solve problems
   generalise
   consider more than one point
      of view
   evaluate?

(b) Collaboration – how well do the children
   initiate a conversation
   introduce a topic
   hold the interest of
      others
   elaborate
   ask questions
   invite others to speak
   discuss
   support others
   keep the group to the point
   suggest ways to approach the
      tasks
   act as leaders
   listen to the views of other
      members of the group
   recognise metacommunication?

(c) Distribution of talk among members of the group –
       is there a dominant member
       is there a non-participant
   or do all members give a fair contribution?

(d) What effect does size of group have
on any of the above
or on success in the task?
(e) What effect does the presence or absence of the teacher have
on any of the above
or on success in the task?
(f) Think about teachers' questions – are they
closed ended, with only one acceptable answer
open ended, thought provoking, with no predetermined answer?

If possible, make time to record one child's opportunities for talk during a whole week in school. Think about:

(a) the size of the groups of which he is a member
(b) the variety of other children with whom he works or plays
(c) the kind of activity which encourages him to talk and listen
(d) are these planned classroom activities?
(e) If so, do you consider there was time enough for sustained language development?

Reading

Every teacher must recognise that real reading requires the reader to think. If this is so, then surely it ought to be reflected in the selection of books the child is offered, even at the very earliest stage. Great care should be given to the choice of any reading scheme – if the school feels it must rely on this method. Every tiny detail in helping a child to read needs attention; even the practice of following a line of print by holding a piece of card across the page militates against the growth of the good reading habit of informed guessing of a word by reading on, as in cloze procedure. It is a minor point; how much more important then is the choice of the beginner's reading material.

Every school should give consideration to the reasons why they feel a reading scheme is essential; is it that members of staff want the apparent safety of being able to 'prove' a child's success in mastering the skill of reading by numbering his steps up through a graded reading series? If so, they should question whether this does demonstrate true ability, which means reading with understanding. Or is this similar to 'reading age' tests which give a numerical answer of little or no value? Many children, brought up in this way, become over-competitive and often the main object in going to books is not for pleasure, or for a search for information, but to finish one book and proceed to another as quickly as possible. The scheme may be linked with supplementary cards, discussion books, exercises and the rest, but the goal remains the same – to beat one's peers. Thereby children are not only developing a questionable trait but are also failing to recognise what reading has to offer them for the rest of their lives. Add to this, if they are with a teacher who uses schemes as the basis for most reading ploys, however well advertised and produced they may be, the children will certainly be denied most of the interesting experiences that happen in and around a school, many of which can be used as a stimulus for reading and writing. There might be science problems, cookery recipes, sequencing cards (carrying, perhaps, instructions for modelmaking, activities, games and experiments), and books on environmental topics to refer to when something in the real world has aroused interest and attention. Why cannot all young children be taught to read using 'real' books as Jill Bennett (1982) recommends. Liz Waterland (1985) describes this approach most helpfully in her book *Read with Me*.

Teachers of young children often find a dearth of good reference books with suitable text. One way of overcoming this difficulty is to make recordings of the relevant passages of the book and have these available to help with (but not to replace) the printed word. Good readers can employ their skills in the making of these useful classroom aids. Another way out of the dilemma is for children to make their own information books; in doing so many skills are learnt, reading is extended and a sense of pride in achievement is guaranteed because the finished product is a valuable contribution to the class reference library. For the child whose actual handwriting is poor, or who needs an added incentive to put pen to paper, a word processor is of inestimable value; his contributions to the topic reference book can be as attractive and as correct as those of his more able companions.

The information book is certainly one good way of storing the laboriously collected data which is so frequently wasted at the conclusion of children's research. Much more use should be made of handouts, articles, books etc. produced for a wider audience and for the recording of information for future reference. Here a computer is of value, if facilities like factfile or database are used. These necessitate the use of reading skills, sequencing skills, and vital question-forming ability. Such challenges give the modern child a meaningful reason for reading.

Another handicap which schools sometimes inflict upon themselves is the ruling – or at least the attempt – 'to hear every child read every day'. With able young readers it would probably be more advantageous to collect together a small group of children who had all recently read one particular book and chat to them about plot, characters, and the deeper meanings the author has embedded in the narrative. Fiction, well chosen and well used, can play a dramatic part in helping a child grow towards maturity, understanding both himself and others. It is, therefore, very worrying to find in the document *English from 5 to 16* (HMI, 1984) that it is not until the objective for sixteen-year-olds that the following statement occurs: . . . children should 'Read whole books of some length requiring some persistence.' If books are selected with the care, knowledge and perspicacity that should be given to this important area then this can be an objective for the very young reader.

Writing

Looking back over the first half of the century it seemed as if children's writing, like all Gaul, was divided into three parts – composition, handwriting and grammar – with no connection between them. Then so-called creative writing burst upon the scene, allowed children freedom, encouraged fresh, original thought, deepened children's awareness of their own abilities and heightened teachers' expectations. Yet the emphasis remained, as in pre-war years, on the end product, the final result. There were, of course, a few teachers on the lunatic fringe who, during the 'creative writing' boom, allowed children to ignore the code altogether so that spelling and syntax were, in some cases, ignored. These are important; nevertheless they must not be the major factor. Throughout at least 70 years of the twentieth century almost all correction has been error marking, highlighting failure instead of pointing to success. Usually in primary schools the writing to be marked was the first and only attempt. Now, at last, teachers are beginning to realise that drafts should be made, worked on, shared with partners and brought to the teacher for conference, edited and redrafted (maybe several times). Then, and only then, should consideration be given by the author as to what to do with the final draft. Perhaps:

(a) Publish it in book form.
(b) Submit it for inclusion in a magazine or newspaper (school edition).
(c) Copy it out for display.
(d) Send it to another school.
(e) If it is a letter, post it.
(f) Put it in the wastepaper basket.

Why write?

All children need to know the answer to the question which must often spring into their minds – 'Why write when it would be much simpler just to say what I want to say'; or, nowadays, with modern technological aids, 'Why write when I could dictate onto tape?' In many cases, in particular with young children making stories, the answer might well be, 'Don't write, do use a tape recorder'. But, despite computers, word processors, tape recorders and the rest, writing remains an important lifelong skill and the writer needs to have both audience and function in the forefront of his mind if he is to see evidence of purpose.

One occasionally sees letters written in exercise books; can there be a more stultifying operation? An audience for children's writing is not difficult to find. The teacher is always there, usually as the chief recipient, but she should do her best to ensure that she is not seen at all times as marker, examiner, critic and the only reader. She must be an appreciative reader who is anxious to seek further information from the author, willing to comment on things which are well expressed, able to help where the writer needs guidance and quick to indicate growth-points to further development of expertise. Sometimes she must be prepared just to say, 'Thank you for allowing me to read this'.

The peer group forms an obvious readership for much of a child's output from poetry and narrative to reports on research and problem solving. The 'response partner' (a chosen friend with whom to discuss the draft) should be the first of the peer group with whom to share work. If the author decides that the final draft is ready for publication then near perfection can be aimed for in the fair copy, especially if it is to be a contribution to the class library where it will be read by others.

The same demand can be made for fair copies of stories written for other classes in school (another ready audience), but if the tales are directed towards the youngest children it is preferable to have them typed out in 'jumbo' type face.

Wider audiences can be found in magazines, letters or exchange of information with other schools.

There remains the most important of all audiences for whom the writer writes – himself!

Purpose

Children need to have explained to them how and why writing is so important, so that they can appreciate the value of becoming masters of the craft. Permanence of the written word can be demonstrated so that children gradually realise that wonderful notions, ideas, remarks, stories or discoveries are ephemeral if only spoken, but can be stored, communicated to someone at a distance and shared far more widely if they are committed to paper. And for true communication they must write legibly and spell correctly.

Young writers should be encouraged to reflect upon how writing helps them order their thoughts in all forms of problem solving (particularly if they learn the skill of flow-diagram making), and how note making aids in the recall and organisation of facts they already know.

'Learning logs' and 'Think books'

It is essential for teachers to know when their pupils have truly grasped a concept and no amount of regurgitated phrases from their own lessons, or text copied faithfully from a reference book, will give them this information. Children's free writing will often reveal a great deal. The introduction of either 'Learning logs' or 'Think books' can be an excellent way of building up a trusting relationship between teacher and taught in which deeper understanding of one another can grow. Another bonus is that they demand that children examine their own learning and evaluate it. Possibly 'Learning logs' are easier to use at the outset. Here children are asked to write freely about their school work, a specific lesson perhaps, or the whole day or even more. It must be understood that they are required to write honestly, not seeking to please, nor creating a piece of polished literature, nor yet struggling to set down badly understood concepts, but to be commenting truthfully on their lessons and their learning. There are really two audiences here; first the self, because these logs help the writer heuristically (often in describing an unsolved problem the light dawns just as so frequently happens in talk). Second, logs help the teacher to recognise fundamental truths about the learning; whether the concept has been fully grasped, partly understood, or whether the whole idea has been completely misconceived. They also reveal whether the learner enjoyed the experience or hated it. And, perhaps most telling of all, they give a clear indication not only of 'how sound was the learning' but also of 'how sound was the teaching'. No teacher should ever be afraid of evaluation, and who are more qualified to do this than the consumers themselves?

It must be stressed that once embarked upon, time for writing these records in depth must be allowed, then they must be collected, read by the teacher, treated with respect, and replied to or acted upon. But not marked! In all, they must be accorded status.

'Think books' differ from 'Learning logs' in a small way; they are more private, but they can be just as useful. Here the pupil is given a book in which to write exactly what he feels about – school, lessons, home, play, friends, himself – indeed, anything he wishes to set down. He may well wish to share his writing with his teacher, but the choice remains firmly with him. A child who keeps his book entirely to himself, at first, may later wish to change his mind and share some of his thoughts on one occasion. In this case he must be allowed to clip together those pages he does not wish his teacher to read, and she should honour his trust.

Any teacher who follows up the idea of either 'Learning logs' or 'Think books' must recognise that they themselves will have to be prepared for candour because, if the reports are honest, and genuine dialogue ensues, frustration, dislike or other negative feelings may well be expressed. This, in itself, can be useful.

Classroom organisation

What considerations need to be borne in mind when planning?

Teachers should be aware of the effect of their surroundings upon all concerned, themselves as well as the children. How then to organise for education in its widest sense, the developing of the full potential of each child? What criteria ought to be considered? What aims should be borne in mind? It can prove helpful to itemise these aims and arrange them under the headings Academic, Social and Emotional, providing it is always remembered that these are not hard and fast divisions. Everything that takes place in the classroom has its effect on the children. The strands are closely interwoven.

ACADEMIC AIMS

(a) to stimulate curiosity and maximise learning;
(b) to demonstrate quality and depth of thought;
(c) to teach independence in the selection and use of resources;
(d) to make readily available a wide variety of sources;
(e) to encourage children to take some responsibility for planning and recording their own work;

(f) to have areas within the room where specialised skills may be developed;
(g) to save both the teacher's and the children's time.

SOCIAL AIMS

(a) to develop social skills through group activities;
(b) to develop empathy;
(c) to organise storage so that all necessary resources are within the children's reach and, as far as possible, to use the return of certain items to reinforce learning (jigsaws, coins, pencils, tools, etc. can be matched to bases and become self-checking; toys, science equipment, dressing-up clothes might be stored under attribute headings which may be changed from time to time);
(d) to encourage care in the use and return of equipment;
(e) to ensure an uncluttered room because untidiness leads to lack of care in all directions;
(f) to so arrange the furniture that movement around the room is easy for teacher and child.

EMOTIONAL AIMS

(a) to allow for differences in children's needs;
(b) to create many varied opportunities so that everyone can find an area of excellence and so gain satisfaction, success and status in the peer group;
(c) to develop independence in all aspects of work;
(d) to develop individuality;
(e) to develop within each member of the class a positive self-image, particularly through work in groups;
(f) to form areas within the room where children may be quiet and undistracted;
(g) to reduce unnecessary noise (perhaps by covering certain work surfaces with blankets to deaden, for instance, the sound of the impact of bricks, etc.);
(h) to pay due regard to colour in relation to space, shape and display;
(i) to make the room attractive and welcoming.

It is noteworthy that many of these aims are directed towards self-discipline and autonomy. In Britain people are given a vote at eighteen years of age and are presumed adult, and schools should be helping children towards independence physically, emotionally and socially from the day they enter the building. Too much teacher dominance hinders growth. With this in mind, continuity of provision throughout the years of schooling should be examined; is there a transfer at 7, 11, from class to class, or indeed at any stage, where this development takes a considerable blow?

Displays

A display of some kind set just inside the room, visible immediately the door is opened, offers a welcome and sets a standard. It should be supplemented by other displays to which careful thought must be given. Consider:

(a) What proportion should be children's work?
(b) How is this to be mounted – beautifully by the teacher or as well as possible by the children or sometimes one, sometimes the other?
(c) Does the background enhance the display; if not, what can be done about it?
(d) Are the displays to be purely decorative or are they to form an integral part of the learning?
(e) How much first-hand material ought to be included?
(f) What interesting artefacts could be meaningfully displayed?
(g) What time will be allowed for studying the displays and how will this be ensured?
(h) How will everything be displayed at the correct height to be studied?
(i) How will you ensure that the children understand why the things are on display?
(j) Is all display to be a kind of record of work completed or will it be used to raise further questions?

Areas for work

Within the room the furniture should be so arranged that working in groups becomes a simple matter. Bays are useful. These should not be too closely tied to the adult conception of subject compartmentalisation, but access to the correct resources can be facilitated and too much movement around the room saved if apparatus is stored near the area where it is most likely to be used. Suggested designations might be:

1. A book corner or reading area, carpeted if possible, and with comfortable seating. The teachers of younger children might wish to segregate fiction from reference books to help in selection and understanding.

2. On the other hand, this area might be made more comprehensive and developed into a language area, complete with everything necessary for writing including such articles as manuscript pens and bookbinding materials for use in perfecting final copies.
3. Art/Craft area.
4. Mathematics area, adjoining the
5. Science bay which, if possible, should be situated in the practical area preferably near a sink and water supply.
6. Cookery bay, also in the practical area.
7. Listening area, for all age groups, not restricted to Infants only, complete with cassette tapes ready for the particular users.
8. Computer/Audio-visual area.
9. Home corner.
10. Drama area.
11. Dressing-up area.

These last three, even more than the rest, need to have their use most carefully thought out. They can so easily become places in the classroom where nothing purposeful goes forward, yet they have a most important contribution to make if well planned.

Choices of area will naturally depend upon the age and maturity of the children and the balance the teacher wishes to have at the time.

Physically it is best to make the bays obviously separate. Wooden trellis work obtainable from garden suppliers, both the diamond style and the square type, can be adapted quite simply to form area dividers. They are easily moved when rearrangement is desired, good for use for holding displays and they provide discreet areas for children to work in while still leaving them visible to the teacher. Such barriers cut down on interference, and thus friction, between children.

Do not overlook the floor space; young children in particular, are perfectly comfortable carrying out some ploys at floor level.

If the room has a door leading to an outdoor area make that, too, part of the plan and use it to the full.

Storage

The storage of equipment, resources and materials needs careful thought. Everything must have a place, clearly marked, self-checking if possible, and tidy return to that place must be insisted upon. There is, on the market, a variety of trays, baskets, boxes, drawers and cabinets that, though not specifically designed for educational use, lend themselves to it extremely well.

Children's time

One of the most effective ways to plan the children's learning is to give children their work for the whole morning session, preferably negotiated with them during the initial period. Seven- and eight-year-olds can cope most adequately with their assignments for a whole day; older junior children enjoy the challenge of planning their own work for at least a week at a time. This method allows the children the opportunity to learn to organise themselves, to allot their time effectively, to record and evaluate a great deal for themselves.

Try to identify what causes those blank periods (if they occur) when children have to wait patiently for the teacher's attention, or when they are of necessity unoccupied because they do not know what is expected of them next. And, having recognised the circumstances, eliminate the chances of their recurrence.

If ever queues form by the teacher's desk, question 'why?':

(a) Has the teacher asked too many children to work at a task which is above their capability when working in an unsupported situation?
(b) Are the children insecure and therefore in need of constant reassurance?
(c) Have they been encouraged to be independent?
(d) Are the resources easy to get at?
(e) Have the children been taught how to use them?
(f) Is there easy access to word banks, dictionaries etc. for their written assignments?
(g) Have the children just formed the habit of depending upon the teacher for all guidance?
(h) Are some children 'professional queuers' who have found that they can enjoy periods of complete freedom from work if they join the end of a queue – and then politely allow others to proceed them?
(i) Do the children know that their teachers should usually be the last resource they turn to?

If there is an occasion when the formation of a queue is essential, try to ensure that the children wait in an area where they can be meaningfully occupied while waiting – near bookshelves, or display areas, for example.

Teacher's time

When assigning work thought must be given to the obvious dilemma that not all children can have attention at the same time. The teacher must plan her own daily timetable and adjust the level of work for those groups she will not be visiting so that they can be independent of her for some appreciable time. She must also know which groups she is going to sit with in a tutorial role, and those children who will need occasional assistance or supervision. A detailed programme of the day, showing both her own and the children's timetable, is essential.

It is a great help to have at least one other adult in the room; teaching assistants, nursery nurses, parents, grandparents, retired friends, grown-ups currently out of a job, school children on 'work experience' can, when available, be most useful partners in the programme. Their share of the day should be carefully timetabled so that they only do those tasks which the teacher plans for them. With adequate forethought teachers can make sure that their time is spent in actually teaching and furthering the learning of their pupils, and not diluted by mere servicing of activities, acting as childminders or even as filing clerks.

All of this means a great deal of time and effort must be put in during the initial stages, but once work in this mode is set in motion it proves a most rewarding method for all concerned.

Interaction

The classroom must be a place where children learn not only academic skills, but social skills and life skills. Grouping should always be considered as an integral element in the learning. For children always to be organised in groups with their peers of like ability, is to ignore the contribution that cooperating with all types of people can offer to their development. They need to experience the making of contact with others across the barriers of IQ, class, creed or race; they need to learn that other children laugh and cry, suffer from fears, troubles and worries in much the same way as they do themselves, even though, at first sight, they may appear vastly different. They must also be helped to appreciate not only the sameness but also the richness that people from different backgrounds can offer them.

> Children's experience is essentially social. From the earliest days in the family, they learn and grow in interaction with others. What is

more, this interaction is itself of central interest and significance for them. It matters to them how they relate to others, for this is crucial to their self-image. ... This social development is a framework within which primary education is developed. (Richards, 1980, p. 132)

The child has more urgent needs than the basic skills, teachers have more to deliberate on than the imparting of factual knowledge or testing and measuring in an engineering mode. They have responsibility for human beings. This chapter has been an attempt to review how all the processes of learning continue to affect individual children and their successes and failures in life.

References and recommended reading

BARNES, D. (1976) *From Communication to Curriculum* (Harmondsworth: Penguin).
BARNES, D., BRITTON, J. and ROSEN, H. (1971) *Language, the Learner and the School* (Harmondsworth: Penguin).
BENNETT, N. (1976) *Teaching Styles and Pupil Progress* (Wells: Open Books).
BENNETT, J. (1982) *Learning to Read With Picture Books* (Stroud: The Thimble Press).
BENNETT, J. (1983) *Reaching Out. Stories for Readers 6–8* (Stroud: The Thimble Press).
BLENKIN, G. and KELLY, A. (1981) *The Primary Curriculum* (London: Harper & Row).
BRITTON, J. (1970) *Language and Learning* (Harmondsworth: Penguin).
DAVIES, F. and GREEN, T. (1984) *Reading for Learning in the Sciences* (Edinburgh: Oliver and Boyd).
DONALDSON, M. (1978) *Children's Minds* (London: Fontana).
GRAVES, D. (1983) *Writing: Teachers and Children at Work* (London: Heinemann).
DES (1975) *A Language for Life* (The Bullock Report) (London: HMSO).
DES (1978) *Primary Education in England* (London: HMSO).
DES (1985) *Better Schools* (London: HMSO).
DES (1985) *Good Teachers* (London: HMSO).
GRIFFIN-BEALE, C. (1984) *Christian Schiller in his own words* (London: National Association for Primary Education/A & C. Black).
HMI (1984) *English from 5 to 16* (Curriculum Matters 1) (London: HMSO).

HOLT, J. (1969) *How Children Fail* (Harmondsworth: Penguin).
HUTCHCROFT, D. M. R. (1981) *Making Language Work* (Maidenhead: McGraw Hill).
LUNZER, E. and GARDNER, K. (1982) *Learning from the Written Word* (London: Heinemann).
MEEK, M. (1982) *Learning to Read* (London: The Bodley Head).
MERRITT, J. E. (1980) *'Who is literate'* in 'Persistent Problems in Reading Education' Eds: McCullough and Inchworm (London: International Reading Association).
RICHARDS, G. (1980) *Primary Education: Issues for the Eighties* (London: A & C Black).
ROSEN, H. (1973) *The Language of Primary School Children* (Harmondsworth: Penguin).
WATERLAND, L. (1985) *Read with Me* (Stroud: The Thimble Press).
WALKER, C. (1974) *Reading Development and Extension* (London: Ward Lock Educational).
WELLS, G. (1985) *Language Learning and Education* (Windsor: NFER/Nelson).
WILKINSON, A. (1971) *The Foundations of Language* (Oxford: OUP).

Chapter 3

A Coordinated Approach

Kenneth David

Much of our work in primary school classrooms is still formal and traditional, but much is intuitive, even unplanned. In seeking to interest children in learning, and to meet the excitement of a primary school child's expanding world, we vary between the normative and the intuitive – we think they ought to learn certain traditional areas of knowledge, but we want to encourage and follow their changing interests and varied enthusiasms. There is, after all, such an overwhelming volume of facts and knowledge and processes in the modern world that it must be argued that a random selection, a 'tasting' and experimenting process, is all we can offer a young child. The curriculum debate is long standing, as Vaughan Johnson (1981) pointed out. 'Teaching by subjects is a mode of instruction which . . . does not always correspond with the child's unsystematized but eager interest,' said the Board of Education back in 1931. In viewing our teaching profession Blackie (1969) pointed out:

> the number of junior schools which had been substantially affected (by ideas of child centred education) was very small, and even in the infants' schools . . . there was still a solid block of conservatism.

Plowden (1967) spoke of 'The inherent conservatism of all teaching professions.' Has the last twenty years brought major change in the planning of junior school education?

The debate continues, of course. E. J. Bolton, Senior Chief Inspector, speaking on 'Current issues in Primary Education' in 1984, said: 'Changes . . . have led to a fundamental questioning of education in terms of what are its purposes; how good and relevant is it to the world in which we live and, more importantly, to that in which children today will be adults?' He continued,

... a primary education that did not set out to lay firm foundations for literacy, numeracy, scientific and technological competence, a sense of time and place, and aesthetic and artistic awareness, as well as developing personal and social competences, enquiring minds and awareness of rights and obligations would be neither a satisfactory experience for primary children living in the here and now, nor an adequate preparation for what comes next – directly in education, or in life generally.

In preparing for 'life generally' in modern times, one faces the same challenge in approaches to teaching. The intuitive approach is attractive, and topics which are important for the socialisation of children ought surely to be dealt with as and when they arise, we may think. This is a modern viewpoint and it fits with ideas of how children truly learn. We can, however, ensure that important themes are followed through, and preparation for the future now merits a more planned and coordinated approach, perhaps against our inclination to work in the more intuitive and child-centred mode. Just as we ensure that mathematical processes are systematically dealt with by recording individual pupil's progression, rather than by constant formal class teaching, so we should increasingly have a basic list of Personal and Social Education topics of which every primary school child should have understanding, either through class teaching, through work with differing groups, or by individual methods. The need to have a planned checklist of essential themes is as important in preparation for adulthood as in Mathematics or language teaching.

How can we presume to select the best 'socialisation topics' when we are faced with the whole of human life and relationships? Family life shapes so much of the young child's approach to life, that it is difficult to select a necessary programme of Personal and Social Education (PSE) or whatever school curriculum title we use, without proper feelings of humility. We plunge confidently into the planning of Mathematics and language, but shy away from the personal programme. This is natural, but it is an attitude we must change, for schooling is now a major support for socialising in families, perhaps the only major support. Schools are guardians of educational standards in traditional subject areas, and increasingly they are the nervous guardians of society's mores. Where else beyond the family are personal attitudes discussed, human relationship knowledge provided, social habits encouraged, basic values proposed and models provided for children to shape their future? Does TV provide these things in competition with our schools, or should one be dubious of TV as society's teacher and setter of values? Can the churches or unions or workplaces or entertainment centres provide the answer to the preparation of children for their future?

There is a three sided approach to children's socialisation. The family itself has the major task, of course, though it appears to be less capable of doing this than in the past; schools then inevitably provide a major support for aspects of family life continuity; society, represented by the media, by law-makers, by authority, by workplaces and leisure settings, provides the third side, perhaps constructively, perhaps destructively. In construction terms the family provides the blueprint, schools help to shape the model, and society accepts or rejects it.

So the school has its socialising role whether we like it or not. The social influence of the teacher can be considerable, depending on the calibre of the teacher, and linked with the quality of leadership in the school, and with the teaching methods and the overt and hidden curriculum. A chief education officer used a memorable phrase some years ago, 'The hidden curriculum is the agenda for the 1980s'.

In attempting to coordinate the approach of the primary school staff to the personal and social education plan of their school, certain procedures appear to follow.

1. The effect of the school as an institution on the pupils must be studied and debated at depth by the whole staff. The aims and objectives must be simple, clear and manageable. Parents' and school managers' involvement in the actual debate is commendable, and at least the cooperation of adults other than the teachers is a high priority. The rituals of school movements between rooms, of assemblies, dining and tuckshop methods and playground arrangements should be studied for their social teaching as well as their convenience for staff. The pattern of staff meetings, of record keeping and of staff communication in academic and pastoral matters must be checked from the viewpoint of child development as well as administrative convenience. If we search our own adult memories of schools, the importance of analysing the institution for its effect on individuals becomes clearer, for our occasionally vivid memories can be positive or negative in their effect on our lives as we look back.

2. The school in its environment will be considered. Are there environmental habits, attitudes, values and events which require the consideration of the school in making its personal and social education outline plan. Are we preparing children for life in a particular setting, with such things as class structures, racial balance, and language and

leisure habits? Or are we preparing children for a different and mobile future in other parts of society and the country?
3. We then consider the preparation for life topics with which we are to be concerned. Some are obvious:
   Responsibility and care for others
   Family life strengths and values
   Safety in home and on roads
   Growth and development
   Understanding emotions, and so on.

Making the lists of topics is not difficult, and material from which schools could make selections follows. What is difficult is reducing the wide choice to an essential list, and to decide at what ages it will be appropriate, in what sequence and at what level. And we will also be considering which topics will fit into various projects, which will arise inevitably from children's interests, and which will have to be raised deliberately. What topics are essential and which are desirable for children's future habits, attitudes and values?

We have to provide information, we have to help children towards social and decision-making skills, offer encouragement in their understanding and true comprehension of PSE topics, and encourage and help them towards seeing their own values and responsibilities.

We are likely then to realise that what we are doing is reviewing the whole purpose of the school and of our lifelong teaching tasks! We probably also need to consider what we mean by 'normal', what would be an invasion of a family's privacy, and what are the limits of our ability to help. Professor Pring (1984) puts it well:

> At the more limited level of the school, there is clearly a need to examine the values which are often hidden in the unexamined methods of teaching, structures of authority, and modes of control, and yet which correlate so strongly with educational and behavioural outcomes. The moral atmosphere of the school or classroom seems to be the key element in translating thought into action and in ensuring the personal and moral growth of the individual pupil. In particular the classroom teacher might consider how he or she might (1) encourage greater mutual respect between teacher and pupil and between pupil and pupil; (2) create a climate of caring and fairness; (3) ensure a sense of achievement, rather than of failure, and of personal worth; (4) develop a habit of deliberation and reflective learning; (5) introduce systematic discussion of significant socio-moral issues; (6) approach learning co-operatively rather than competitively; (7) foster care for the

group and eventually the wider community rather than for self-interest; and (8) increase group responsibility for decisions taken.

4. Detailed management and professional tasks remain.
   (a) What division of work among staff may be necessary? While primary teachers can reasonably be expected to deal with most PSE topics, there may be value in exchanging classes, or groups of children, at times. An enthusiastic non-smoker may do better than a smoker on a tobacco topic, or perhaps the two could work and discuss this together with a larger group of pupils. One teacher may be less than comfortable with a particular section of the work, and an exchange may be helpful, while not permitting a total withdrawal by one teacher from the PSE and personal aspect of education.
   (b) What materials will be required? While resources are secondary in much PSE work, commercial curriculum materials or teacher-made materials will probably be prepared in advance. Pictures, cards with newspaper cuttings, questionnaires, fact cards and books can be aids to teaching and to discussion with children.
   (c) A pattern of visitors will be planned, not to come in as experts to take over sensitive parts of the curriculum (which is often an admission of teacher failure or cowardice?), but rather to be 'interviewed' by the pupils who will have prepared for the visit beforehand, and who will discuss it with their teacher afterwards. A policeman or a professional footballer could be interviewed by the children who are dealing with the topics of aggression and violence, or of leisure or, indeed, of authority?
   (d) Recording of the work done, to enable evaluation and change to be routinely arranged is of great importance, and is not always a characteristic of all primary school work. The school will be moving as a whole, with the efforts of all teachers interlinked year by year, class by class, topic by topic, and leading in a flexible and facilitating way towards an agreed set of aims and objectives in preparing children for a different future life, work and leisure. So the work which will be implicit in the curriculum, and which will be done in occasional special projects, by all staff, by selected staff, by a team approach and by reinforcement by visitors, will be a flexible but purposeful package.
   (e) The size of pupil groups will be considered. Most teaching and discussion will take place in classes of the normal size, and

smaller groups can talk together after an opening class presentation of some kind, returning to the full class and breaking off again into small groups as required. The purpose is to get children talking and thinking as well as listening; children live in families and have a considerable and pragmatic knowledge of adult life at times, and can contribute shrewder thoughts than we sometimes admit. Surely we can improve our ways of making children more articulate of their feelings, hopes and experience, in a way which is supportive, and without an invasion of individual or family privacy? Small groups are an important aid in this, and sometimes classes ought to be joined for some sessions, with a teacher taking small groups of six or eight in turn. Discussion techniques and a knowledge of group dynamics are not always as well understood as they should be in the profession of teaching, nor are they much considered in basic teacher training, which is strange and disappointing.

(f) Confidentiality needs to be discussed by the staff. If we are to encourage children towards greater articulation and thought on their development towards adolescence and adulthood in a challenging society, then they will talk about themselves and their families and community – they do now, in fact, in incidental ways. Teachers will need to prevent children from revealing too much of their families' secrets and successes and troubles, and sometimes we will need to counsel and talk with children individually rather than in class or groups. Teachers are competent to know the sensible limits of individual and family life discussion and how much ought and ought not to be revealed. What does the staff see as 'normal' family life, what is solely a family's business, and what is an invasion of privacy, in fact? The danger is that to be safe we avoid all mention of the personal and family life of a child, yet we may be the only adults who can listen in compassion and sympathy to a child's view of his or her home life. The question perhaps fines down to what is and is not appropriate in class and group discussion, for surely nothing is barred in a teacher's talk with an individual child?

The following summary of topics may be helpful to a school in reviewing the appropriate contents of a coordinated school PSE plan. Much work is being done already. What is missing that ought to be considered in the primary school curriculum in general? What is inappropriate?

It can be said that certain topics are difficult to find in some primary schools. Consideration of the following might be made:

Aggression, assertiveness, and violence
Mental illness
Sex education and sexuality
Drugs of all kinds, tobacco, alcohol, household and illegal drugs and chemicals
Bereavement
Safety in the home
First aid
Obesity and diet management
The handicapped
Prejudice
Happiness, perhaps?!

What we are trying to do is to work out a basic survival course of topics for children of primary school age. Which topics are appropriate for that child, that school, that area, and which are we avoiding or dealing with superficially, or concentrating on too much? What is the core of preparation for secondary school and adolescence? What habits, attitudes, values and knowledge are newly essential in the pupils' future adult life, and do they or do they not start in the primary school?

A checklist for work in Personal and Social Education

1. A possible general aim
   To help pupils to find information about human behaviour and to examine the habits and values which people have found lead to personal happiness and stability in our society.
2. Possible objectives of the teacher:
   (a) To inform the pupil about himself and his growing powers of mind and body.
   (b) To help the pupil develop stable relationships with others, accept other people and appreciate the value of tolerance.
   (c) To widen pupils' horizons to the problems of humanity and to awaken an awareness of responsibility towards neighbours and community.

(d) To encourage pupils to explore and appreciate other people's beliefs, while developing their own.
   (e) Occasionally to act as counsellor for individuals, recognising those who require special help.
3. Personal development
   (a) The body and how it works.
   (b) Reproduction and birth in the setting of family life and caring relationships.
   (c) The growth and development of babies and children.
   (d) Puberty.
4. The individual
   (a) Special advantages Man has over other animals.
   (b) Learning processes and memory.
   (c) Development of individual personalities.
   (d) Moods and emotions.
   (e) The influence of heredity and environment.
   (f) Self-control and cooperation as essentials for a civilised life.
   (g) Conscience and personal standards of responsibility.
   (h) How important is it to be an individual?
5. Personal behaviour
   Standards of personal behaviour with reference to the following:
      Exploitation of others;
      Bullying;
      Disobedience and rebellion against authority;
      Jealousy and vindictiveness;
      Shyness;
      Facing adversity;
      Fear;
      Desire for security;
      Conceit and possessiveness;
      Greed;
      Respect for others in the family and circle of friends;
      Codes of behaviour;
      Why do people behave badly?;
      Good manners and courtesy;
      Social responsibility in a community.
6. Personal and community health
   (a) Personal fitness and exercise.
   (b) Personal discipline and responsibility.
   (c) Personal hygiene and health habits.
   (d) Food and diet.

(e) Suitable clothing.
(f) Foot care and shoes.
(g) Dental health and fluoridation.
(h) Care of skin and hair.
(i) Care of eyes.
(j) Hearing.
(k) Dirt and danger in smoking.
(l) Common illnesses. Major diseases and community health.
(m) Handicaps.
(n) Alcohol and drugs education. Solvent abuse.
(o) Road safety.
(p) Home safety.
(q) Safety in outdoor pursuits.
(r) Elementary first aid.

7. Personal relationships
   (a) Need for affection, recognition and acceptance.
   (b) Self-understanding and knowing one's strengths and limitations.
   (c) Need to live and cooperate with others.
   (d) How do we behave towards people we dislike and like?
   (d) Loneliness in ourselves and others.
   (f) Making friends.
   (g) Recognising roles and attitudes, and the need to present oneself well to others.
   (h) Boy–girl relationships. Socially acceptable behaviour. Recognition of courtesy and respect.

8. Friendship
   (a) What is a friend? What is an acquaintance?
   (b) Discuss the meaning of true friendship – giving as well as taking.
   (c) What qualities do you expect in a friend?
   (d) What qualities do you have which make you a good friend?
   (e) Discuss changes in friendships of group members.
   (f) Friendships in groups, gangs and clubs.

9. Relationships with others
   (a) What is a group? Types of groups. The family group.
   (b) Unorganised groups. Mass thinking and mob law. Irrational behaviour in a crowd. Gang bravado and panic in crowds. Formation of public opinion.
   (c) Deviant groups. Minorities. 'Not our sort' – our reactions. Stereotyping.

(d) The handicapped and their needs.
(e) Class, racial and religious prejudices in relationships.
10. Sexual relations
    (a) Sex education and human biology.
    (b) Sexuality, attitudes and values.
    (c) Sex roles.
    (d) Love and affection.
    (e) Sexual behaviour and courtesy; mutual respect; exploitation and selfishness.
    (f) The effect of alcohol, group pressures and drugs on behaviour.
11. Family life
    (a) Growing up in the family – the importance of play for pre-school children. The family socialises children. The family as a sheltered environment.
    (b) Foster children, adopted children, only children.
    (c) What is family loyalty?
    (d) Parents' rules – understanding parents.
    (e) The family as a social institution. Family trees. Comparison of British family today with that of other cultures.
    (f) Extended and nuclear families.
    (g) Differences between social classes, religious denominations and countries.
    (h) 'Problem' families.
    (i) The elderly.
    (j) Are the traditional roles of men and women changing?
    (k) School and home cooperation.
    (l) Home making.
12. Marriage
    (a) Teenage and arranged marriages. Ideals of love. Child, adolescent and adult viewpoints. Differing cultures.
    (b) Commitment and companionship.
    (c) Rights and duties of wife and husband. Changing roles of men and women. Mothers at work.
    (d) Home making. Mortgages and hire purchase. Family and personal budgeting. Pocket money.
    (e) Divorce and separation. Living alone by choice.
13. Intolerance
    (a) Prejudice – how is it formed? Family background? Mass media? Stereotyping?
    (b) Sense of security of belonging to a group. Do we reject what is outside our group?

(c) Racial problems. Anti-racist attitudes.
(d) Amicable relationships at school, work or leisure, with people having different views on politics and religion.
(e) Jealousy, hatred, conceit, bullying.

14. Leisure
    (a) What is leisure?
    (b) Constructive and destructive uses of leisure.
    (c) Social obligations.
    (d) Rest and relaxation.
    (e) Boredom.
    (f) Laziness.
    (g) 'My time's my own.'
    (h) Local leisure facilities for the various age groups.
    (i) Individual and shared leisure activities.
    (j) Wasting time – has inactivity a value?
    (k) How does use of leisure make work for others?
    (l) Misuse – pornography, gambling, drunkenness.
    (m) Voluntary work.
    (n) Future happiness compared with present satisfaction.

15. Work and parents/older siblings
    (a) Working conditions of today and yesterday. Technological change and its consequences for the individual and society.
    (b) Problems of leaving home. Problems of living at home.
    (c) Careers for girls and married women. Equal rights legislation.
    (d) The value of further education and training. The problems of friends who ignore this and in the early years earn more money. Ambition.
    (e) Getting on with people at work. Understanding work discipline.
    (f) Rewards of standards of work – job satisfaction. Training.
    (g) 'Only mugs work.' Is work a good thing in itself? Economic incentives alone produce neither willing workers nor good craftsmanship.
    (h) The need for personal convictions and standards of one's own.

16. Authority
    (a) Imagine yourself in a position of authority. What difficulties might you encounter?
    (b) What is the basis of authority:
        Within home?
        Within the community?
    (c) Self-control, willpower and conscience are bases of authority.

A Coordinated Approach 67

(d) Why do authorities impose standards of behaviour?
(e) Young people and the Law. Age and legal status.
(f) Petty and organised crime. Delinquency. Vandalism.

17. Freedom
    (a) How important is freedom? How is it related to responsibilities?
    (b) The reasons for rules.
    (c) Does 'becoming an adult' depend only on size and age?
    (d) Discuss respect for other people and their ideas. Balance between 'my' freedom and 'their' freedom.
    (e) Behaviour with older people, parents, opposite sex, one's own friends.
    (f) Changing standards and values. Does absence of manners denote immaturity?
    (g) Why do people behave badly – insecurity, ignorance, fear, nervousness?
    (h) Is freedom a privilege or a right?

18. Environmental control and community care
    (a) Pollution of the environment: its causes, effects and methods of control – air, water, food and living conditions.
    (b) National Health Service and local health and welfare services.
    (c) School Health Service and local health and welfare services.
    (d) Social services, both voluntary and statutory: voluntary organisations, voluntary social service work by young people.
    (e) World health and welfare: WHO, FAO, UNESCO, UNICEF, Red Cross, Oxfam and other international organisations that deal with poverty and lack of education in developing countries. UN Charter.
    (f) Awareness and development of critical faculties. Creating a good environment. The development of critical awareness. Exploitation and manipulation by the mass media. Influence of film, radio, TV advertising, press and literature. Straight and crooked thinking.
    (g) The 'affluent society'. What is affluence? The development and problems of affluence. Possessions or people? Poverty in an affluent society. Gambling. Charity.

19. Social environment
    (a) Population growth, morality, disease, diet, medicine.
    (b) Responsibilities to society: cultivating responsible attitudes.
    (c) Conservation of the environment: the individual's contribution as well as the efforts of authority and industry. Conflicting needs and demands.

(d) Disease: history, infectious and non-infectious, control, common vectors of infection. Health hazards both in kinds of disease and precautions against them.
(e) Chemical substances used in medicine: purpose of drugs in medication, dangers of self-medication, misuse and abuse of drugs and the dangers arising.
(f) Addictive practices: alcohol, tobacco, and other drugs. Gambling, physical and social effects. Social attitudes.
(g) What is a good neighbour? Samaritans, Marriage Guidance Councils, Alcoholics Anonymous, NSPCC, RSPCA.

20. The environment affects everyone
Man as a technologist and as a farmer. World demands for energy. General development of machines and transport. Individuals and the state. Conservation movements. Urban problems. Effects of pollution. The future evolution of humans. World problems: population, hunger, poverty, disease, housing, apathy. Immigration and emigration. Ideologies and religions. Nationalism and internationalism. The need for 'communities'.

21. Morality and human behaviour
    (a) Qualities men and women admire in others:
        Love
        Patience
        Faithfulness
        Sacrifice
        Courage
        Faith
        Qualities men and women do not admire in others:
        Hatred
        Prejudice
        Greed
        Revenge
        Sloth
        Cowardice
    (b) How do we decide what behaviour is right?
    (c) Who should make the rules? Church, State?
    (d) What moral codes do we follow?
    (e) What does it mean to be human?
        What are we for?
        Religious and non-religious views.
    (f) Does every human being have problems?

(g) Why is there uncertainty?
Overthrow of traditional value systems based on authority; religious authority; authority of moral codes.
22. Health education as a general theme
   (a) Personal health
   Personal hygiene
   Fitness: exercise and rest
   Personal appearance
   Dental health
   Internal working of the body
   Care of feet, ears, hair
   Nutrition
   Standards of personal behaviour
   Growth and development
   Understanding ourselves
   Decision making
   Personal values and attitudes
   Responsibility
   (b) Community health
   Diseases
   Alcohol and alcoholism
   Drug taking
   Smoking
   Health services and public health
   Medicines and common illnesses
   Handicapped people
   First aid
   The elderly
   Mental health and stress
   World health
   Food hygiene
   Noise
   Multi-cultural aspects of health
   (c) Health and the environment
   Road safety
   Safety in the home
   Safety at work
   Water safety
   Conservation
   Pollution

Law and order
Mass media and its effect
Consumer education
(d) Family life and personal relationships.
Feelings and needs of other people
Tolerance
Friendship
Anxiety and stress
Life within families
Care of young children
Home making.

Conclusion

The approaches suggested in this chapter can easily be misunderstood, and certain points must be emphasised. It is not being suggested that the checklist is a recommended curriculum – it would occupy the whole of a primary school career! It is literally a checklist to enable teachers, parents and pupils mutually to discuss what they feel are useful topics in preparing for adolescence and adulthood, and for life in a secondary school as well.

Hamblin (1986), writing of secondary schools, warns vigorously and correctly of the futility of foisting ready-made 'pastoral programmes' on schools. The same applies to the planning of primary school pastoral programmes. While the need to have more planning and purpose in such programmes is increasingly seen – the recent debate about how we can best help children sexually abused, for example – each school will have the task of negotiating such programmes, and of constantly evaluating and developing the work. We also need to remember that the skills of observing, caring, discussing, evaluating, clarifying, thinking logically, and so on, are the longer lasting aims, and are more important than the details of facts within topics.

References

BOARD OF EDUCATION (1931) *The Primary School* (The Hadow Report) (London: HMSO).
BLACKIE, J. (1969) *Inside the Primary School* (London: HMSO).
CENTRAL ADVISORY COUNCIL FOR EDUCATION (England)

(1967) *Children and their Primary Schools* (The Plowden Report), (London: HMSO).

COWLEY, J., DAVID, K., and WILLIAMS, T. (1981) *Health Education in Schools* (London: Harper and Row).

DAVID, K. and WILLIAMS, T. (1987) *Health Education in Schools* (London: Harper and Row).

HAMBLIN, D. (1986) *A Pastoral Programme* (London: Basil Blackwell).

JOHNSON, V. (1981) 'Health Education in Primary Schools' in *Health Education in Schools* Eds: Cowley, J., David, K., Williams, T. (London: Harper & Row).

PRING, R. (1984) *Personal and Social Education in the Curriculum* (London: Hodder and Stoughton).

Chapter 4

School Routines and Administration

Jim Abraham

> There are many different things that could be done in schools; there are so many things that are done. How are we to decide what should be done? It is particularly important for British teachers to ask this question for our system is noteworthy for its relative lack of central direction. (Schools Council, 1975)

Education is not a matter of throwing children into life at the deep end. We select experiences which we believe will be of benefit to children and we try to help them make sense of them. Most children have already learned a great deal from their pre-school experiences of the world, and looked at analytically, many of the skills acquired before school are enormously complex; skills such as walking and talking. Yet, despite the fact that the vast majority of children learn these skills with no formal training and so demonstrate their natural talent for learning, schools are still thought to be necessary; it is interesting to note that many schools claim that teaching their pupils 'how to learn' is one of their main objectives. Perhaps the most fundamental reason for the existence of schools is that society makes a clear distinction between the knowledge and skills acquired 'naturally' through 'experience' and that which is transmitted in formal, intentionally didactic contexts with large groups of children.

The value of routines and rituals

Reading through the 'statement(s) of aims' that are now required of all primary schools, one is likely to be struck by the degree of similarity. It would seem that the majority of schools share remarkably similar ideas about the aims of primary education. Equally remarkable, though, is the degree of difference that occurs in the short step from aims to the realities of classroom practice. It must be said, however, that in all too many cases even the most articulate teacher would have difficulty justifying some practices in relation to the expressed aims of the teachers who use them. Given that our education system allows for difference (and long may it be so), there are certain routines and rituals that can be common to all schools. Just as the regular routines of family life can help to provide an element of stability, so can the routines and rituals of school life. They can help to construct a framework within which clear roles and identities are readily established and maintained. Since constant change is what we expect of our pupils it is essential to provide a secure base from which to grow. There are times when considerable changes are expected of teachers; they too need a secure base which clearly defines their professional roles and responsibilities.

These routines and rituals encompass many facets of school life, such as the daily completion of the attendance register, the timing and form of the Assembly, clear understanding about the standards of behaviour expected in the playground, the maintenance of pupils' records and clear and concise statements about duty rosters. It is all too easy to take for granted the extensive and detailed knowledge of such things that the long-serving teacher accumulates, and thus to overlook the stresses that can be caused to new members of staff who will be totally at a loss as to what is expected of them. With no clear statements to inform a new member of staff it is hardly surprising that it can take as long as two years for a teacher to feel fully part of the school. This can be of no advantage to either teacher or school.

The purpose of this chapter is to provide examples of the way that some routines can be defined and given structure.

Obligations and procedures

Our education system has become enormously complex. It is often claimed that the responsibilities of Heads and teachers have widened dramatically in recent years. In fact, it is true that there are a surprising number of obligations on Heads and teachers, some of which are determined by law. A *Head's Legal Guide* (Howarth, 1984) has been compiled to delineate some of these obligations, and the contents are listed in Figure 1.

Taken as a whole they describe procedures and routines by which a school can fulfil its statutory obligations. Some of these procedures and

PART I — STRUCTURE AND ADMINISTRATION OF EDUCATION

A. Management structure of education
Central Government
Local Education Authority
Diocesan Education Committee
Governing Bodies
Ancillary Services
Accountability of Schools
The Stages of Education

B. Management structures within the school
The Head
Deputy Head
Senior Teachers
Heads of Department
Other Scale Posts
Administrative Staff
Support Staff
Maintenance Staff
Outside Contractors

C. Accountability and auditing
District Auditor
Internal Audit

D. Other internal administrative procedures
Record Keeping
School Day, Term, Year
Admission of Pupils
School Leaving Dates
Information for Parents

E. Management of the curriculum

F. Reorganisation of schools

PART II — EMPLOYMENT OF STAFF

A. Appointments
Definition of Types of Appointment
Appointment of Staff

B. Terms and conditions of employment
Contract of Employment
Holidays and Leave
Industrial Relations/Employee's Rights
Disciplinary Procedures
Termination of Employment
Disqualification of Teachers
Redeployment
Early Retirement
Industrial Action
Injuries Suffered by Teachers

PART III — DAY TO DAY RUNNING OF THE SCHOOL

A. Health, safety and welfare
Health and Safety at Work etc. Act
Responsibility for Security/Safety of Premises
Health
Welfare Services
Environmental Requirements
Fire
High Risk Areas

B. Daily routine
Travel
The School Day
Religious Education
Rules

C. Teachers 'in the course of duty'
In Loco Parentis
Powers, Duties and Responsibilities
Negligence
Powers and Duties Combined
Supervision
Special Issues
Testimonials and Confidential Reports

D. Children out of the classroom
Employment of Children
Part-time Employment of Pupils
Work Experience
Children in Trouble
Problems Caused by Marital Breakdown

E. Parents' duties and rights
Duty to Secure Education for their Child
Parental Choice of School
Parents' Rights under the 1981 Act
  (Special Education)

F. Schools and external agencies
Schools and Solicitors
Schools and the Courts
Schools and the Police
Schools and Juvenile Bureaux
Schools and Education Support Services
Schools and N.S.P.C.C.
Home/School Associations

Relationships with the Press
External Examination Entries

G. Reports
Teachers
Pupils
Confidentiality
Data Protection

H. Insurance and finance
Insurance
Tax
Financial Procedures within the School

PART IV EXTERNAL DEALINGS

A. School journeys and educational visits
Preparation
Organisation
Approval
Parents Meetings
Financial Arrangements
Pupil–Teacher Ratios
Parental Consent
Letters of Indemnity
Taking a Party Overseas
Passports
HM Customs

B. School minibuses and coaches
Putting a Minibus on the Road
Using a Minibus on the Road
Operator's Liability
Taking a Minibus Abroad to E.C. Countries

C. Use of premises for other than normal Teaching purposes
Licencing
Use of School by Outside Bodies

D. Copyright

PART V SPECIAL EDUCATION

A. Assessment of Special Educational Needs
An introduction to the concept of special education
The Warnock Report 1978
Abolition of statutory categorisation of handicap
Multi-professional assessment of needs
Teacher training

B. Integration
The process of integration
Variety and range of special educational provision
The role of the ordinary school
Education Act 1981; conditions to be met when deciding placement in ordinary school(s)

C. Education Act 1981 in Operation
Stages of Assessment
Reviews under the Act
A suggested checklist for pupils with special educational needs
A designated unit within an ordinary school
A Head's sources of guidance in relation to special educational needs

D. Microcomputers and Special Educational Needs
Curriculum implications
The contribution of the microcomputer
Special educational needs
Word processors
Special education micro electronic resource centres

Fig. 1

routines are further defined in the forms and documents relating to them. Registers are a good example: the correct procedure for the maintenance of the attendance register is defined by instructions from the LEA and by the form of the register itself. The Head and teacher can be sure that their personal obligations in respect of attendance registers will have been fulfilled if they have followed the instructions and filled in the register accurately. Any departure from the established procedure could result in complications, as occurred recently when an LEA took a parent to court for failing to secure an adequate education for his child by not ensuring regular attendance at school. The attendance register was submitted as evidence, but was ruled inadmissible because entries had been made in pencil, contrary to LEA instructions.

Monitoring children's progress

There are, however, areas of responsibility which are much less clearly defined, or, in some cases, not defined at all. These, in the main, relate to the content and management of the curriculum.

The rapidly changing demands that our modern society makes on the education service, especially in the context of what is often described as a 'knowledge explosion', have resulted in an approach to the curriculum in which there is a definite emphasis on the needs of the individual child in relation to his dynamic role in the learning process rather than on content. This 'new' approach is very demanding of teachers. The sheer complexity of a classroom catering for the needs of 30 or more individuals invariably results in compromises. Too many compromises can lead to dissatisfaction and frustration for both children and teachers. The teacher requires the support of 'control systems' which will help him to maintain a balance between what is intended and what is practicable. The 'control system' in this sense is an organisational device which enables the teacher to monitor both the child's progress and his own attempts to help. Traditional methods of record keeping either plot a child's place in a textbook or scheme, or provide comment so detailed that the next teacher can never find time to absorb it. The result is that many teachers openly admit that they prefer not to look at children's records but would rather wait until they can form their own judgements about ability and progress. There are alternatives.

A pre-school profile

In our present system most schools know very little about their reception infants when they first arrive at school. Only in exceptional circumstances will any information be officially relayed to the school before the child arrives, and this will nearly always be of a strictly medical nature. The extensive knowledge that the parents have of their own children is rarely tapped by schools, and where it is it is often thought to be unreliable. However, the experience of the medical profession suggests that with careful questioning in an unthreatening situation the majority of parents can be both accurate and perceptive in describing their child's development.

The home visit of the health visitor on the occasion of the child's third birthday can provide an opportunity for the school to establish its first contact with the child and parents. The following questionnaire (Figure 2) has been designed to provide the health visitor with the information she will need, and the reception teacher with the information that will help her prepare for the needs of individuals and the reception class as a whole. It can also point to the need for intervention before the child is due to start school. It might become clear, for example, that a large number of the three-year-olds are lacking in a particular area of development and that their needs might best be met before school by the establishment of a nursery or pre-school playgroup. Furthermore, the items in the questionnaire may help to inform parents of the kinds of experience and opportunity that they should try to provide for their children. The nature of this early contact with the parents will hopefully establish the beginnings of the kind of partnership which is so necessary to the success of early schooling.

It is possible to use a pre-school profile such as this to investigate the feasibility of identifying children who, because of certain factors in their development, may be at risk of educational failure by the time they are seven. If an investigation of this sort were to prove successful it should then be possible to plan intervention programmes both before and during early schooling that might help to prevent that failure. If for some reason a pre-school profile is not practicable, there are other instruments available which are aimed at identifying children at the age of six years who may, without specialist intervention, be at risk of educational failure by the time they are seven. They are usually designed to be completed by the reception teacher, based upon her observations of the child's behaviour over a period of time. The instrument that follows (Figure 3) is an adaptation of the Rhode Island Profile of Early Learning Behaviour

A Pre-school Profile

(Section from a six-part profile completed by parents on or near the child's third birthday)

A

My Child..........	Rarely	Often
1. Puts on and takes off his/her clothing.........		
coat or jacket		
jumper or pullover		
dress or shirt		
socks or tights		
shoes on correct feet		
2. Fastens his/her clothing		
zips		
buttons		
3. Drinks without spilling		
from a cup		
from a glass		
4. Feeds him/herself		
with a spoon		
with a spoon and a fork in each hand		
with a knife and a fork in each hand		

	Not Yet	Needs a lot of help	Needs a little help	Needs no help
5. Washes his/her hands and face without help				
6. Goes to the toilet by him/herself				
7. Tells what he/she wants or needs				

School Routines and Administration 79

B

My Child . . . .

	Not Yet	Occasionally	Often	Usually
1. Takes turns with other children.				
2. Takes good care of things he/she uses.				
3. Remembers rules of games he/she plays.				
4. Finishes a game if he/she is losing.				

	Usually	Often	Occasionally	Seldom
5. Fights or cries when he/she doesn't get his/her way.				
6. Bullies other children.				
7. Is bullied by other children.				

C

My Child . . . .

	Not Yet	Just Beginning	Well	Very Well
1. Jumps off steps with both feet together.				
2. Skips on alternate feet.				
3. Hops on one foot.				
4. Goes up and down stairs.				
5. Colours pictures within lines.				
6. Builds with blocks.				
7. Enjoys fitting things together: puzzles, construction sets etc.				

8. Plays with a ball . . .

	Rarely	Often
throws it		
bounces it		
catches it		

Fig. 2

SCHOOL:

Name _____ Sex _____ Age _____
Date of Admission _____ Date of Birth _____

	Column	Means
INSTRUCTIONS	1	Always
For each item on the Checklist tick the appropriate	2	Frequently
column	3	Occasionally
IF UNSURE ABOUT ANY ITEM LEAVE IT BLANK	4	Rarely
	5	Never

Part 1

			1	2	3	4	5
A	1	Gives appearance of being tense					
	2	Unable to focus on task at hand					
	3	Tends to be discouraged and gives up easily					
	4	Cries easily and is unable to take reprimands					
	5	Tends to avoid group activities					
	6	Shows no concern for younger siblings or sympathy for playmates in distress					
	7	Fails to understand taking turns and being cooperative					
B	8	Bumps into objects					
	9	Trips over self					
C	10	Has difficulty using a pair of scissors					
	11	Has difficulty pasting					
	12	Has difficulty hopping					
	13	Has difficulty catching a ball					
	14	Has difficulty buttoning buttons					
	15	Has difficulty threading wooden beads					
D	16	Has difficulty sitting still					
	17	Has difficulty standing still					
	18	Has a short attention span					
	19	Is easily distracted from task assigned or task immediately at hand					
		Sub-totals					

PART 1 TOTAL ☐

Part 2

			1	2	3	4	5
	20	Has difficulty repeating four numbers					
	21	Has difficulty understanding instructions					
E	22	Has difficulty with names of letters/numbers					
	23	Has difficulty recalling events of the previous day					
	24	Has difficulty retelling a simple story					
	25	Has difficulty colouring within lines					
	26	Has difficulty following between lines					
	27	Has difficulty copying triangle and square accurately					
	28	Has difficulty constructing a house from a rectangle and triangle					
F	29	Work varies in quality					
	30	Work is untidy					
	31	Work has many errors					
	32	When copying, mirrors or reverses letters/numbers					
	33	In free writing, mirrors or reverses letters/numbers					
	34	Has difficulty arranging five objects in order of size					
	35	Has difficulty in building three steps with six cubes from a model					
G	36	Is unable to string beads to an ordered pattern					
	37	Runs words together in copying					
	38	Omits or substitutes letters or words or numbers in copying					
	39	Has difficulty repeating matching numbers to objects up to five					
	40	Has difficulty naming four colours					
H	41	Has difficulty matching eight colours to colours					
	42	Has difficulty completing assignments in allotted time					
	43	Has difficulty remembering daily routine					
	44	Has difficulty remembering serial lists or picture pairs					
		Sub-totals					

PART 1 TOTAL ☐

PART 2 TOTAL ☐

OVERALL TOTAL (PARTS 1 & 2) ☐

Fig. 3

82 *The Caring Role of the Primary School*

INFANT RATING SCALE *Level 2* G. A. Lindsay

Name ....
School/Class ....
Date of rating ....
Date of birth ....
Chronological age ....

Notes: This version of the Infant Rating Scale is suitable for children of about 7–7½ years of age.

The detailed instructions should be read before the Scale is used (see page 2 of the Manual).

Once the Scale has been completed, the results should be transferred to the Profile/Record sheet.

LANGUAGE/EDUCATION

(i) Expressive Language

(a) Articulation
5	4	3	2	1
Excellent articulation; very rarely makes an error	Good articulation; occasional errors	Satisfactory	Many words mispronounced	Poor articulation; difficult to understand or does not talk; marked speech defect

(b) Vocabulary
5	4	3	2	1
Excellent vocabulary; uses precise words to convey thoughts; uses abstract words with ease and understanding	Uses many descriptive words and phrases	Satisfactory	Limited vocabulary; precise descriptive words only rarely used; descriptions tend to be vague because of lack of vocabulary	Very limited vocabulary; uses very few abstract words

(c) Sentence Construction
5	4	3	2	1
Always or nearly always uses grammatically correct sentences; uses all parts of speech correctly; sentences may have several sub-clauses	Few grammatical errors; uses long sentences with sub-clauses	Satisfactory	Uses incomplete sentences; longer utterances are usually strings of statements joined by conjunctions (e.g. 'and I went out and I had a game and I ...')	Often uses incomplete sentences with many grammatical errors; short utterances are common

(d) Expression
5	4	3	2	1
Excellent ability to recount stories and relate ideas in a logical manner. Stories show well developed imagination and richness of thought	Good recall of stories; generally uses a logical sequence to recount events	Satisfactory	Has difficulty relating a story in a logical sequence, except with teacher's help	Stories and news, etc., are poorly recounted with confusion of sequence of events; much help required to produce comprehensible story

Level 2 of the INFANT RATING SCALE covers the following areas: LANGUAGE/EDUCATION – Articulation, Vocabulary, Sentence Construction, Expression, Comprehension of Instructions, Understanding of Words, Memory for Oral Information, Writing-Content, Spelling, Reading, Number; FINE MOTOR SKILLS – Fine Coordination, Drawing; BEHAVIOUR – Temperament, Attitude to Teacher, Kindness to Peers, Concentration & Ability to Organise, Approach to Learning, Attention & Distractibility; SOCIAL INTEGRATION – Participation in Class Activity, Acceptance by Peers, Desire to Mix; GENERAL DEVELOPMENT – Gross Motor Skills (e.g. running, climbing), Response to New Situations, Level of Concern Felt.

Fig. 4

(Novack, et al., 1972) and is currently in use in all Gloucestershire primary schools. It was developed by a working party consisting of experienced head teachers, advisors, an educational psychologist, and a Senior Medical Officer over a period of two years. The classroom teacher's observations are translated into scores from which it is possible to predict the degree to which the child may be considered to be 'at risk'. When an instrument of this kind has been rigorously validated, as is the case with the Rhode Island Scale, the information can be used by an authority as the basis for the allocation of its resources for 'children with special educational needs'.

Continuous monitoring through the infant years

The average infant classroom is a hive of every imaginable activity. The infant teacher needs to be a master of organisation. It is neither practicable nor necessary in this situation to catalogue the individual child's every activity. The aim of monitoring is to describe the progress of the child in a comprehensive and meaningful way which lends itself to either detailed or more general analysis. A rating scale, such as Lindsay's (1981) *Infant Rating Scale* (Figure 4), can fulfil this aim and at the same time be very easy to administer.

Rating scales are criterion referenced, but do not require specific tests to determine the child's capability or stage of development. Unlike traditional tests, rating scales do not sample behaviour or performance at one point in time, but rather require the teacher to observe the child over a long period. Since the scale requires the teacher to look at a wide range of the behavioural factors which have been found to be significant to educational progress, its use will help to prevent the possibility of overlooking them.

In order that the information from the rating scale is readily accessible it can also be represented in a graphical form (Figure 5). In this way strengths and weaknesses are immediately apparent. Individual strengths or weaknesses may not be significant, whereas in combination they may well be. This can only be determined by reference to the norms that have been established for the scale. The resultant profile gives a very clear picture of the significance of particular combinations of strengths or weaknesses and therefore the degree of concern that needs to be shown. (It is possible to use the school's computer to help in the production of these statistical profiles so that a complete profile can be returned in less than three minutes.)

84 The Caring Role of the Primary School

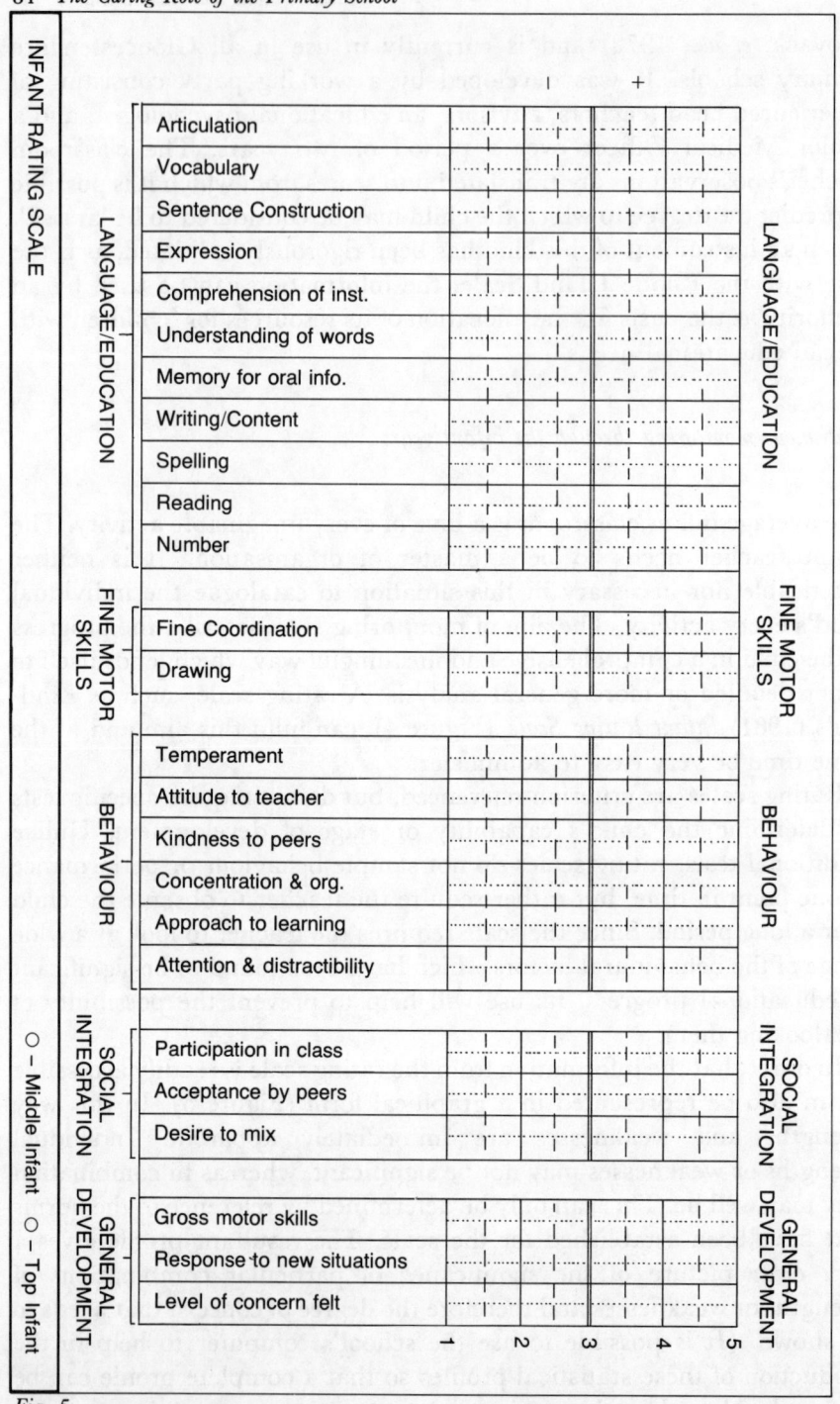

INFANT RATING SCALE			−		+		
LANGUAGE/EDUCATION	Articulation						
	Vocabulary						
	Sentence Construction						
	Expression						
	Comprehension of inst.						
	Understanding of words						
	Memory for oral info.						
	Writing/Content						
	Spelling						
	Reading						
	Number						
FINE MOTOR SKILLS	Fine Coordination						
	Drawing						
BEHAVIOUR	Temperament						
	Attitude to teacher						
	Kindness to peers						
	Concentration & org.						
	Approach to learning						
	Attention & distractibility						
SOCIAL INTEGRATION	Participation in class						
	Acceptance by peers						
	Desire to mix						
GENERAL DEVELOPMENT	Gross motor skills						
	Response to new situations						
	Level of concern felt						
		1	2	3	4	5	

O – Middle Infant   O – Top Infant

Fig. 5

When teachers have become familiar with a rating scale it is a relatively easy matter, though time consuming in the initial stages, to organise the school's resources to enable rapid response to particular types or combinations of difficulty.

Continuous monitoring through the junior years

Rating scales have the same advantages for teachers of junior age children. The items on the junior scale may differ from the infant scale although there will be many similarities. Where both infant and junior teachers are using similar scales the information passing between them can be far more meaningful and useful than is often the case. A graphical representation of the results not only helps interpretation but can make possible comparisons to the results of the objective, point-in-time tests with which most schools are likely to be more familiar.

There are basically two types of such tests: norm-referenced and criterion-referenced. Norm-referenced tests can tell the teacher where an individual child stands in relation to other children of the same age. Criterion-referenced tests measure the individual's performance against a specified set of skills or objectives. Both types are valuable, but it is important to establish whether the test in question is measuring achievement or capability. As every teacher knows, they can sometimes be very different. Careful consideration should be given to the adoption of any test. There are many norm-referenced tests available which will certainly produce interesting statistics but have little or no further value. The experienced teacher will also wish to satisfy himself that the questions in criterion-referenced tests are, in fact, measuring the defined criteria. There are occasions when the relationship between the two seems somewhat tenuous.

The most useful tests are those that measure the widest range of either achievement or ability with a minimum of writing required. A multiple-choice format is ideal since it usually requires no writing at all and, therefore, does not disadvantage the child who writes very slowly. And, since the answers will usually include several possibilities, the child with a history of reading difficulty seems also to be less disadvantaged than with a more traditional type of test.

The results of tests of this type can be useful at several levels. For the classroom teacher they can indicate whether a child is continuing to make satisfactory progress. As with rating scales, they identify areas of strength and weakness. If a number of children in the class have failed to make satisfactory progress in the same areas, it may be reasonable to assume that the teaching is in some way at fault. When discussing children's progress with their parents it is important to be able to give a clear indication of the standard achieved relative to national standards. Some published tests have been shown to predict, to a reasonable degree, future performance in public examinations. This can be helpful to parents when considering secondary school placement. For the head teacher concerned to assess the effectiveness of different schemes, teaching styles and methods of organisation, the results of objective tests can be a very valuable source of 'evidence'. However, tests must never be regarded as ends in themselves, nor must the information they provide be regarded as absolute. Test results are merely pieces in the jigsaw puzzle. Sometimes they give important clues and help to clarify the overall picture while at other times they seem of little value. They should always be viewed with caution and always need to be interpreted by a teacher.

Organising resources to meet individual need

If the resources of a school are not sufficiently well organised some of the needs of many individual children will not be met. The ideal is to establish a system which will allow a rapid, if not immediate, response to the perception of a need. What follows is a description of just such a system for the teaching of Mathematics. It has been in operation in one large Gloucestershire primary school for over three years.

The Mathematics scheme at the heart of the teaching programme has been very carefully structured in terms of its conceptual content (*Holt School Mathematics*, Nicholls *et al.*, 1978). It is organised on a spiral basis with central themes being returned to at ever-deepening levels. The children's work programmes are divided into three levels:

Level 1 is a 'minimum course' for children of lower than average ability,
Level 2 is an 'average course' for children of average ability, and
Level 3 is an 'enriched average course' for children of above average ability.

The central themes are present in each 'course' but at different levels of complexity.

When a child is ready to start a new 'course' he will complete a criterion-referenced test related to the conceptual content of the new 'course'. It is a multiple-choice type test and when complete is ready for diagnostic marking by computer. The child will identify himself to the

DIAGNOSTIC/CHAPTER TEST RESULTS	
TEST NUMBER 1310	DATE 01/16/86 STUDENT: MATTHEW MATTIX STUDENT 9990J2
OBJECTIVE MASTERY % = 66	
NUMBER OF OBJECTIVES TESTED 10	NUMBER OF ITEMS TESTED 27
NUMBER OF OBJECTIVES MASTERED 3	NUMBER OF ITEMS CORRECT 7
PERCENT MASTERED 30	TEST SCORE % = 25

OBJECTIVES NOT MASTERED
    PRESCRIPTION/ASSIGNMENT

13085 DIVIDE MULTIPLES OF 10 AND 100 (A)
       T238–239 PE339 WB100

13087 DIVIDE 2-DIGIT NUMBER NO REMAINDER (B)
       T246–249 PE340 WB103 104

13088 DIVIDE 2-DIGIT NUMBER REMAINDER (B)
       T250–251 WB105

13091 DIVIDE 3-DIGIT NUMBER QUOT > 100 W/WO REMAINDER (C)
       T258–259 PE340 WB108

13744 ADD HOURS AND MINUTES (D)
       T262–263 WB109

13607 SOLVE WORD PROBLEMS / (E)
       T261 PE345

13903 NOW DO THESE
       T240 245 256 257 260 261

COPYRIGHT (C) 1982 BY HOLT, RINEHART AND WINSTON, PUBLISHERS/ENI.

Fig. 6

OBJECTIVE GROUPING REPORT			
JW MR WALKER	YEAR J2	ARTHUR DYE	
MATHEMATICS	CLASS 200	01/16/86	

13004 IDENTIFY PLACE VALUE OF A DIGIT TO 999 (D)
STUDENTS WHO HAVE NOT MASTERED OBJ 13004 ARE:

		TEACHER PLANNING SCHEDULE	
STUDENT	NAME	GROUP	INDIVIDUAL
999000	ANDERSON JULIE	_____	_____
5840J2	ANDJELIC JOVAN	_____	_____
621000	BARNES IAN	_____	_____
5970J2	BEST LAURA	_____	_____
805000	GRIFFITHS GEMMA	_____	_____
796000	WADWORTH CAROLINE	_____	_____

COPYRIGHT (C) 1982 BY HOLT, RINEHART AND WINSTON, PUBLISHERS/ENI.

Fig. 7

computer and type in the number of the test to be marked. He then types in each of his answers, a maximum of 36. The computer will complete the diagnostic marking almost immediately and will respond with a printout (Figure 6) of the results indicating the number and percentage of answers correct, and the number of 'concepts mastered'. This information heads a sheet, including the child's name and class, which details a work programme tailored to the child's understanding and attainment as indicated by the test. The teacher confirms that the programme is appropriate and the child starts work.

The test results are recorded by the computer and can be used to generate a progress report between dates specified by the teacher. Since the records of all the children are held, the teacher can instruct the computer to list the names of all children who have 'failed' on a specific concept (Figure 7). This is clearly useful for group teaching.

Manual diagnostic marking of the tests is both time consuming and tedious. The use of a computer releases the teacher to help the child at the threshold of his difficulty and not at some later stage when the child is not present to explain his thinking. Furthermore, the needs of the able, fast-working child need not make undue demands on the teacher. The able child need not, therefore, wait for the teacher's attention in order to progress.

This is a very brief overview of a management or 'control' system currently in use in one large primary school. Its main feature is that it allows each pupil to find his own pathway to understanding. A number of different experiences are made available to the child by the expertise of the teacher, and each will require the child's active participation. The character and detail of these experiences may well, of necessity, differ markedly from child to child. Some compromises will be inevitable. Efficient 'control' systems of the kind described will help to minimise those compromises because the individual needs of individual children are more readily perceived and understood in relation to the process of learning and development and the resources available to the child.

The following case studies may help to show how this can be achieved in other areas.

CASE STUDY NO. 1: SARAH AINSLEY

The Junior Rating Scale graphical profile for Sarah Ainsley (Figure 8) indicates quite clearly that Sarah has difficulty in a number of areas. The relative significance of the difficulties is more apparent from the computer-generated statistical profile (Figure 9). The Language/

90 *The Caring Role of the Primary School*

JUNIOR RATING SCALE — SARAH AINSLEY			
LANGUAGE	Oral	Expression	
		Vocabulary	
		Comprehension of instructions	
		Understanding of words	
		Memory for oral info.	
	Written	Content	
		Spelling	
		Sentence construction	
	Reading	Reading Level	
		Attitude to Reading	
	Maths	Number	
		Problem solving	
MOTOR SKILLS		Fine coordination	
		Gross motor skills	
BEHAVIOUR		Temperament	
		Attitude to teacher	
		Approach to learning	
		Attention & distractibility	
SOCIAL INTEGRATION		Participation in class act.	
		Relationships with peers	
GENERAL DEVELOPMENT		Response to new situations	
		General assess. of maturity	
		Creativity	
		Level of concern felt	

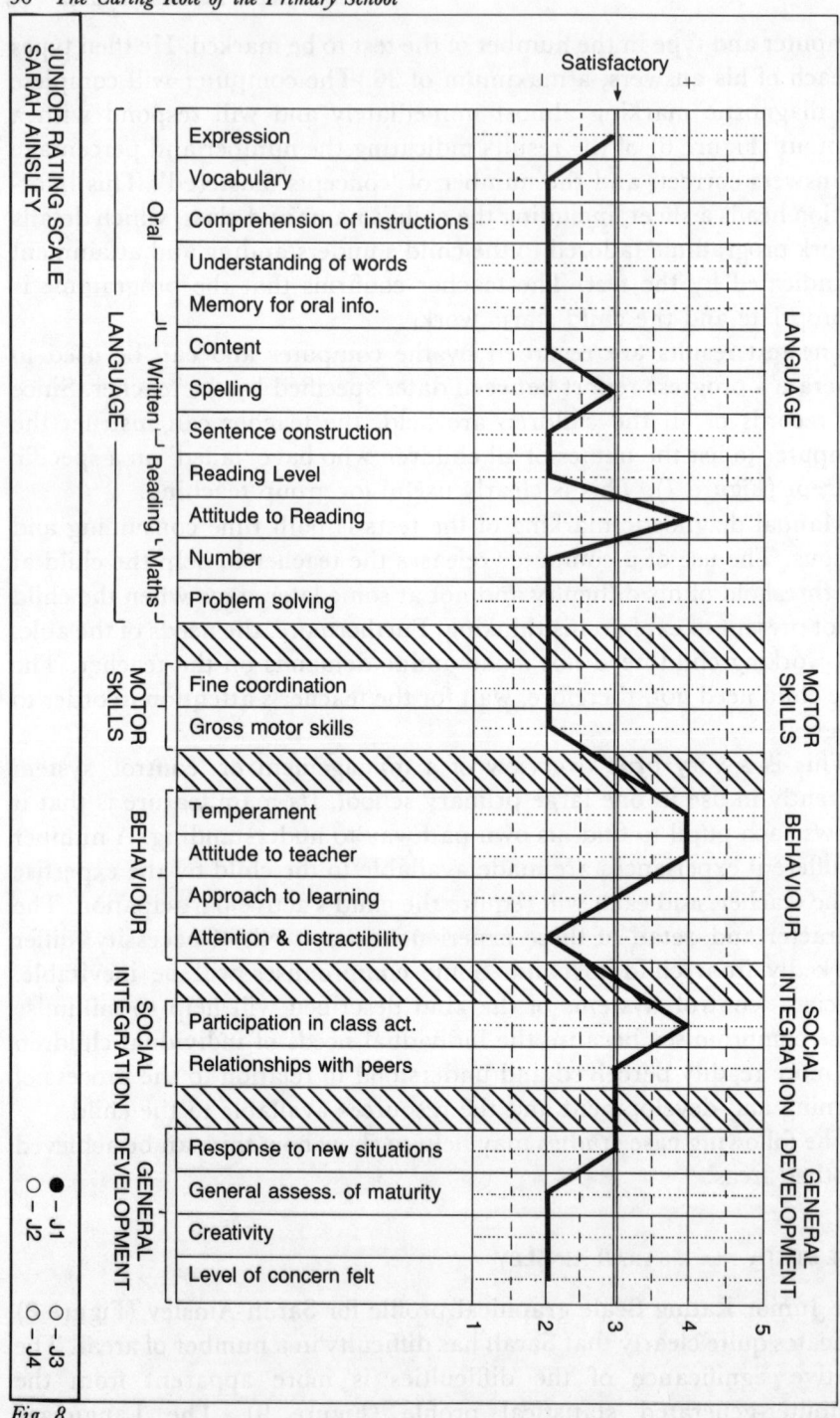

Satisfactory ↓ (scale 1–5)

● – J1
○ – J2
○ – J3
○ – J4

Fig. 8

| **JUNIOR RATING SCALE** | | | | **PROFILE/RECORD** | |

NAME OF CHILD: SARAH AINSLEY DATE OF BIRTH: 13/04/77
SCHOOL/YEAR GROUP: ARTHUR DYE PRIMARY/J1 AGE: 8 YRS. 2 MTHS.
RATED BY: MRS. STAMP DATE OF RATING: 15/06/85

	RAW SCORE	% OF CHILDREN RATED			SUBSCALE	
		SAME	LOWER	HIGHER	SCORE	%ILE
EXPRESSION	3	41	14	45		
VOCABULARY	2	16	2	82		
COMPREHENSION OF INSTRUCTIONS	2	15	3	82		
UNDERSTANDING OF WORDS	2	12	2	86		
MEMORY FOR ORAL INFORMATION	2	12	2	86		
CONTENT	2	21	7	72		
SPELLING	3	40	27	34		
SENTENCE CONSTRUCTION	2	23	5	72		
READING LEVEL	2	12	5	83		
ATTITUDE TO READING	4	36	50	14		
NUMBER	2	20	4	6		
PROBLEM SOLVING	2	19	6	75		
LANGUAGE/EDUCATION TOTAL	28				28	14
FINE COORDINATION	2	9	1	90		
GROSS MOTOR SKILLS	2	9	1	90		
MOTOR SKILLS TOTAL	4				4	5
TEMPERAMENT	4	39	40	21		
ATTITUDE TO TEACHER	4	38	33	29		
APPROACH TO LEARNING	3	38	13	49		
ATTENTION AND DISTRACTIBILITY	2	21	4	75		
BEHAVIOUR TOTAL	13				13	41
PARTICIPATION IN CLASS ACTIVITIES	4	42	47	11		
RELATIONSHIPS WITH PEERS	3	41	12	47		
SOCIAL INTEGRATION TOTAL	7				7	60
RESPONSE TO NEW SITUATIONS	3	50	17	34		
GENERAL ASSESSMENT OF MATURITY	2	20	3	77		
CREATIVITY	2	13	3	84		
LEVEL OF CONCERN FELT	2	19	5	76		
GENERAL DEVELOPMENT TOTAL	9					
OVERALL TOTAL	61				61	14

Fig. 9

Education and Motor Skills totals give real cause for concern. But, while the areas of difficulty are identified, the exact nature of the difficulty is not. A series of diagnostic tests were then administered by the head teacher to try to discover more detail about Sarah's difficulties in order that appropriate steps could be taken to help her. The Head's summary of the results includes a sample of the recommendations as to how the teacher and/or parent can respond to the 'findings' of the tests. Reference is made to complete 'training programmes' already held in the school's resource bank, but it is not intended that they should be used in isolation from everyday activities. It is important to include the detail of such programmes, however, so that the teacher and parent can learn to recognise the types of activity that are appropriate for Sarah. In this way, opportunities to include or emphasise these activities in the context of everyday activity are less likely to be wasted.

CASE STUDY NO. 2: STEVEN MARTIN

Steven Martin came to the school at the beginning of the spring term in his final year in the junior department. There were no standardised test results in the records sent from his previous school, but several examples of his work were included, accompanied by numerous comments on his attitude and progress throughout his primary school career. As had been suggested by his previous teachers, his new teacher soon felt that his general performance fell significantly below his ability. The results of the Junior Rating Scale (Figure 10a & 10b), obviously influenced by his teacher's intuition about his ability, suggested that he was of above average ability. The results of the Richmond Tests (Figure 11), however, confirmed that, in general, his attainments were below average. It is worth noting, though, that the results of the Tests W1, W2 and W3 and 'Mathematics' sections were substantially above average. The Head teacher had administered the Richmond Tests and had noticed that Steven had shown clear signs of panic during each of the five administrations. After subsequent discussions with his teacher and parents it was revealed that Steven had always been 'anxious' about 'school work', although he was very happy at school and enjoyed excellent relationships with both adults and children.

To gain further insight into his ability, he was given a non-verbal intelligence test on which he achieved a quotient of 130. He also subsequently showed considerable ability with lateral-thinking type problems. These results seemed to suggest that the traditionally language-based mode of learning employed in schools was not suited to Steven's cognitive style, and that he had not learned how to impose his

School Routines and Administration 93

JUNIOR RATING SCALE
STEVEN MARTIN

Satisfactory

	LANGUAGE		
Oral	Expression		
	Vocabulary		
	Comprehension of instructions		
	Understanding of words		
	Memory for oral info.		
Written	Content		
	Spelling		
	Sentence construction		
Reading	Reading Level		
	Attitude to Reading		
Maths	Number		
	Problem solving		

MOTOR SKILLS
- Fine coordination
- Gross motor skills

BEHAVIOUR
- Temperament
- Attitude to teacher
- Approach to learning
- Attention & distractibility

SOCIAL INTEGRATION
- Participation in class act.
- Relationships with peers

GENERAL DEVELOPMENT
- Response to new situations
- General assess. of maturity
- Creativity
- Level of concern felt

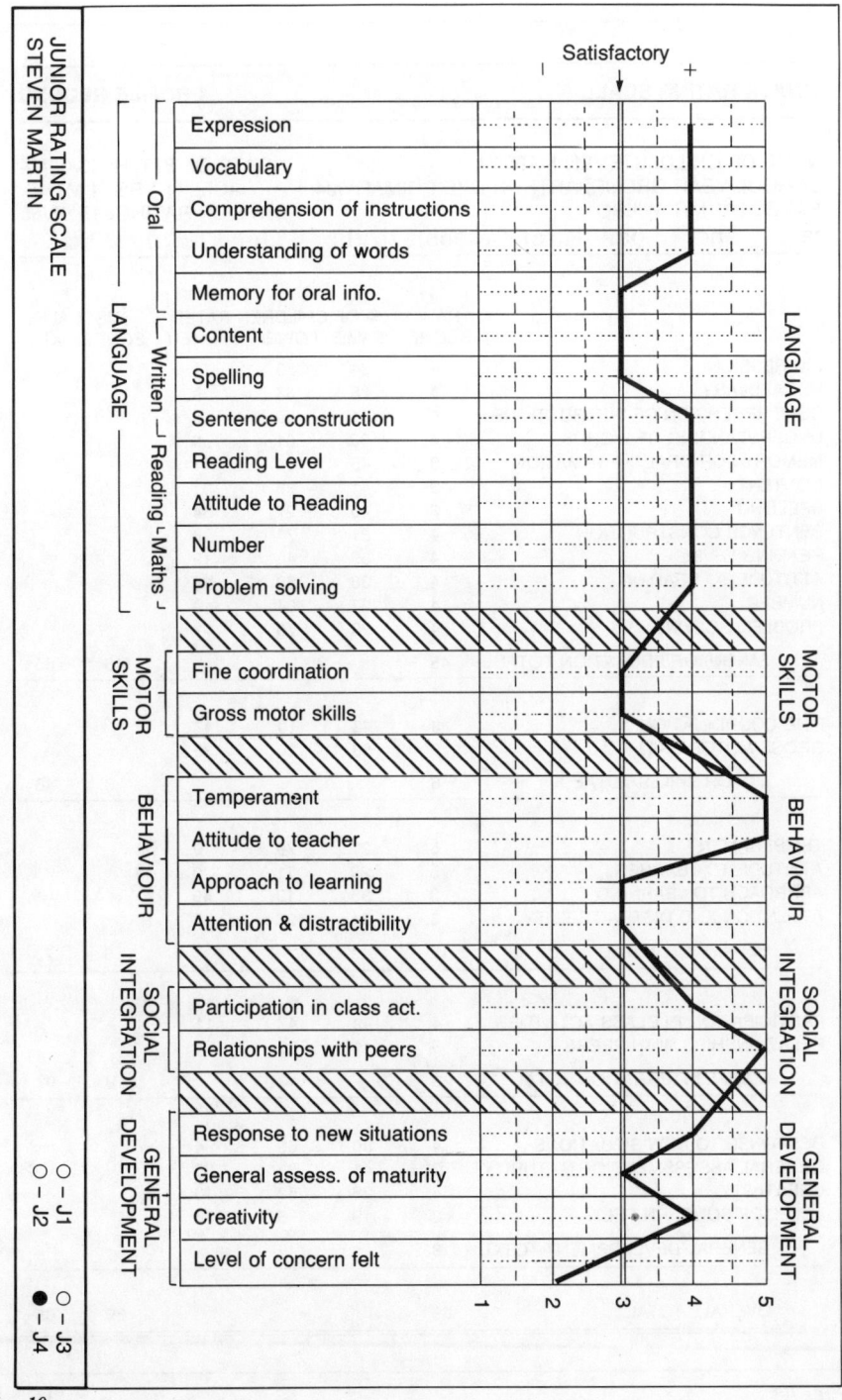

1 2 3 4 5

○ – J1
○ – J2
● – J3
○ – J4

Fig. 10a

JUNIOR RATING SCALE   **PROFILE/RECORD**

NAME OF CHILD: STEVEN MARTIN   DATE OF BIRTH: 03/02/74
SCHOOL/YEAR GROUP: ARTHUR DYE PRIMARY/J4   AGE: 11 YRS. 4 MTHS.
RATED BY: MR. WILSON   DATE OF RATING: 15/06/85

	RAW SCORE	% OF CHILDREN RATED SAME	LOWER	HIGHER	SUBSCALE SCORE	%ILE
EXPRESSION	4	34	55	11		
VOCABULARY	4	28	63	9		
COMPREHENSION OF INSTRUCTIONS	4	31	59	10		
UNDERSTANDING OF WORDS	4	30	61	9		
MEMORY FOR ORAL INFORMATION	3	45	14	41		
CONTENT	3	41	28	31		
SPELLING	3	40	27	34		
SENTENCE CONSTRUCTION	4	21	71	8		
READING LEVEL	4	35	46	19		
ATTITUDE TO READING	4	36	50	14		
NUMBER	4	27	64	9		
PROBLEM SOLVING	4	23	70	7		
LANGUAGE/EDUCATION TOTAL	45				45	65
FINE COORDINATION	3	43	10	47		
GROSS MOTOR SKILLS	3	53	10	38		
MOTOR SKILLS TOTAL	6				6	46
TEMPERAMENT	5	21	79	0		
ATTITUDE TO TEACHER	5	29	71	0		
APPROACH TO LEARNING	3	38	13	49		
ATTENTION AND DISTRACTIBILITY	3	34	25	40		
BEHAVIOUR TOTAL	16				16	73
PARTICIPATION IN CLASS ACTIVITIES	4	42	47	11		
RELATIONSHIPS WITH PEERS	5	11	89	0		
SOCIAL INTEGRATION TOTAL	9				9	92
RESPONSE TO NEW SITUATIONS	4	30	66	4		
GENERAL ASSESSMENT OF MATURITY	3	41	23	35		
CREATIVITY	4	28	62	10		
LEVEL OF CONCERN FELT	2	19	5	76		
GENERAL DEVELOPMENT TOTAL	13					
OVERALL TOTAL	89				89	65

Fig. 10b

School Routines and Administration 95

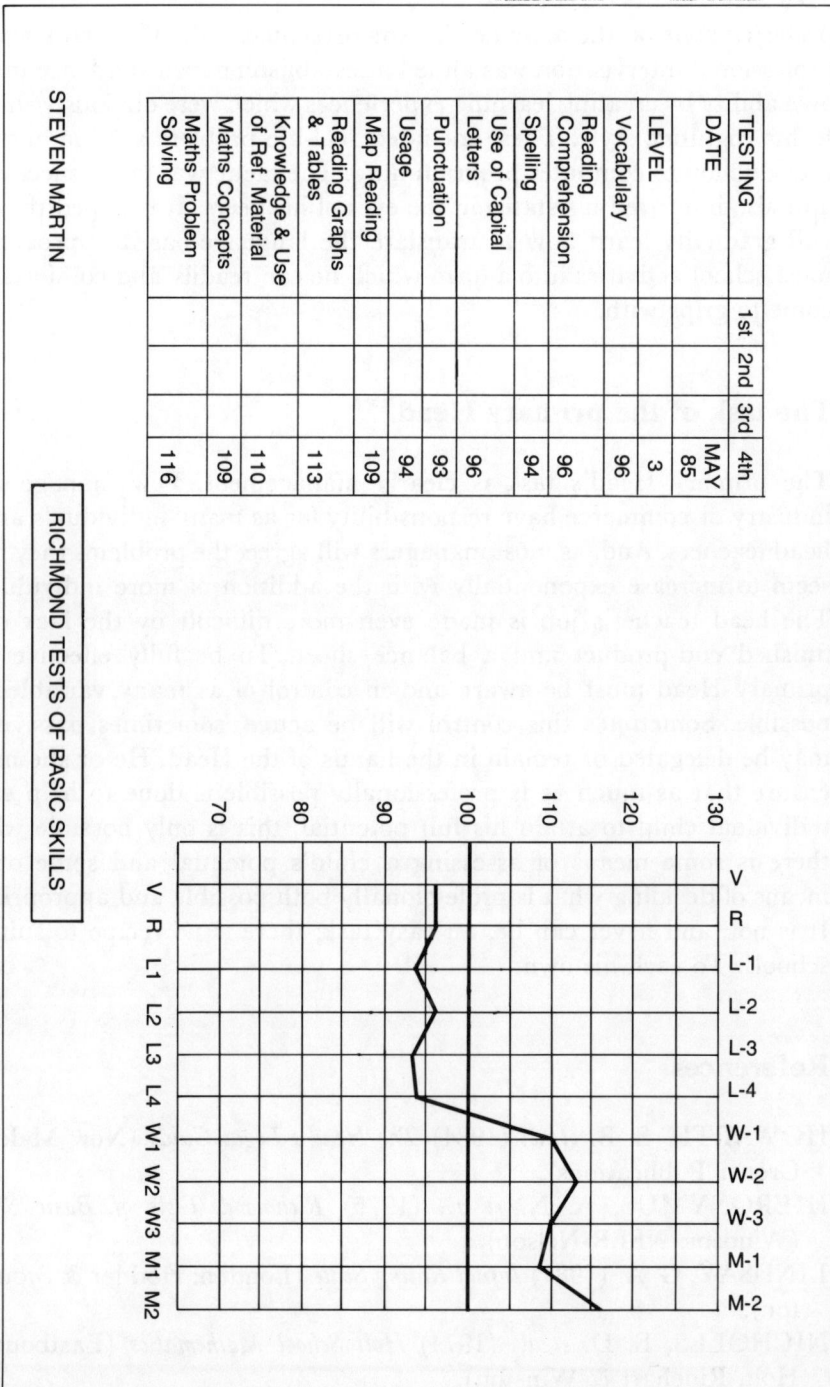

STEVEN MARTIN

TESTING	1st	2nd	3rd	4th
DATE				MAY 85
LEVEL				3
Vocabulary				96
Reading Comprehension				96
Spelling				94
Use of Capital Letters				96
Punctuation				93
Usage				94
Map Reading				109
Reading Graphs & Tables				113
Knowledge & Use of Ref. Material				110
Maths Concepts				109
Maths Problem Solving				116

RICHMOND TESTS OF BASIC SKILLS

Fig. 11

preferred style on the activities he was presented with. The first stage of professional intervention was aimed at establishing his confidence in his own ability by creating learning experiences which were obviously suited to his cognitive style. These included real-life problem solving and an introduction to computer programming. The tactic was fairly successful and also improved his status in the eyes of his peers. It is hoped that he will gradually learn how to translate the language-based approach of most school activities into a form which he can readily and comfortably come to grips with.

The task of the primary Head

The primary Head's task is clearly management. Few managers in industry or commerce have responsibility for as many individuals as do head teachers. And, as most managers will agree, the problems they face seem to increase exponentially with the addition of more individuals. The head teacher's job is made even more difficult by the lack of a finished end-product and a balance sheet. To be fully effective the primary Head must be aware and in control of as many variables as possible. Sometimes this control will be active, sometimes passive; it may be delegated or remain in the hands of the Head. He or she must ensure that as much as is professionally possible is done to help each individual child to attain his full potential; this is only possible when there is some means of assessing a child's potential and some other means of deciding what is professionally both possible and appropriate. It is not, and never can be, an easy task; there is no recipe to suit all schools. To each his own.

References

HOWARTH, S. B. *et al.* (1984) *The Head's Legal Guide* (New Malden: Croner Publications).
HIERONYMUS, A. N. *et al.* (1975) *Richmond Tests of Basic Skills* (Windsor: NFER-Nelson).
LINDSAY, G. A. (1981) *Infant Rating Scale* (London: Hodder & Stoughton).
NICHOLLS, E. D. *et al.* (1974) *Holt School Mathematics* (Eastbourne: Holt, Rinehart & Winston).

NOVACK, H. S. et al. (1972) *Rhode Island Profile of Early Learning Behaviour* (Providence, USA: Jamestown Publishers).
SCHOOLS COUNCIL Working Paper 55 (1975) *Curriculum in the Middle Years* (London: Evans/Methuen Educational).

Chapter 5

Welfare and Liaison

Frank Coombes
Bill Horton

Introduction

One of the controversial issues developed over the past two decades is the recognition of the need to bring social care into teaching as a prerequisite to effective learning, based upon the premise that a child needs to be emotionally and psychologically adjusted in order to gain maximum benefit from the learning situation. The difficulties that prevent this are often subtle and difficult to assess or observe. Teachers are in the front line of social and personal observation of children. Society now expects schools to have a compassionate pastoral role. The open door policy now available in most schools will determine, to some extent, the dialogue available between teacher and parent and contribute to the mutual understanding of each other.

While some schools may have the time, the resources and the desire to handle such problems from within, it is professional wisdom to know where the support services are based and when and how they might be able to employ their resources to assist the school and family with a particular concern. Within the present-day social structure a large number of helping agencies exist, all with differing tasks, with a variety of roles to play and employing a wide range of social, medical and psychological skills.

As education is a major influence in producing tomorrow's society, there is a need to ensure that the teacher's knowledge and understanding of the variety of services available to support families and their children, is kept up to date. This chapter will look at those services involved and will act as a guide to the teacher when the need arises to make appropriate referrals. All of these support services are aimed at assisting each individual to live as full a life as is commensurate with his/her potentialities and therefore all have a rapport with the education service whose role is based on the same concepts.

The range of welfare matters in the primary schools

What are the kinds of concerns in the primary school that might initiate a referral from school to an outside agency? Changes in both demeanour, health and behaviour of the child in the classroom are the early warning signs of things going wrong at home and/or at school. Absence from school, so often regarded as an affront to school and the law, also has to be viewed by the teachers with the same enquiring mind. Lack of adequate clothing, money for meals, disputes with friends, introverted or nervous children, together with an anti-school attitude by the parent, can all lead to absences which are amenable to good social work intervention and cooperation between school, the support agencies and parents. The social work frontline is, in fact, in school, with the teacher as the observer of change in the child, while the school register and the period set aside for registrations can be a sensitive barometer of the child's health and difficulties.

The need to avoid terms which confuse and which are not applicable in law when discussing or reporting absences, and the need for accurate reporting cannot be over-emphasised. Should serious social breakdown occur, requiring a legal decision or advice, accuracy in registers and terminology then becomes very important indeed. One piece of useful advice we should offer is not to use the term 'truancy' for absence until it is established that the child is acting contrary to the parents' wishes. The word 'truancy' has become a generic description for all absence, most of which has social causes rather than the assumed avoidance of parents' wishes. There exists a wide variety of publications on issues of school attendance and the complex causal factors. A publication by the National Youth Bureau (1985)[1] gives an annotated bibliography of some 450 publications on a wide range of educational difficulties.

The most common causes of failure to attend school are still child ailments. The side effects of absence are often greater than realised. Children, once free from the school routine, find difficulty in readjusting unless there is good parental awareness of the need to overcome school reluctance caused by temporary absence. The next most common cause is the primary pupil's anxiety about leaving home to attend school. The problems many families encounter in attempting to provide meals, clothing, and other school-oriented extras can in some cases cause sporadic absences from school in the same way as children with anxieties or dislike of certain subjects or teachers, will in fact become unwell, or feign illness or avoid issues with which they have failed to come to terms.

Children who have frequent changes of homes, or schools and teachers, or who have suffered loss of friends, also tend to become less enthusiastic about attending school and will be more likely to be disinterested in the subject matter being taught. Children whose parents are in hospital, or who are in trouble in the courts, and those whose parents are in marital distress or disharmony, are all vulnerable to loss of education, either by being unable to produce a sufficient attention span or by school refusal, or by a fear of returning home due to parents threatening to leave home. There are, at times, children who dislike school for no easily discernible reason. They are reluctant to attend school, and easily kept at home, and they are a constant worry to parents about attendance. Quite often a different discipline has to be found to create attendance, based upon close social case work and consultation between school and home. The smallest group, contrary to most reports, are those that absent themselves from primary education, without their parents' knowledge or consent. These are the only real truants, and this problem often can be easily overcome by a system of daily reporting by the home to school and vice versa.

The special issues brought to notice recently of children being physically/sexually abused by parents or members of the family or others, has introduced a national scheme of care and cooperation between all the agencies. Where these issues affect children at school, and signs of changes in behaviour or physical or emotional ill-treatment are suspected, the Education Authority, the Social Services' Department, the Health Department, the NSPCC, the Probation and After-Care Service, and the police are all provided with corporate plans of action to deal with such incidents. All schools are made aware of the procedures through the Head of the school and in all cases education welfare officers, social workers, school medical officers, school nurses and health visitors are able to give immediate help, support and advice.

The Education Welfare Service

One of the services most directly concerned with schools, and in the majority of authorities in this country employed within the Education Department, is the Education Welfare Service, sometimes known as the Education Social Work Service. This body of people are in regular contact with schools and often act as the main link between schools, homes and other agencies.

Their work involves providing day-to-day fieldwork support to schools and families and includes:

(a) Establishing regular liaison between school and home in all matters relating to the child's well-being and, where necessary, providing support to children and their families showing signs or experiencing symptoms of a variety of problems.
(b) Coordinating channels of communication and consultation between school staffs and agencies concerned with the education, health and care of children.
(c) Seeing that children of compulsory school age receive an appropriate education. This may involve the use of persuasive or disciplinary means to ensure regular attendance at school for those pupils who are frequently absent for reasons other than illness (e.g., school refusers, school phobics, school truants).
(d) Ensuring that children and their families are aware of, and draw maximum benefit from, the welfare rights available (e.g., free school meals, clothing grants, travel assistance).
(e) Maintaining close involvement at all levels with children whose problems have caused them to be suspended or excluded from school.
(f) Providing appropriate support for children with special educational needs.
(g) Initiating and coordinating necessary action concerning child/sexual abuse.
(h) Arranging home tuition where appropriate (e.g., where a child's ill health prevents attendance at school).
(i) Arranging transport to school where appropriate (e.g., where a child cannot walk because of injury).
(j) Escorting children to and from residential schools, clinics and hospitals.
(k) Providing reports on children coming to the notice of the police and courts (in conjunction with the school).
(l) Preventing the exploitation of children in employment and entertainment.

The central role of the education welfare officer or social worker is based on the assessment of social, emotional, and educational problems affecting a child's ability to benefit from the educational opportunities offered.

The EWO deals with faults and failings in children who fail to attend school for numerous reasons. His role demands that he plans his work on a preventive model in order to reduce educational loss, and may involve sometimes invoking the law and, where there is a need, maintaining harmonious relationships between school and home. The officer is able to counsel parents, conveying the school's situation to the home and the home's problems to the school. He is able to marshall the resources of the Education Department by providing aids for children with clothing problems, and free school meals, where appropriate. Working with children at risk of suspension because they are presenting behaviour problems in school (in some cases necessitating a change of school) is another of his tasks. The provision of transport where a child under eight lives more than two miles from the nearest school or, if the child is over eight years three miles from the school, is another of his aids to ensure regular attendance. The prevention of absence due to long-term illness requiring the use of home tuition also comes within his remit. In cases where intractable problems occur and where absence is due to factors which will not respond to social work preventive methods, the officers are empowered and trained to take the matter for a decision into either the Juvenile or Magistrates' Court (usually only after considerable work with the family and consultation with other agencies). The condoned absence of children by parents using the child for employment purposes, either in regular businesses, or in market trading, is also a matter for the education authority and comes within the education welfare officer's role. He is required to see that the law protecting children at school from illegal employment is enforced. In this matter, children under thirteen are unable to be employed whether paid or not.

Similarly a head teacher may not grant leave of absence for a child to be so employed, except those who have a local education authority certificate for stage or a broadcast entertainment. To facilitate easy access to schools for those children with special education needs, the education welfare officers are able to provide escorts to those children needing to travel to schools in a residential setting, and to support and counsel parents on matters affecting the child and school.

The summary of the work as provided by the Local Government Training Board's recommendations (Ralphs Report, 1973)[2] are: school attendance – lateness – poverty – behavioural problems – children with special needs and rehabilitating children returning from residential care and special schools.

In carrying out his role the officer needs to develop a supportive relationship with teachers, children and parents in order to contribute toward the alleviation of such problems that are referred to him. The mobilisation of the resources available in the Education Department, together with liaison with the other statutory and voluntary agencies, often enables him to be an effective helping agency for both family and school. It will be generally recognised that his work will take him into homes where most serious problems are present, including child abuse and other social ills. His role will bring him into contact with the Social Services Department, the NSPCC and the police, together with all the other agencies that form a multi-disciplinary team to deal with severe social problems.

Communication and conflict

There may well arise, in certain cases where the child's education has broken down and has not been successfully resolved by normal counselling and social action, a need to invoke legal proceedings in a juvenile court. In such cases there is a legal requirement in the Children and Young Persons Act (1969)[3] for both Education and Social Services Departments to consult prior to such action being taken.

It is very often at this stage that departmental conflicts emerge due to the differing philosophies of the two departments and their legal duties. The educationalist on the one hand is seeking the continuity of the child's education, while the social services often have to follow a policy of retaining children within the home environment, rather than removing a child into care. It is usually the severity of the problem that causes the Education Department to seek a solution in the courts, due to the unlikelihood of the child receiving full-time education while remaining at home. The policy and practice of the Social Services' Department may well be in conflict in such cases, and may rely upon supervision and parental counselling to remedy the difficulty, a procedure which has already invariably been carried out by the education welfare officer without success.

It has to be accepted that there are sometimes widely differing views between the Social Services Department, which has to accept responsibility for the child's future care and accommodation should a care order be made by the courts, and those who seek to provide appropriate education. Such differences should not be underestimated or ignored. It is a strongly held belief, developed over recent years, that the removal of the child from his/her home environment, no matter how critical the situation may be, may have a severe and lasting psychological effect upon the child. As a result, such removals are only approved of in the most severe cases. Consequently, teachers will find very often that little educational improvement occurs in the child, despite interventions by the services concerned.

For all these reasons it is essential to have an equal understanding of both views. The internal organisation for consultation in schools and the local authority's system of multi-disciplinary conferences need to be well known to all concerned, and the representatives selected to attend should be well briefed.

The Social Services Department

Social services are the main local authority service for social work with families dealing with the elderly, the handicapped, the homeless, and the care and protection of children. The Local Authority Social Services Act (1970)[4] formed this central department, providing social workers to families and young people, in order to alleviate problems and encourage individuals to live as full a life as is possible in the community. In Scotland there are some differences and the service is known there as the Social Work Committee. The provision of homes for the elderly and disabled, those suffering from mental disorder and the chronically sick comes within the purview of the Social Services Department. The work is usually carried by district social work teams. The department provides social workers to hospitals and to child guidance clinics, and in two authorities in England they, and not the LEA, provide the school welfare service (Somerset and Coventry).

The parameters of the social services' responsibility are wide and varied and a policy of citizen involvement in a number of caring services is an essential part of the social work development. The need for family guidance and personal supervision of children before the courts is also an essential part of social work. In cases of children with problems directly related to education breakdown, the supervision may be carried out either by a social worker from the social service section or by the education welfare worker. The essential elements are the close and harmonious relationships built up between workers in various departments, and the cooperation extended to all caring agencies by schools and education workers.

The Educational Psychology Service

The Education Department employ educational psychologists, all of whom have teacher-training qualifications in addition to their professional qualifications as educational psychologists.

The service provides help with the educational problems of children from the pre-school stage right through the period of schooling. Support is given individually to children with learning and behaviour difficulties and by discussion with their parents and teachers.

In a number of cases, the educational psychologist is the main link in collating assessments of a child's special educational needs, leading on to a statement being issued by the Education Department. Inevitably this brings the educational psychologists in close contact with the special educational provision provided by the local education authority and therefore to a prime position to advise parents and teachers.

Schools may well seek the advice of the educational psychologist in a consultative capacity or as an advisory service to teachers either in talks to schools' staff, in-service training or workshops.

The educational psychologist works closely with other professional agencies in the welfare field and, in most of the country, forms part of a multi-disciplinary team in a child and family guidance section working with individual children and their families. Referrals come to the service from a variety of sources (see Child and Family Guidance Service below) and may be made under their educational psychology role or as part of the wider child and family guidance team.

The Child and Family Guidance Service

Generally speaking, the function of the child and family guidance clinic is one of prevention, diagnosis and treatment, aiming to relieve anxiety and distress where these work to the detriment of the child. While the service tends to be child centred, work is also directed at those adults who form an integral part of the child's life (e.g., parents, relatives, teachers and other significant adults).

The problems of children referred may be broadly categorised as developmental and management problems both at home and school, and these form a fair part of the work, as do children who have difficulty in managing their own emotions and who might well have problems in forming relationships. At the more extreme end of the problems to be dealt with, are urgent cases relating to suicide attempts. Other problems involve anti-social behaviour, problems related to school attendance, children having physical symptoms such as enuresis, encopresis, obesity, or asthma, all of which may have a psychological component.

Referrals to the child and family guidance clinic come from a variety of agencies including schools, education welfare officers, social workers, health visitors, GPs and parents themselves.

Treatment is usually effected by a multi-disciplinary teamwork approach involving a consultant child psychiatrist (Health) who specialises in children's problems, an educational psychologist (Education) with experience of children's intellectual and emotional development, and a psychiatric social worker (Social Services) with experience in family, as well as individual, therapy.

Help offered takes many forms and is concerned at first with the evaluation of the problem and then with suggesting ways of promoting the child's healthy development. The traditional 'tool' in the treatment of emotional problems is psychotherapy, which can take various forms. Fundamentally they have the same aim and that is to affect basic change in the intra-psychic equilibrium of each patient. This may be achieved through insight catharsis, warmth, sympathy, empathy and the ability to listen and respond on the part of the therapist within a relationship with the client.

In addition to the treatment methods described, another important function of the clinic, in conjunction with the educational psychologist, is an involvement in the assessment of children with special educational needs. Recommendation for placement at a special school might well be part of the treatment plan for a child.

As well as giving direct help to individual families, the service has a consultative and educational function and staff are generally available for advice to other professional groups concerned with the good development of children and their families.

The Local Health Authority

The health service is provided to promote health and well-being and to forestall illness and disability by preventive measures. Where illness occurs the aim is to provide care in the community, at home, at centres or in residential accommodations and hospitals. The service available to schools is based within the local health department, with a senior physician in charge of the service. The National Health Service Act (1977)[5] provides for medical and dental inspections, and the treatment of pupils at school. Treatment has to be given with the sanction of a parent; it is an important ethic of those who care for children that treatment has to be discussed and agreed with the legal guardian or parent. It is also worth remembering that it is the health authority, under Regulations 8 and 9 of Education (Teachers) Regulations (1982)[6], which requires a satisfactory health report before a teacher can be appointed.

The regular inspection of children attending school is vital and an important part of preventive medicine is the early discovery of all kinds of emotional, physical or mental difficulties. Medical inspections are sometimes routine at certain ages or may be required or requested by the Head of the school. Similarly, parents may also request medical examinations. Children in need of special educational help are also dealt with by the medical officer or psychiatrists employed by the health service. The latter provide mainly for children in the child guidance clinics.

The routine eye or scalp inspections are now carried out either by health visitors or by school nurses from the Health Department. Many health visitors are attached to the local general practitioners' clinics and surgeries and are likely to have knowledge of most children and their families prior to entering school. All health visitors are qualified midwives with training in social work practice, and are a resource available to schools on questions of parenting and general health education. The school nurse also plays an increasingly valuable role in all aspects of health promotion.

The Probation Service

Although the probation service is not designed to assist schools directly, the wide and varied role of the probation officer will, at times, bring him or her into contact with schools, particularly when a marital supervision order exists. The service's full title is the Probation and After-Care Service as it is also responsible for the after-care of those released from prisons or detention centres, and in some areas carries out the supervision of children made subject to a supervision order by the juvenile courts (usually children over the age of fourteen years). The concern of the Social Services' Department, the Education Department and the probation service in children of school age who are affected by the law in the courts, brings all three services into close contact in matters affecting planned approaches to offending children and their parents. The position of the probation service in Scotland is different from the rest of the country – probation officers in Scotland are an integral part of the social work service.

The Department of Health and Social Security

The DHSS, as it is known, provides financial and material aid to those who are sick, unemployed, homeless and beyond normal working age. It is the local office of the DHSS where most benefits paid to those groups takes place. The service employs home-visiting officers, and special enquiry officers whose task it is to see that benefits are necessary and adequate. The main beneficiaries affecting schools are those parents receiving supplementary benefits, or child benefits. The provision of school meals under present legislation is tied specifically to those who receive supplementary benefit, family income supplement, and housing supplement benefit, all of whom are entitled to free school meals.

Voluntary societies

There are two main voluntary organisations with whom teachers will come into contact. The National Society for the Prevention of Cruelty to Children (NSPCC) was formed in the 1880s and is funded by voluntary subscription and employs officers in each district to whom parents, police, and other agencies may appeal for help in preventing or forestalling the suffering of children in their own homes. Such is the reputation of the NSPCC that they are one of the agencies recognised in the Children and Young Persons Act (1969) as being authorised, together with police and local authority departments (Education and Social Services) to bring parents and children before the courts in respect of child-care offences.

The other society which assists families, particularly in matters of inadequate school clothing, is the Women's Royal Voluntary Service. They have served as a resource for social workers with insufficient finance to provide holidays for deprived children, and the WRVS Holiday Hostess Scheme has been often used in cases of need.

There is a great number of voluntary groups which deal with children, one-parent families, and handicapped people. Most areas have voluntary service centres or an information bureau where all the local services can be discovered. The school social worker or education welfare officer will also have this information.

The law, the parent and the school

Education is surrounded by a number of enactments dating from 1944 when the principal Act was introduced. There are some 24 Acts of Parliament between 1944 and 1986, dealing with the administration of schools, supply of teachers, regulations for schools, government of schools, structures of managing bodies, and parents' rights and duties in the education of their children.

We do not intend to enter such a complex field in this chapter, except to outline the basic tenets for teachers and parents and to advise careful reference to the known legal departments of the local education authority and local libraries where the short but explicit Citizens Advice Notes, published by the National Council for Voluntary Organisations[7], are available.

The main theme of education law and practice is contained in the Education Act (1944). Parents' duties are contained in Section 36, which requires all parents to seek full-time, efficient education suitable to their child's age, ability and aptitude by attendance at school, or otherwise. Thus there is parental choice, to choose a state school, or to educate the child privately by tuition at home or at a school where fees are charged. Once having accepted the state school registration, both school and parent have entered into a contract to observe the school rules, whether they are verbal or written. Children are not of compulsory school age until they reach five years of age and would then normally be admitted at the commencement of the term following their fifth birthday. Some local authorities may, and often do, admit children earlier than this, either to nursery or primary school, but there is no requirement in law for them to do so. Where disagreements occur, LEAs have to make arrangements for an appeal's procedure.

Where the nearest school is more than two miles from the pupil's home and the child is under eight years of age (or in the case of a child over eight, three miles) the local education authority is responsible for the provision of reasonable transport arrangements.

The LEA may, where they are satisfied that extraordinary circumstances permit, arrange for education to take place other than at school either full-time or part-time (e.g., where children require long-term hospital stay or are excluded from school on health grounds). Transport can also be arranged to school in special circumstances, such as where a child has an injury or a broken leg, which prevents him walking to school in the normal way.

The school sessions also are legislated for, and there must be 400 in each education year (i.e. half days); this may be reduced to 380 sessions by ten days' occasional holiday in the year. It is often found to be difficult to comply with this clause where accidental damage to schools occur or industrial action prevents the governors of the school complying.

The registration of pupils has to come within the law as laid down in Section 80 of the Education Act (1944)[8] and the Pupils' Registration Regulations (1956)[9]. An admission register has to be kept showing all the children, whether of compulsory school age or not, their names and addresses and date of admission, together with the names of their parents or guardians. In addition, an attendance register must be kept and marked by the teacher at the beginning of morning and afternoon sessions showing those present and those absent. Registers have to be made available for inspection during school hours by duly authorised officers. Usually the authorised officer is the education social worker or welfare officer. Registers must be kept in ink and corrections must not obliterate the original entry. Regular returns must be made of children who do not attend school regularly, or who are absent for more than two weeks except where such absence is due to certified illness.

It is of interest to note that where children have to leave one school to transfer to another for any reason, the governing body of the first school should supply the educational records if so requested. It is important to remember that records of children entering a school from another, will only be obtained if the receiving school requests them. The system has often failed in the past due to the failure of the receiving school to apply, or because some pupils have been continually moving from one place to another.

Leave of absence from school can only be given by the Head of the school delegated to that duty by the governors under the Education (Schools and Further Education) Regulations (1981)[10]. Leave must not be given to allow a child to be employed. Employment means any work, whether paid or unpaid. There are exceptions to the leave issue; one is that a child may be granted time off to pursue a properly licensed appearance in a theatrical, radio, TV or film performance. Another is that pupils may be given leave of absence to accompany parents on their annual leave. Similarly, where pupils are ill they will not be expected to attend school. Such licenses are granted at the discretion of the education authority and come within the role of the education social/welfare officer.

School admission arrangements

The principle enshrined in the main Education Act (1944) that children should be educated in accordance with the wishes of the parent (provided it does not cause unreasonable public expenditure, or conflict with efficient education) is further enforced by the Education Act (1980)[11], which requires schools to publish for each school year, particulars of their arrangements for the admission of pupils to schools maintained by them. In the case of aided schools and special agreement schools the governors of each school are responsible for publishing such arrangements.

School attendance orders

If it appears to any local education authority that the parent is not undertaking the responsibility laid upon them under Section 36 of the Education Act (1944), the education authority must serve a notice on the parent that they intend to make a school attendance order if, after 14 days, the parent has not satisfied them that proper education arrangements have been made. A period of time is given for the parent to comply, but should they not do so, the remedy is only possible through the courts, and in this matter the education welfare service takes the necessary action.

Children with special educational needs

The Education Act (1981)[12] makes it a duty for the local education authority to ascertain which children require special education provision, either in the ordinary day school, or in some other special day or residential setting. There are very complicated rules and regulations setting out procedures for making assessments and for ensuring that the parents are involved in discussions and decisions from the outset. The whole procedure requires knowledge of the Education Acts (1944, 1980 and 1981) together with the 1985 Education (Special Educational Needs) Regulations (SI, 1982, No. 106). The right of all education authorities, and all parents to require an assessment of the child's educational needs from the age of two years and throughout the school life of every child, is an extremely important part of education law, involving school staff, education psychologists, health workers, education social workers, and education administrative workers. The general principle of retaining the child in the normal day school, is often considered, and where some unusual or unprovided facility is needed, the decision to place the child in a day or residential special school setting, other than the normal day school, has to be taken step by step in line with the procedures set out and in line with parental wishes.

Offences against the Education Act 1944 to 1981

The parent is likely to be counselled, and advised over some period of time should any part of the Acts be ignored and children are not, (1), attending an appropriate school, (2), not receiving full-time efficient education, (3), being continuously late for registration (being the period set apart in the curriculum prior to the commencement of secular education at each session), or (4), being withheld from attending due to parental neglect. Where parents engage in a trade or business of such a nature as to require them to travel from place to place, there is a requirement that the child must have attended as regularly as the nature of the trade permits and have recorded at least 200 sessions in the year. In most cases social action is effective, but where circumstances indicate that the restoration of education is unlikely by this method, the local education authority has the duty to ensure that a parent is brought before a court (either juvenile or adult) to seek a remedy. This may result in the making of a supervision order over the child, a care order (see Supervision/Care Orders below) or imposing a fine upon the parent for an offence against the Acts; the education welfare officer in such cases acts on behalf of the local education authority in the courts. Where supervision orders for children are issued, they may be managed by either a social worker, education welfare officer or probation officer, depending upon the child's age and other circumstances peculiar to each case.

The most recent review of the Law of Education[13] is passing through parliament as we write and will introduce new concepts for school government, including a minimum number of parent governors, teacher governors, and co-opted members of the governing bodies. It is intended to allow parents to stand for election to school governing bodies, and for the school governors to hold an annual meeting to which all parents have to be invited. The removal of corporal punishment, and the control of pupils subject to exclusion from school is contained in the 1986 Act, together with regulations that will apply in the new appraisal of teacher performance. Schools will produce a report through the governing body each year and this must be made available to parents. All of these changes are to be dependent upon regulations made by the Secretary of State in the months ahead. The two Advisory Councils for Education, and the Annual Report to Parliament by the Secretary of State will no longer exist after 1986. Those whose tasks are more onerous, and those who interest themselves in the study of the law, will be helped by the publication, *The New Law of Education* (pub. Butterworth Press)[14].

Children subject to cruelty or abuse

In recent years, the area of child/sexual abuse has become one of serious concern to all agencies in the field of child care. Agencies such as the police, NSPCC, social services, education welfare and community health department staff (i.e. school medical officers, health visitors and school nurses) work closely together with school staff in the prevention/ treatment of cases of abuse.

In recent years emotive cases, such as those of Maria Colwell and Jasmine Beckford reported in the media, have highlighted inadequacies in communications between these multi-disciplinary agencies, with serious consequences for the children concerned. Government reports which followed these tragedies, advocated that everyone concerned should re-examine their agency policy for dealing with cases and strengthen their liaison arrangements with fellow professionals.

Such cases are dealt with under child care legislation and, where necessary, actioned through the juvenile court, under the 1969 Children and Young Persons Act, where an order is likely to be made to protect the child concerned. A Place of Safety Order can be taken before an application is made to the juvenile court. In certain cases, voluntary care arrangements can be made by the Social Services, under Section 2 of the Child Care Act (1980)[15].

Place of Safety orders

Where there is serious concern about the physical, moral or emotional well-being of a child or young person, a Place of Safety Order can be taken by the local authority for a period not exceeding 28 days, or by the police for up to eight days. To take a place of safety means to remove the child from his parents or guardian, and the undesirable situation, and place the child with foster parents, in a children's home or maybe in hospital.

In facilitating such action, the case must be brought to the attention of a local magistrate and agreement reached that a Place of Safety is in the best interests of the child or young person. However, the child must then be brought before a juvenile court before the 28 or eight days expire, with a plan of action, otherwise the child or young person must be returned to his/her parent or guardian.

Taking such action and placing the child in the juvenile court, might well lead to the making of a supervision order or care order depending on the nature of the case.

Supervision orders

A juvenile court may make a Supervision Order for any period not exceeding three years in respect of any child or young person under the age of seventeen years who is proved to have committed an offence, or who has been found to be in need of care or control.

The effect of a supervision order is that the child or young person will be supervised by a social worker from the Social Services Department or in certain cases, by an education welfare officer, or by a Probation Officer.

The decision as to which service will supervise will be made by the court, but generally a child under fourteen years will be supervised by a social worker. Supervising officers aim to befriend, guide, advise and counsel the child, and will keep regular contact with them and their family in an attempt to resolve the problems that made it necessary for a supervision order to be made.

Care orders

A juvenile court may make a Care Order committing a child or young person up to the age of seventeen years to the care of the county council, where a criminal offence has been proved or where the child or young person has been found to be in need of care or control. Care orders made in respect of children and young persons under the age of sixteen years remain in force until their eighteenth birthday. If made after their sixteenth birthday they remain in force until they reach nineteen years.

The making of a care order has far wider implications than a supervision order and gives the county council the same rights, powers and duties as the parent or guardian.

Parents have a right of appeal and a juvenile court can discharge a care order on the application to do so by the county council, the parents or the young person concerned, if it feels that it is in the best interests of the child or young person. However, while in force, a care order allows the Social Services Department to make a wide range of decisions about the child or young person, generally in consultation with them and their families.

In the present climate and at the time of writing, the move is clearly towards reintegrating the child or young person back to his natural family wherever possible. Sometimes, for a variety of reasons, this is not practicable and in certain cases the child or young person will be placed for long-term fostering or adoption.

Case histories

The unending variation in the causal factors for loss of education makes all case histories little more than an interesting guide to what may occur, and alerts the observant teacher to small changes in child behaviour, and reactions to school which may point to one more unique incident which requires sympathy, understanding and action. Even in the primary school some children become unteachable due to behavioural difficulty or extreme anxieties about issues outside the school, sometimes very real and at other times exaggerated by nervous anxiety sparked off by some unwelcomed and unexpected happening. It is wise also to remember that such unexpected and unwelcome happenings may also spark off similar anxieties in the parent, making advice and recommendations that much more difficult.

PETER AND THE PRIMARY SCHOOL BLACKBOARD BLACK-OUT

Peter was the youngest of three children and the only son. He had attended the local primary school for three years, and was almost eight years of age. His repeated questioning of the teacher, or any of the children sitting near him about the words or figures on the blackboard, had been assumed as part of his determination to be noticed, until one day, his new teacher sent him to the headmaster for his persistent talking and disturbing other children's ability to concentrate on the lesson in hand. After a suitable ticking off for being 'inattentive', 'disruptive', 'disobedient' and 'a damned nuisance', he returned to class quite unchanged. On his third visit to the headmaster he stoutly defended his behaviour by saying, 'I can't see the blackboard from where I sit'.

The weekly visit of the education welfare officer coincided with the headmaster's decision to write to the parents inviting them into school. Peter was losing ground, his work was poor and he was becoming aggressive and at times morose. The education welfare officer, after discussion with the headmaster, was persuaded on the urgency of the matter, and his home visit was most welcomed by the parents. Both parents were concerned at Peter's dislike of the school and all the teachers, as he did not want to go and felt ill each morning. His father had to smack him the previous evening and send him to bed for sitting up so close to the television set, that no one else could see the programme. The EWO decided to return when Peter had come home from school and father's long day on the farm was over.

Peter was small, shy and speechless at first, and his father could not understand why he had changed in the past year. Previously he had been getting on well and was no trouble at all. The school seemed to have a down on Peter, but his mother was not so critical of the school, as she had the advantage of having a friendship with one of the teachers and had heard the story that 'Peter could not see the blackboard'. After a one-to-one session with Peter, the EWO supported Peter's defence as not being able to see the blackboard, and suggested that Peter took time off from school the following day for an eye test by the family doctor, to save time waiting for the next school medical. The following day the GP referred Peter to an eye specialist, and the eventual report, plus a confirmation by the school doctor later, was that he was partially sighted. An application was made for Peter to be classified as needing special education and he finished his education at the Exeter School for the Blind and Partially Sighted. It may seem quite strange that a boy who entered a school with what was regarded as adequate vision should, after three years, and at least one school medical, suddenly need special education for failing sight. Peter's strenuous and sometimes defiant words in his own defence had been unavailing, but the need to sit close to the television set had convinced the EWO that something was amiss. The efforts of the school to obtain help and advice to change his education situation, once the problem was known, is remembered by a grateful family.

THE DIY SYNDROME AND COMMUNITY COMMUNICATION

It was becoming more than common talk that Esme, who lived on the nearby council house estate, was not going to go to school when she was five. While Esme's father, an eccentric man, was unemployed, both parents had good family backgrounds but had come upon hard times. Esme was their first child, who was valued, protected, and spoilt. Her association with other children was restricted, and she was taught from the age of three by her mother.

The Head of the primary school, a man with a heart and social conscience, confided in the visiting education social worker, and asked what would happen should the child not be registered at his, or any other, primary school when she became five years of age. His long experience and training as a teacher had not included the finer details of the law and policy on children who did not attend school, and here was an opportunity for him to test the local education authority with whom he had a distant tenuous relationship. He preferred, in the main, to be independent of authority and conduct his school in his own way which was, to say the least, well liked by the community, though somewhat critically appraised in the distant Education Department.

The school staff as a whole were wondering what was to happen when Esme reached the first day of term after her fifth birthday, which is the first day of every child's legal right to full-time efficient education, according to their age, ability and aptitude, Education Act 1944 (Section 36). The last few words of this Section say 'by attendance at school or otherwise'. Esme's mother had chosen otherwise. The headmaster was informed of this after the first day of the term when Esme should have met the world outside and joined her friends in school.

It was pointed out to the headmaster that there was no authoritative method of checking when children became five, and no direction of parents and children into school. The matter was one for the parents entirely. This was quite unsatisfactory for the head teacher and his staff, as they were concerned for the girl's effective, efficient education. The Head's challenge went out to the education social worker in the words, 'what are you going to do about it'? Consequently, the EWO undertook to visit the home to talk with the parents.

On this visit the officer was made welcome. Having made discreet, but direct enquiries of both parents, as to whether they had qualifications to teach, the school social worker then advised them that if they wished to continue to educate Esme at home, they would have to make their home and workplan available for inspection by the local education authority advisors. The education welfare officer cautioned the parents that the result of educating children at home, without proper safeguards, inspection, and qualified advice, meant that the question would be decided in the courts by a prosecution under Section 37 of the Education Act

(1944). This required the local education authority to serve notices upon both parents to satisfy the local education authority in not less than fourteen days or such period as contained in the order, that the education was full-time and efficient according to Esme's age, ability and aptitude.

The parents preferred to take a line of least resistance and ask the LEA advisors to call and make their report after one term had been undertaken at home. The report was adverse and a notice was issued requesting the parents to choose a school for Esme by the beginning of the following term.

Esme's entry into school was very special to her, and the staff invited parents and child to a social event at the school before the day of entry, and offered Esme's mother a task as a teacher's aide. Esme's entry into school, although one term late, was prompted and propelled by a group of interested and curious teachers at school whose concern for 'the one that was lost', made it possible to avoid long term anti-school feelings in a family whose do-it-yourself ambitions failed in the face of community concern.

THE EARLY DIAGNOSIS OF EDUCATIONAL DIFFICULTY

Probably the greatest test of observers of children at school is to relate patterns of behaviour while at school to underlying causal factors. While most children suffer anxiety and stress, within the school attendance period, there is a vulnerable group who react by absence from school.

Norman and Ronald were two brothers attending the same school. Norman was seven and Ronald a year younger. Both parents were apparently interested in the boys' general progress and attended the school regularly to see reports and discuss matters with the teachers.

Both parents were employed. The mother worked part-time and was at home to tend to the children before and after school. The marriage appeared to be stable. One morning the father of the boys appeared in the school just before assembly and asked if the Head could help him get both boys out of his car as they refused to enter the school. After a violent struggle both boys were carried into school and remained there all that day. The following morning they were absent again and a note from the mother was sent, asking for help in getting both boys to school. The Head decided to offer to pick them up the following morning, and when he arrived at the house these two, once docile and withdrawn characters, were wild and aggressive, kicking and struggling in an attempt to avoid being taken into the car. The bruised headmaster withdrew and 'phoned for the education welfare officer.

The EWO visited and obtained the entry of the eldest boy by persuading him to try and attend for a morning only and being taken quietly and gently into the school before assembly each day. This only lasted for two days, and after very long and detailed conversations with both parents, it became clear new initiatives were needed to ensure education. The matter was referred to the child guidance clinic, and labelled 'school phobia'. The EWO was visiting almost daily to maintain contact and to look for some element in the family or the boys, which would account for the problem. The clinic decided that this was a case of school phobia that would pass after a careful restart had been made, using home tutors to maintain education while all the medical and psychological factors were looked into. This continued for a full year, until the deadlock needed to be broken by referral to the juvenile courts in the hope that removal from home and into the care of the local authority would remove what was diagnosed as a constant nervous stress factor in both children which exaggerated imagined home problems. One of these was that the mother would suddenly disappear while they were at school.

Both boys spent the whole of their school life in the care of the local authority. Later, it was discovered that the boys' father took them every week to the home of his wife's sister with whom he was having an affair. The boys had told their mother of the affair, but were threatened not to disclose the matter to anyone. Even the clinic and courts failed to elicit this piece of information, and only after the boys had gone into care, did the mother tell the education welfare officer of the violent marital quarrels that had occurred during the period of school attendance difficulty.

THERE'S A BOY HERE WHO HASN'T COME

Ralph sat unconcerned when the EWO entered the classroom to see the head teacher. His ample figure gradually subsided like a deflated lifebelt sinking lower and lower below the desk top, however, as the Head greeted the EWO with the words, 'I am glad that you have come today as we have a boy here who hasn't come'. The EWO's initial embarrassment showed some sympathy towards the targeted Ralph. To the Head and the class this was a friendly and amusing game. But not to Ralph. The Head's next question to Ralph was, 'That's right, isn't it, you are here but you have not been with us at all?' Ralph's sullen nod of agreement called for some relief from this stressful classroom situation and the EWO asked if Ralph could accompany him outside for a chat.

The EWO elicited, in private, from the Head that Ralph was not attending well and, when in school, was making little progress and appeared unable to concentrate on his work for more than a few minutes. Reports had been constantly passed to the Education Department asking for a psychological assessment about his lack of ability to learn, but to date nothing had happened. A surprised headmaster then agreed to allow the boy to be taken home for a one-to-one discussion between the parents and the EWO. The EWO was well known to the family and assured of entry. Both parents knew Ralph had a reading difficulty and both accepted the advice of the school and wanted him sent to another school where this problem could be rectified.

Knowing the weekly itinerary of the educational psychologist the EWO asked for an early assessment, and within a few weeks Ralph was in a school for the educationally handicapped, following an investigation into the headmaster's lost reports and letters.

Conclusion

The love, support, and encouragement that a child receives at home is the most powerful of all the forces that affect a child's behaviour. But although the influence of home is paramount, the concern which a school shows for the individual pupil can affect the child's learning and development. Particularly important is the early discovery of difficulties in learning, or inter-personal relationships and behaviour patterns. Early warnings of trouble in children, which enable early identification and suitable provisions being made for those with learning, behavioural, emotional and social handicaps, may also require a wide area of support from helping agencies trained to deal with them. The Education Welfare Service, being school centred and developed to support the child, the family and the school, is the first line of help, advice and action for schools and families, working in partnerships with many other agencies that make up the modern social work network.

Notes and references

1. National Youth Bureau: 17–23 Albion Street, Leicester.
   Publishers of *Disaffection from School* by Alison Skinner, Hilary Platts, and Brian Hill: a compilation of written works affecting schools and parents, with an impressive index of book lists and articles on school problems.

2. Local Training Board: 8 The Arndale Centre, Luton, Beds.
   Published the Ralphs Report in 1973. A national review of the Education Welfare Service, it also made recommendations as to the future role and training to a professional social work level.

3. The Children and Young Persons Act, 1973: HMSO.
   Amended the previous 1933 Act with regard to children appearing before the courts, and introduced new procedures for care orders and supervision of children in trouble with the law, including children affected by absence from school.

4. The Local Authority Social Services Act, 1970: HMSO.
   Provides the legal framework for the Social Services Department and Committees in England and Wales, and combined services for children, the aged, the handicapped, and mentally ill into one service. Also contained an option to include the Education Welfare Service.

5. The National Health Service Act, 1977: HMSO.
   Requires health authorities and social services to cooperate together in the advance of health and welfare of the people and to appoint joint consultative committees. Also contains the provisions of school medical and dental regulations, including the provision by the local education authorities for suitable accommodation. The legal requirements are laid down in this Act.

6. Education (Teachers) Regulations, 1982: HMSO.
   Regulates the employment of teachers and other persons employed by the education authority and other workers employed as workers with children, including teacher qualifications, and the need for health examination; also contains the powers of the Secretary of State to bar teachers on health or disciplinary grounds.

7. Citizens Advice Notes. Published by the National Council for Voluntary Organisations
   Available at most libraries; comprehensive abridged notes on law, education, social services, the health service, employment, social security, and consumer services.

8. The Education Act, 1944: HMSO.
   Contains the basic principles and duties of local education authorities in both England and Wales, together with the responsibilities of governors of schools and parents. The Act has been amended by numerous Acts between 1946 and 1986.

9. Pupils' Registration Regulations, 1956: HMSO.
   Sets out the rules for keeping both admission registers and class registers and the deletion of pupils' names from the register. Applies to both state and independent schools.

10. Schools and Further Education Regulations, 1981: HMSO.
    Regulation 11 prohibits the employment of children, whether paid or unpaid, during schools hours, except under the Work Experience Act (1973). It also deals with leave of absence granted by schools, and sets out the minimum number of school openings per year required by law.

11. The Education Act, 1980: HMSO.
    Under Section 8 of this Act local education authorities are required to publish each year their arrangements for admissions to schools maintained by them. Regulation made under this Act (School Information Regulations, 1981) requires the LEA to publish information concerning policy for primary and secondary education.

12. The Education Act, 1981: HMSO.
    Local education authorities are required to ascertain which children require a special provision in education. This includes assessment after identification and cooperation with parents.

13. The Education Act, 1986 (yet to receive the Royal Seal of Approval)
    Will exclude all corporal punishment from schools. Sets out the constitution of future governing bodies for schools. It introduces minimum numbers of teacher and parent governors. The provision of a system of teacher performance appraisal is also suggested.

14. *The New Law of Education* (published by Butterworth Press, London)
    This is a comprehensive book on all education laws and regulations previously published. Is revised and updated from time to time.

15. The Child Care Act, 1980: HMSO.
    This Act consolidated previous legislation and brought together parts of the 1963, 1969 and 1975 child care legislation.

16. *The Long Walk from the Dark: Frank Coombes OBE and Dave Beer*
    Published in April 1984 by National Association of Social Workers in Education.

Chapter 6

Body and Mind – Sources of help for young schoolchildren

Anthony Fairburn

Only three generations ago there was, simply, no school health service for British schoolchildren. The surprise finding at the beginning of the twentieth century of the Boer War recruits' deplorable health and stunted growth did, however, trigger off some rapid and effective action. By 1904 the first school meals were introduced and then, in stages, a sequence of three physical checks aimed especially towards the poorer children who had somehow survived malnutrition, rickets, and the killing infections such as pneumonia, diphtheria and streptococcal scarlet fever.

Eighty years further on, with the predicted small up-turn in our depressed birth rate just beginning to show, the newspapers and science reports describe how new health checks are being invented for the foetus as it is growing in the womb, and how high technology is used for monitoring babies for defects at birth.

Young people are, on the one hand, learning about the new DNA probes and the idea that they may be offered checks on their own genes before, or when, they decide to start a pregnancy. At another extreme, they can watch the reduced numbers of minority communities in relatively deprived inner-city areas describing on television their impoverished lives, and citing their children's poor health in claiming better social conditions.

Parents and teachers expect a superlative health service for the under-elevens and, they ask, will they get it?

This chapter addresses the question: 'Have we yet evolved a "superlative service"?' It looks at the detection of handicap that has not yet emerged, and the monitoring of body growth, physical well-being and some psychological needs. It indicates who is there to help the teacher when a child is malfunctioning or ill, and helps route the enquirer to a specialist service, but it also warns that we have not yet solved the problem of having two separate services for health – one which does most of the treatment, the other for prevention and monitoring.

A particular stress is laid on how good contacts between teachers, doctors and nurses just do not happen automatically, and that any interactive liaison has to be worked for, as is proper between professional people.

A standard, 'off-the-peg' school health service?

It is important first to realise that there is no such thing as a standard school medical service. The 201 district health authorities created in 1982 in England and Wales are still evolving their own policies in response to local circumstances. In some areas, notably the London Borough of Tower Hamlets, and in Nottingham and Newcastle, experiments in integrating the child health services across the board are well under way and are being evaluated (Russell, 1984).

A low take-up rate of health services by people living in a deprived inner city, where there may be higher incidences of psychiatric disablement and misuse of drugs and alcohol, raises the priority for selective physical checks and screening before their children are five years old, compared with other children whose parents use health services to the full.

In one town, a concentration of immigrant West Indians, South Asians and others from the Eastern Mediterranean makes necessary specific screening arrangements for hereditary sickle cell blood conditions, especially in pregnancy, teeth extractions and injuries (Health Education Council, 1983). Immigrant Chinese or Vietnamese with a possible 80 per cent risk of being Hepatitis B carriers may require screening for this when undergoing such procedures.

Immigrant communities may also be watched more closely for tuberculosis whereas, generally in Britain, Heaf tests and routine childhood inoculation with tuberculin may soon be a thing of the past. We are reassured – though this is challenged (Pollock, 1985) – that we need no longer keep up our 'herd immunity' to that dreaded crippler and killer, well remembered, along with the wretchedness of poliomyelitis, by doctors who qualified in the 1950s.

A flexible local medical response to children's needs is essential. An epidemic of, say, meningitis among school children in a small county town which, puzzlingly, just refuses to go away and whose origin cannot be traced, will entail diverting doctors, nurses and laboratory and environmental hygiene staff to trace the source of the dangerous microbe.

Services for the special senses of vision and hearing, and for language testing, hitherto concentrated more in 'special needs' schools, are moving steadily towards a more individual, pupil-oriented pattern following the 1981 Education Act. This Act proposed in Sections 2(2) and 2(3) that pupils with handicaps '. . . are to be educated in ordinary schools so far as is practical'.

Children of average intelligence who have special disabilities such as malformed or short limbs; or who have chronic coughs, low energy and retarded growth from fibrocystic lung disorder; or congenitally malformed hearts (making their fingernails and lips look blue); or damaged kidneys (making their skin pale, yellowish or wizened); should now be receiving better health support services to allow and encourage them to remain integrated with their friends in the local school community.

The anomaly that none of these changes was previously funded may be eased by means of new education support grants for two out of the five special programmes for schools, which were aimed specifically at such reintegration.

Options for all kinds of health staff to specialise more in children's work is another change, highlighted in 1976 by the Court Committee report, *Fit for the Future* (DHSS, 1976). The growth of the extra pre-qualification and in-service training programmes needed to support this has been slow. Certain staff, notably audiometricians and speech therapists, are still in very short supply. The first, rare, hearing therapists were appointed in 1984.

Professor Court's Committee also recommended that the (mainly) hospital-based consultant paediatricians rearrange their ward and hospital out-patient workload to take on a more community-based role. This has happened, for instance, in the Isle of Wight.

The Royal College of General Practitioners, whose Members and Fellows are essentially extremely broadly based, generalist doctors, turned down the Committee's other radical idea – to create a new specialism of 'general practitioner paediatricians' who would concentrate chiefly on the children in their practices. A trend towards better integration of these family doctors with the community child health services has happened in some counties such as, for instance, Somerset, but most felt that such total specialism would isolate them from treating the whole family.

A related proposal (Gray, D. J. Periera, 1982) that family doctors learn more about positive child health, routine surveillance and disability screening has been well received, and many more established family doctors do go on child health courses. More of the young GP-trainees are taking up this child health option in their first three years of community-based in-service postgraduate training.

The next section, therefore, emphasises how these truly family doctors can, with better child health skills and an intimate knowledge of the children's family backgrounds, prove themselves to be the teachers' great allies. It also develops the idea that, for immediate advice when in a quandary, *every* teacher should create a 'confidential health contact' list, and suggests how.

Using the family doctor

Before exploring how teachers can use the hospital and community health staff (school doctors, nurses, child specialists, paramedical and technical staff) as allies, let us recapitulate how a family doctor's knowledge of the background can be crucial in understanding the interaction between a child's health and behaviour. For this, he or she, naturally, calls upon the others in the primary care team – health visitor nurses, district nurses and, increasingly, some attached social workers. One important factor is that they have accumulated knowledge throughout a child's life, sometimes back a generation or two, whenever the family has consulted them for personal help with physical and mental health problems. The doctor and nurse are trusted for their discretion.

Another is the medical tradition that doctors who are concerned always try whenever possible to improve their patients' adverse home and social circumstances. A few, like Dr Barnardo, are well known from accounts of their humane activities in the eighteenth and nineteenth centuries. Others are exemplified in fiction, as when Cronin's hero, young Dr Manson, in *The Citadel*, one night blew up the town's main sewer that was propagating typhoid among his miner families.

It has been estimated that there is a sufficiently small, manageable group of roughly twenty handicapped children (say, 5 per cent of 400 children in most practices) for each family doctor to get to know well and review regularly (Gray, 1982).

Why, then, is so little use made by schools of the 'GP' as a potential, valuable resource for understanding the child's vulnerability and his or her extra needs? Some say that '... doctors are so busy, they can't be disturbed'. Regrettably, this is occasionally based upon inexcusably defensive behaviour on the telephone by a curt receptionist, though most are chosen very carefully for their personal qualities. Another fear arises from doctors seeming to be rather awesome, clever and powerful people, perceived to discourage approaches which are not to do with personal illness, and to be 'just the sort to rebuff a mere teacher'.

An interesting technique is used by some psychiatrists and psychologists to explain how such destructive misperceptions can arise in people's thinking, with the result that good communication is biased and blocked. It is called 'cognitive therapy', and it uses positive, logical thinking to help break down barriers (Burns, 1980). One of its uses is to demonstrate that, although a notion is sometimes based on an earlier, really bad experience, it has progressed to become illogically over-inclusive by a process of extrapolation from a number of small assumptions (like those about doctors). The technique also explores what important ideas might lie just beneath the surface of these apparently simple notions; whether they are tied up with earlier life experiences with, say, in this case, figures of authority such as bank managers or even certain teachers in one's childhood!

If that sounds rather abstract, the truth of the matter is that most doctors when approached during working hours, are found to be exceptionally glad to make time to help a child of a family in their practice. Equally, they know that teachers are just as busy and hard-working fellow professionals as themselves.

Out of hours, to get some time off, a third of doctors switch their telephones over to a medical deputising service whose locum doctors will not know the families.

But all good inter-disciplinary liaison requires a stage of careful preparation. This was done in some interesting 'teachers-meet-doctors' schemes in such provincial towns and cities as Yeovil, Somerset, and Plymouth, Devon, where the initial exploratory talks fortunately revealed that each had for some time been wishing informally to meet the other. A joint forum was evolved: the educationalists offered their Teachers' Centre, the doctors their Post-Graduate Medical Centre. An initial, small group, perhaps warily drinking coffee in each others' houses, turned into a regular, but not too frequent, well-planned evening seminar at which topics of common interest (such as 'Bereavement, Loss and Grieving', or 'The Latest on Test-tube Babies and the Pill') were presented, and useful health educational ideas explored. Each found, besides human interest and a liking for the other, areas of relevant knowledge and mutual expertise which they could not have predicted.

Doctors have another special use. From their student days they have become assiduous observers, 'people-watchers', trained to notice the slightest change in a person's condition – the dilated pupils, the flush creeping up the neck. This may sometimes be embarrassing but they are also trained rigorously to adduce proper and restrained conclusions from these observations in a scientific way.

Clinical examples

'IS SHE PUTTING IT ON, DOCTOR?'

Kim, aged ten, had complained of faintness a couple of times before leaving for school, had been irritable and off her food, but she was normally a bit choosy in eating matters. Some minor unpleasantries at school might have accounted for any of this.

There was no anaemia, and her heart, blood-pressure and central nervous system were in good order but – even though she had not been noticed to be jaundiced – there, in the white of her eyes, could be seen with difficulty the very faintest tinge of yellow. Tests revealed that Kim was, in fact, just getting over a 'subclinical' bout of Hepatitis A.

Her behaviour could quite easily have been ascribed to an emotional state or some life event, by such of those who find it easy and impressive to see and to state categorically what is cause and effect, on inadequate and unproved grounds.

A TODDLER HEADING FOR DANGER

Gary, only 18 months, was brought by his mother with an obvious fever. He had a raised temperature but little in the way of overt local disturbance in his various systems. The doctor noticed, however, that he was making tiny movements which slightly flared his nostrils, the 'alae nasi', as he breathed in. He knew then, from this important sign – which could so easily have been missed – that he had to look even more closely to discover whether Gary was not already entering the early, incipient stages of a developing broncho-pneumonia.

THE LOST CHILD NO ONE TALKED ABOUT

Another crucial contribution from a family doctor came near the end of a rather long child-abuse case conference. It had reached the rallentando stage when everybody was beginning to wonder whether the expensive presence of so many professional people round the table, including teachers from three schools, could clarify any further the degree of what seemed rather lesser risks to the children in a very complicated family. Members were still bemused, after an hour, by uncertainties somewhat redolent of the Old Testament, as to 'who had begat whom', and other marital and cohabital intricacies.

The elderly doctor, who had built up a certain loyalty over the years with these difficult and unpredictable people, was the sort sometimes described as 'coming from the old school'. He had been sitting quietly with all the National Health Service cards of the ramified family on his knees, listening but saying little. Then: 'I wonder if any of you know this, but surely this is the "XX" family whose second baby died in late 197x under very suspicious and totally unresolved circumstances?'

Nobody in the room had ever heard of this essential and highly significant risk item. None of the files in which five agencies had accumulated data over a number of years of history taking, monitoring and helping, had any mention of this dead child.

While professional confidentiality should be broken only to save a child from risk, in Britain we are moving rapidly towards full disclosure of medical and social work records to the individual patient or client and, at the same time, discussing with them more freely and seeking permission for the necessary, limited, inter-professional exchange of sensitive personal information that makes the basis of a coordinated service to children. Verbal permission for this should always be recorded. If in doubt, one can ask for written permission but, in practice, this will rarely be found to be necessary.

Identifiable personal data stored on disk or tape have now to be statutorily declared, and one should take great care with photostated material since it inevitably gets into the wrong hands at some time. Any document can, of course, be subpoenaed later for court use.

School nurses

The school nurse who has managed to maintain continuity in a school is worth her weight in gold. What are her tasks? Prevention can sound mundane (the 'responsibility to monitor and to maintain health') but when put into action is rather more exciting. In an initial health interview with parents and child on entering infant school – at five years in Britain, and possibly even earlier – she and the school doctor will pick up most of the important defects of vision, speech and language, and any problems of psychological development which may not have emerged earlier, including clumsy or mildly mentally handicapped children. Up to two-fifths of these five-year-olds may be found to have a health problem of some sort.

By plotting selectively those children whose growth deviates most – the exceptionally heavy and largest (above the '90th centile') and the ultra-light and shortest (below the '10th centile') – a comparison with the imaginary hundred representative British children of exactly the same age and sex pictured on the centile chart can be made.

Cases of obesity, skin disease, upper respiratory and ear infections are generally picked up earlier by the family doctor but, as Bax has cogently pointed out, a significant number are missed before school age especially in disadvantaged inner city areas, where uptake is lower (Bax, 1976). Roughly equal numbers with defects of posture and poor musculo-skeletal development, sleeping and eating problems, persistent bed-wetting, and overactivity, aggression and poor emotional adjustment are identified by school health staff as by family doctors (OPCS, 1974).

The spinal deformities have a nasty way of progressing from a hardly noticeable, slightly S-shaped curvature to a very unyielding scoliosis. These must not be missed, so the child must be adequately stripped and examined with the mother or father present and, if possible, the teacher.

A further check two years later at the age of seven-plus with the emphasis on growth, vision (including colour blindness) and hearing defects, is generally agreed to be timely. The principle of these continuing function-surveys is to be selective if appropriate. In Bax and Whitmore's study in London, one in five parents were glad to take up the offer of a further nurse interview because of health worries in their seven-year-olds (Bax and Whitmore, 1981).

It goes without saying that decent premises for all health activities are essential – for physiotherapists (who will advise and train parents and teachers to carry on their physical mobility and postural coordination practices) and speech therapists, and for vision-testing (with the room blacked-out). The present pervasive lack of facilities for treatment, as well as for examination, is said ruefully by all such medical staff to '... give us real, major problems'. This will apply increasingly to ordinary schools, as to special needs schools.

Further checks at nine or ten years may show up significant handicaps in one in seven children. More are done at eleven-plus, and usually in '4th-year pre-career medicals'. Nurses taking up community jobs are becoming more experienced at recalling pupils, with 'hands-on' experience of computer terminals and, if the proposed English Nursing Board's new training schedules are adopted, will start with earlier community experience as learner nurses. Their training in the management of child-abuse, including sexual abuse, is particularly helpful to school staff and education welfare officers, not least as extra support if staff later find themselves involved in court hearings.

In the Netherlands and Sweden, as an example of 'whole-population screening', health checks (which may include checking for rubella – German measles, which damages the growing foetus – and giving polio-booster inoculations) may allow also for blood-pressure and urine examination. Here, they are not so much looking for adult-type hypertension, as for certain reversible cardiac defects.

Clinical examples

A REASON FOR BEING LITTLE

Tim was small in infant school, but then so were his parents. Only when, in the hard winter of 1981, he seemed to the nurse to be unduly out of breath, with very obviously poor skin circulation, was his arterial blood-pressure measured. Although the heart beat heftily against his rib-cage on exertion, there were unequal and poor pulses at both wrists and hardly anything to be felt in his groins, where the femoral arteries go down through the thigh muscles.

An injection of X-ray-opaque contrast fluid into the big veins flowing towards the heart showed that there was already a dangerous back-pressure effect on the overloaded lung circulation, with what looked like a niche at the arch of the great aortic artery after it left the heart. The shadow projected on to the film plate showed a severe narrowing in the aortic tube size, running for about 2 cm. Advanced blood-flow studies, using the latest computerised picture synthesis of Tim's mass of heavy vessels in that area, allowed the cardiac surgeon to plan an exact plastic repair deep inside the chest, which freed the high-pressure arterial flow for the first time in his life.

Improvement was dramatic in small-boy energies. The heavy, overdeveloped left heart chamber decreased in size, and serial weight and height checks later showed that Tim was well in line to be bigger than his parents when he grew up. The school nurse treasures on her mantelpiece a blurry photo of Tim threatening one of his friends in a histrionic, 'macho' posture.

School doctors

The 'school MOs' are changing focus, too. Gone in many areas are the routine, or even 'collective' (group), clinic medical examinations. A doctor's time will be more firmly based in school premises, with the emphasis on chronic handicap and on maintaining the contacts with family doctors and other health and specialist child-help agencies. They will be much more available to staff, parents and children for advice and health counselling and, if they are used properly, the better will be their response. A teacher who can get a doctor to come into the staffroom to advise on health education – particularly as it affects the curriculum – will get the best out of that doctor and will help to fulfil the aims of prevention in the child health services (DHSS, 1980).

A practical example is that of rubella (German measles). This is a mild and unimportant virus infection unless a pregnant woman catches it in the first three months of the growth of her foetus, when the foetus will almost certainly be profoundly damaged (yet may, tragically, live). The senior doctor in charge of school health services finds out from special nursing staff what are the uptake figures for inoculation of pre-pubertal girls: 95 per cent plus would be excellent. If the local rate is badly down, the signal will go out to all the health educators and the teachers who can inculcate good practice in their girls and their parents.

The school doctor's other prime value is to route a child towards the appropriate services, to certain fieldwork personnel or a very specialised medical service. If that does not happen, teachers must learn to insist that gaps be filled so that they get nothing but the best. A set of possible questions are appended in a checklist on p. 148, to act as a mind-jogger. This whole topic, the variations in children's health services and in particular the schools' services are discussed in a new, important, accessible, research-based and inexpensive book by Dr Kingsley Whitmore, which is highly recommended (Whitmore, 1985).

The way was indeed smoothed, in the cases of Amy and Jake:

Clinical examples

DISFIGURED, BUT GETTING WELL

Amy had, at the age of nine, developed acute leukaemia and was being treated at the big city teaching hospital. Leukaemia is now most often curable and, to give a child the best chance, complex routines of powerful 'cytotoxic' drugs (toxic to cells) are necessary which can have distressing, but temporary, side effects.

Amy was doing well on this chemotherapy and would soon be going back to school. The high-tech doctors in the city had, at her school MO's suggestion, arranged for a nurse from their hospital team to call at the school to explain it all to the staff and to the children. In particular, she told them how Amy had lost her hair. As the senior physician put it, '... caring and curing are not alternatives'.

A SAD BEREAVEMENT

Jake's father, Rod, was killed while turning right on his 4-cylinder 650cc Kawasaki in heavy rain, on the way to his factory via the local killer three-lane road.

Jake's mother did not hear immediately that it had been totally the fault of a criminally impatient commuter who had attempted a head-on, illegal overtake along the white-striped safety box at the junction. Her first feeling was of horror in recalling the row she and Rod had had as he left home, slamming the door, and it left her bitterly and deeply preoccupied with guilt that their fracas had been contributory. Rod had been a good provider, but was immature relative to his wife.

Jake and his two sisters had by now set off for their local primary school, which was positive and well run. They had been vaguely aware of recurrent rows during an episode of infidelity, but were less affected by the marital stresses through the protective effect of the wider family, good friends and pastorally sensitive teachers. Jake, now aged eight, had needed some extra help six months previously, during a spell of becoming withdrawn and soiling.

The small school moved into the emergency mode. Jake's teacher was able, since she knew and liked Rod and knew quite a lot about the background, to share her personal grief as she drove the three stunned children home and this they found to be impressive and reassuring. Upon reaching a desolate house where their mother was trying to cope with her own equally stunned relatives and friends, and a succession of bewildered and tearful in-laws, it was soon evident (contrary to the beliefs of many people who have not taught bereaved children) that Jake and the older sister wanted to get back as soon as possible into the familiar school routine, to their friends, classroom pets and projects. This was arranged for the following day. The younger girl clung to her mother and a favourite Nan, for several days.

The question on the minds of these very caring teachers was, 'Do the children need something magical called "bereavement counselling"?' Several of them had been on a course which included a day-seminar on many aspects of loss of parents and relatives, and they didn't think so.

They decided to contact their MO for advice. She was fortunately accessible over the telephone; and she also thought not. However, remembering that, during a period of in-service training she had opted to give some supervised assistance to families going through emotional difficulties using the local child and family psychiatric team, she contacted the psychiatrist – a fully trained medical doctor – direct.

He had been one of the speakers at the bereavement study day, and remembered Jake's family well, and the dead father Rod. He speedily identified the expert child and family psychiatric social worker who had joined him in treating that family as cotherapist, and they both knew the mother's strengths. It was therefore proposed that this family expert would (as consultant in her own right) advise and support the teachers in what they were already managing very competently, but only as they felt they needed it, as the crisis progressed. The school MO remained in the picture, mainly to keep the family doctor and community nurses informed.

The psychiatric social worker sent for an extra copy of the dedicated booklet for teachers, *When a Child in Your School is Bereaved*, and this was also enormously reassuring (The Compassionate Friends, 1985).

The end result, which worked out to be supportive for the bereaved young widow and her children, enhanced not only the teachers' self-confidence, but also their future use of 'health advisory contacts'.

In another local primary school – 'Hillfields', which included the infant age group of five to seven years – the informal consultative process had developed further. The background was as follows. The houses in the school's catchment lay in a bowl on the edge of the city. Demographic and other data pieced together showed that the families living in the area had a higher rate of probation orders, social work calls, and child and family psychiatric referrals than in other suburbs. They had more unpaid debts for rent and electricity, a higher rate of juvenile and adult crime, and higher minor illness rates and accidents to small children.

Amenities for that part of the city were, conversely, skimpy. Few of the professionals serving the area chose to live there; it was not unpleasant or threatening, just dull and repetitive.

So a Hillfields scheme grew up. Besides voluntary ventures, one agency contribution was to attach a special infant nurture group to the school, not least in acknowledgement of the Infant head teacher's strong, warm and realistic qualities. Since this unit would take the half-dozen most over-alert, bumptious or generally underfunctioning five- or six-year-olds who had already missed or failed to respond to enriching services for the under-fives, extra support to the teacher and her assistant was clearly called for.

The educational psychologist for that part of the city was a good communicator, had an unusually peripatetic outlook, and she believed in getting very early assistance to young children in special need.

It happened also that there was in the team a specialist child therapist, a young, highly experienced man who, although his esoteric training might have been expected to prepare him mainly to select individuals for lengthy personal psychotherapy, shared decided views on early intervention. He also took immense trouble to make himself known as someone who could be rung up directly on first-name terms for informal advice.

Between these two, the infant, junior and special unit teachers can quickly obtain consultative advice and, as a corollary, the number of formal child and family psychiatric clinic referrals from them has dropped. An extra bonus has been that, between them, they feel that they have also made inroads into the problem of the non-compliant families of Hillfields. These teachers now feel that they are partners in a 'superlative early, preventive mental health service'.

Child mental health services

Other categories of specialists are at hand if teachers feel that families could benefit from help with children who are having emotional or behavioural problems in school.

(a) *Psychiatrist*
This is a consultant who, starting as a fully trained medical doctor, has gone on to gain a minimum of six years' specialist experience under the high standards specified by the Royal College of Psychiatrists, whose advanced Membership examination has to be taken. Some have useful paediatric experience as well.

Needless to say, it is implicitly necessary to offer some explanation and get the parents' permission before referring a child. It helps if you can explain to parents that a psychiatrist does not have 'X-ray eyes' which can see right into a person's thinking processes, but will invite families to talk in confidence about problems and feelings. The same techniques of careful and rigorous history taking are used, as by all doctors.

Very few of the 400 or so child and family psychiatrists stay in their clinics solely to see children and adolescents referred for individual psychotherapy (which helps an individual to change in attitudes and behaviour) though this can be a powerful part of the treatment. They accept referrals from anybody, including directly from the client families, but it is important that the family doctor, who may already be working with a family's psychological problems, knows and can comment.

Many psychiatrists make liaison visits to schools to confer with teachers on site, preferably if the time is allocated well beforehand. Like the family doctors, their secretaries are always chosen most carefully to facilitate informal calls for brief consultations by 'phone, ringing back when the doctor or teacher is free. Getting the clinic gaps to coincide with school break periods requires a little patience! The full range of their clinic and 'liaison' work is well described in Dr Derek Steinberg's excellent paperback, *Using Child Psychiatry* (Steinberg, 1981).

These doctors are used to working with the most seriously disturbed, or mentally ill, damaging or alienating parents, some of whose very harmed children may never have made any attachment to an adult even by the age of leaving junior school at 11-plus. They deal also with all types of broken families, and children taken into care and fostered, and so are much consulted on long-term intervention plans at the earliest stages before irreparable harm can be done to a child.

This is a good use of their time. Early referrals are welcomed, if only for short, often quite pragmatic, active interventions, getting the family to use its latent strengths to work together to support flagging, or hostile, or scape-goated members. In crisis intervention the principle is to pull out when the clients are just over the hump and, having survived being temporarily de-skilled by the stress of the crisis, can with encouragement take back full control of their own affairs.

The wide range of the child and family psychiatrists' work makes them worth considering for advice in such familiar difficulties as the handling of a non-custodial parent who, as part of the continuing bitterness and hostile manipulations that can follow separation and divorce, has been cruelly excluded from seeing a son or daughter or even from receiving school reports. Such parents sometimes (in genuine grief) misguidedly force themselves on to the child at the school gates to try to resolve a prolonged separation, may try to bribe schoolfriends, or foolishly seek a showdown with the teacher.

Psychiatrists will also advise, for instance, on working with apparently non-compliant parents, or teach consultation skills, if invited. They have a policy to help train up all possible fellow professionals to enable children to get help *in situ* from someone they know and, as can be said of their other three groups of professional colleagues, will willingly pass on their expertise.

Besides the educational psychologists, who work directly with schools, many clinical psychologists, the various therapists (child-, family-, and play-therapists), working in the teams with child and family psychiatric social workers, are committed to peripatetic and liaison work, as described in the Hillfields scheme (p. 134).

Naturally, their individual special interests vary. Examples, not necessarily exclusive to each discipline, might be as follows.

(b) *Clinical psychologist*:
 'Social skills' training (for shy or diffident people).
 Overactive children.
 Retarded language development.
 Children with facial grafts after extensive burns.

(c) *Educational psychologist*:
 Modifying behaviour.
 Special investigations for minimal brain damage.
 Dyslexia and related literacy difficulties.
 Parent-and-child reading schemes.

(d) *Therapists*:
 Conjoint treatment, with colleagues, of the whole family.
 Depressed children with sleeping problems.
 Children in a kidney-grafting unit.
 The dying child.

(e) *Social worker*:
 Discussion group for children or parents in adoption.
 Outward (domiciliary) work in acute school phobia.
 Children with deaf-and-dumb parents.
 Families with another child who is mentally impaired.

The helpful secretaries at the child and family guidance clinic or, if there is a hospital base, at the department of child and family psychiatry, have all the telephone extension numbers and hold copies of their diaries.

Some of the wide range of health professionals mentioned in this chapter like to be encouraged to come among school staff more than others, and it is worth establishing this clearly from time to time as staff move, or posts rotate. This will ensure maximum use of both their huge teaching potential, and their willingness to act as informal, personal, 'health advisory contacts'.

Health problems

(a) Some common conditions (excluding simple colds and accidents) are very familiar to school nurses. Every type of virus illness in the throat or chest can develop during the day. Headache is one of the more common complaints. The experienced nurse has then to decide whether to refer a child on to the family doctor via its parents.

Accidents vary from acid spilled on a finger, or a tight ring, to wood chips, copper sulphate or grit in the eye – which must always be taken seriously. Tight rings tend to be sent on to the jeweller. Sprains usually have an athletic history, but are occasionally because, '... my wrist was bent back by a friend'!

(b) *Obesity*

Overweight children often have at least one obese close relative and, as the problem is generally one of family motivation and eating habits, it is best handled by the child's ('primary care') family doctor and nurse team.

Having checked the child's physical status, they will assume responsibility for referral on to the hospital-based dietician if weight gain is intractable. Sometimes, a mother and daughter will agree to diet together.

The school nurse's job is to pick up and record overweight (on the centile chart), and liaise with primary care team colleagues on management, including advising the school kitchen and who checks serial weighings. She may also promulgate health education literature about obesity, for school staff and families.

(c) *Life-threatening conditions*

Diabetes is a life-threatening condition requiring daily, closely controlled medication, with the occasional emergency thrown in. Although a school nurse or doctor may help initially to diagnose this condition, and will certainly have some equipment to test urine for sugar (a sort of dipstick), the regime and specialised reviews will already have been worked out between the hospital paediatrician and family doctor.

With epilepsy the same principles apply, as in the following case study exemplifying worthwhile ideas and good practice.

Clinical example

FITTY PETE – A COLLABORATION

The first signs in toddlerhood of Pete's epilepsy were a couple of febrile convulsions (short seizures at the height of any short feverish infection) which did not worry his foster parents, for they had been reassured that febrile convulsions usually do not recur. In his case they did, and the genesis was known.

Pete was now a solid, rising ten who, at the age of eleven months had been found to have suspicious bruising to the cheekbones, arms and trunk, a cigarette burn from the very unstable mother's third cohabitee (which was to punish him for pulling over some expensive video equipment) and, before this cruelty could be stopped, a massive skull fracture claimed to be from falling from a high chair.

When faced with the paediatrician's and radiologist's expert views that this in no way matched the degree of force necessary to spring the skull inwards and crack three contiguous skull bones right across their separating 'suture' lines, Pete's mother, now alone again, admitted that she had seen, but could not prevent (because she was too frightened), the third cohabitee throw her small son across the room. This, and her wretchedly poor, neglectful standards, and her inability to make use of a contracted period of intensive professional support, led to placing Pete into long term foster care. This was, unfortunately, not the end of it.

Although the fostering was the very best the county's adoption and fostering experts could find, Pete could not overcome some definite, small handicaps. Because the main brain injury had been on the left side, his football-kicking right leg was weak and operated jerkily. Holding a pen was a trial. His speech area (and its multiple connections) was harmed in a way which made forming words smoothly and serially an effort, though he knew what he wanted to say and, given time, he performed in the low average range of intelligence.

Pete's friends got tired of waiting for him to complete what he was trying to say, and could not resist finishing it for him as a leg-pull. Despite vigorous warnings from the deputy Head, this unkind ragging went on behind the scenes and Pete gave up being patient and waiting for it to stop and, having considered whether to pour some of his foster father's weedkiller into the worst offender's stew, settled for lighting a small fire in the bully's desk-space.

During these periods of heightened tension, or at the start of a cold, he would sometimes have a spell of about four or five epileptic seizures within two or three days. It followed a similar sequence. With hardly any warning, he fell forward and to the right, completely unconscious, sometimes knocking his nose or forehead. The body was held rigid for about five seconds; then a fine, symmetrical trembling developed all over and gave way to synchronous convulsive jerkings of the arms, legs and head, including his face. Because the breathing organs could not operate naturally, he became frighteningly blue after about another fifteen seconds of this. Then, there was a shuddering deep breath, pinkness all over, and a brief, snoring sleep, from which he woke fairly gently.

Those who knew Pete had learned that

(a) He was not in danger of the hypothetical old wives' tale of 'swallowing his tongue'.
(b) During the seizure there was no point in trying to restrain him.
(c) The airway was all important, so one had to keep his jaw gently, but firmly, supported from underneath with one's hand once he was relaxed enough, and then roll him into a comfortable semi-prone position, half on his side on a flat bit of carpet or coat (definitely *not* a cushion) to wake when he was ready.
(d) Calling the ambulance wasn't necessary, but his identification tag gave the home telephone number so that he could be collected when well enough to be moved home, which was in about twenty minutes.

Unless the trigger for this typical 'grand mal' seizure was a fluey cold, Pete would probably be back in school next morning. He might be a little bit slowed-up for a further day, and this needed to be understood.

Between these spells, he was free of epileptiform seizures for anything up to ten months, but took a maintenance dose of an anti-convulsant tablet called Carbamezapine, for which occasional blood-level checks were felt to be helpful. Being an active, and not too scatty, ten-year-old who loved to lead a vigorous, normal life, Pete was furious and miserable about the restriction on bicycling in the road and swimming, and began to ask increasingly frequently when the family doctor and the paediatrician (who had a special interest in neurological disorders) would let him cycle and swim with his friends.

The foster parents were good about giving him as much normal freedom as possible, but both they and the school staff worried, as all conscientious parents do, whether they might lay themselves open to criticism if, in the course of living this normal life, he had a fit and died or injured himself badly.

Sensing this at just the right time, the family doctor and paediatrician offered them a joint consultation – the GP dropping in to the friendly hospital paediatric clinic for coffee with them and the sister, at the end of his morning calls. They rehearsed with Pete's form teacher, his specialist remedial teacher and deputy Head, and the foster parents, the three restrictions: swimming, cycling in traffic and climbing at heights. They approved the sensible way the seizures were being managed, checked that Pete's anticonvulsant medication levels were just about right and asked them to make a note if the seizure format changed significantly.

It was made absolutely clear to the teachers and foster parents that the medical people would firmly support them in the event of anything going wrong, and any risks they ran were reviewed realistically together.

The final task was to confirm their rapid availability, at a visit or direct over the 'phone, as 'confidential health contacts' whenever advice was needed between appointments. The paediatrician's personal secretary Sue came in with his letters for signing, and introduced herself so that they would know her voice on the telephone. Pete no longer thinks (of dying accidentally in a seizure) '... well, I might as well be dead, anyway.'

Schools can now expect more children with the more serious physical handicaps and deformities to attend in the normal way.

(d) *Less common chronic (long-lasting) conditions*

Fibrocystic disease consists of being born with an irreversible problem of thick, clinging mucus in the lungs which collects into infected clusters and gradually destroys the lung tissue. The sufferer will have had a great deal of hospitalisation, has greatly reduced exercise tolerance, and looks sallow and ill much of the time. Help is given by physiotherapists, who show them and their parents how to cough up the mucus and drain the various lobes of the lungs. Many have a pretty good idea that early death is a possibility, and it is important for the teacher to be fully briefed by parents and the consultant paediatrician.

With kidney failure some children are on twice-weekly dialysis which processes their own blood slowly from arm veins, removing unwanted salts and breakdown chemicals which the diseased kidneys cannot take care of. Whether done at home or on day visits to the hospital, the routine is a great strain and a disruption for all the family, who never really quite know when grafting might be possible.

Some children with chronic renal failure become anaemic and need a top-up blood transfusion from time to time, which can have a marvellously revivifying effect.

There is also a period of uncertainty after the graft, until it is clear that there will be no late rejection of the donor kidney. The specialist surgical team and the dialysis nurses at the hospital take care to pass on their own high morale, giving constant support to the families, and they will always gladly liaise with teachers.

(e) *Skin and other cosmetic disabilities*

Eczema appears to have an element of allergy, without a clearcut cause. It usually starts in babyhood, decreasing as the child becomes older to leave areas of rough, itchy skin in the flexures – the folds of the elbows and the backs of the knees – maybe a roughening of the wrists and some traces round the back edge of the neck and forehead.

Some children with eczema get worse when they are hot and bothered, and they may have other allergic conditions like asthma.

Psoriasis, whose cause is also not understood, varies greatly from person to person and in its periodicity. Blotchy, sometimes quite large, red patches of thicker skin may appear all over the body in an irregular pattern, totally unpredictably. Fortunately, local energetic treatment with ointment containing steroid hormones from the adrenal glands often reduces the patches, but the condition may recur throughout life. Bumps can be felt in the skin of the scalp. One form with the graceful Latin name of raindrops ('guttate' psoriasis) has uniform tiny spots all over.

Many other cosmetic disfigurations, from the 'port-wine stains' made up of a myriad of tiny capillary blood vessels (haemangioma), to moles and other unwanted patches of dark brown or black pigment may be seen on the face or body. The former are hard to bleach out with laser heat treatment without causing some residual fine scarring or paling of the skin. Plastic surgeons will always advise about the latter; should a child's mole seem to grow an extra outer margin rather quickly or begin to bleed, this may be a sign of (rare) malignant change and ought to be checked by the skin specialist immediately.

Children with such markings on them, or with scarring from burns which may have needed skin grafting, need to know that one caring, immediately accessible adult knows all about it and can counter silly questions or nicknames with matter-of-fact, accurate information.

This gives teachers another opportunity to make use of an 'advisory health contact'. Although the family's or the school doctor can brief teachers (with the family's permission, of course), it is perfectly in order to seek clearance for the teacher to speak direct to the consultant dermatologist, having explained via the personal medical secretary, (a), that it is with their express permission and, (b), how a brief consultation might help.

(f) *Children in wheelchairs*
Broadly speaking, these may be:
  (i) those with permanent neurological handicap, either from early brain damage resulting in weak, stiff or uncoordinated limbs, or from lower spinal damage caused by an accident or from being born with spina bifida – in which the lowest parts of the spinal cord were incompletely formed. The latter may have lifelong problems of bladder control.
  (ii) those with deteriorations in nervous tissue, including certain puzzling systematic destructive processes going on in nerve tracts (the 'neuro-dystrophies'), and quite unrelated processes in muscle fibres themselves (the 'myo-dystrophies'); children with tumours in the spinal cord which were found to be too diffuse to remove fully; and haemophiliacs whose blood lacks a clotting factor so that the slightest injury can start bleeding into (in this case) the leg joints, necessitating a short time in a wheelchair. [Please note: at the time of publication, a small number of haemophiliac children had been discovered to be infected with the AIDS virus from therapeutic blood extracts. The Department of Health and Social Security's (1985) booklet *Children at School and Problems Related to AIDS* reassures teachers that ordinary social contact poses no risk of infection, provided normal hygiene precautions are observed, and advises that they should be free to play football and take part in cookery and science classes with other pupils.]
  (iii) some children with a built-in abnormality of the skeleton – some symmetrical, with short or badly aligned limb bones; others born with fragile, easily injured, shafts and joints.

These children, except the minority with an originating brain injury, are of usual intelligence and they experience the same feelings, curiosity, angers and impatience of all of us when young.

(g) Each person's handicap is different, even if the diagnosis sounds the same. For teachers' briefings, the school doctor will collate information as to any special risks and what to do about them, how normally the child should if possible be treated, what are the parents' knowledge and coping skills, and whom to contact if in doubt. The specialists will hold regular reviews in either the hospital paediatric (out-patient) clinic or in a larger group (to which the teacher should always be invited) loosely entitled the 'community handicap team', which is really a network of professionals got together by the community doctor, with the parents, to review the child's current status and update its predictable needs. This is, despite the jargonistic name, useful and practical.

At these meetings the parents are encouraged to question what is going on so that they understand how forward plans are made for their child's education and management, and can give their assent.

Most paediatricians based, with their speech therapy, physiotherapy and other colleagues in county or city general hospitals, have been able to install some type of childrens' multi-handicap centre, some of which have overnight hostels for distant families. The centres have been given cheerful, humanising names and are staffed, as in all childrens' units, by people who are welcoming and helpful to all comers.

Even though minutes will have been circulated with the names of those convened for the team meetings, a teacher on unfamiliar hospital or clinic territory will at first feel disoriented – just as parents (and doctors) do when visiting a school. The hospital doctors, nurses, physiotherapists, psychologists and others realise this and will respect a visiting teacher who asks, '. . . excuse me, I didn't quite pick up what you said when we all introduced ourselves, could you explain that again?' Someone else in the room and new to the experience, will be grateful for this.

These meetings can help originate the educational statements for the local education authority to allocate places (and funding) for 'special needs' school placements and the 'annual reviews of statemented children', but will, increasingly, be used to service the arrangements for keeping more handicapped children assimilated in their local schools.

They will determine what the handicap means in educational terms: whether a child will require continuous attention and a curriculum geared to the handicap – a 'constant environment' – or whether partial withdrawal into a special unit within an ordinary school will suffice, and will cover such practical matters as the installation of a lift in the school.

LEAs are still working out these new patterns, and those currently operating the systems with few extra resources deserve some sympathy and understanding, until the new methods and improved facilities fall into place.

For more detail of the handicaps outlined above and of others, the reader will find a growing number of sympathetically written books for non-clinical staff. Paediatrician Dr Bernard Valman's (1982) series of *British Medical Journal* articles, the *ABC of 1 to 7*, giving straightforward, orthodox advice with the emphasis on practice rather than theory, have been collected into book form (1982). His references include useful addresses such as the Muscular Dystrophy Group of Great Britain, the British Epilepsy Society and the British Diabetic Association. These specialist groups will always supply or suggest highly practical and up-to-date information sheets or booklets for teachers who wish to set up a file about the handicap.

Another similar approach, giving the parents' angle and multiple useful references, is that of the clinical psychologist Dr Richard Lansdown in his short and readable book *More Than Sympathy* (Lansdown, 1980). The Royal Association For Disability and Rehabilitation (RADAR) has also just brought out a teachers' guide describing 29 different disabilities with their educational and social implications, so that positive action can be taken to help handicapped pupils (RADAR, 1986).

Treatments

From the child's point of view, the main handicap of a school health service which grew separately over 80 years is the inability of the school and local authority based cadre of doctors and nurses to treat children directly, except for relatively minor remedies. This has not immediately been solved by the latest round of health reorganisation in 1984, which has squarely put the running of nearly all health services in the hands of the local professionals. Teachers will need patience and understanding for a while with their health colleagues, until the new work patterns settle down.

The treatments currently available are, with variations, roughly as follows. A small number of so-called 'soothing' lotions and antiseptic creams and mouthwashes are kept in the clinic room, whose efficacy depends mainly upon suggestibility and kindness – which are very important attributes in treating small children – and they at least do no harm.

Some more useful active agents are usually kept in school medical rooms. These include:

Painkillers ('analgesics') – of which Paracetamol is first choice, since it does not inflame the stomach lining like aspirin. When discussing these two home-remedy tablets with older children, a couple of useful notions might help some avoid later difficulties of misuse: neither has any sleep-inducing property, and Paracetamol in overdose (the most popular para-suicidal choice of distressed adolescent girls) is a serious and potentially fatal liver poison, which few people realise.

Clove oil, applied to a painful tooth with root infection, acts as an actual local anaesthetic for an hour or two, and may get a child through its day.

Cough-suppressants, of which Pholcodeine linctus is better than ordinary codeine because it does not also induce constipation, are a great boon to a young person with a dry, irritant cough, but it must be remembered that coughing is essentially for getting up the phlegm (mucus) from the bronchial tubes.

All known asthmatic children, who can quite obviously be heard wheezing when breathing out in particular, ought to have their own anti-spasmodic inhalers or other effective treatment available and, if not, this needs reporting back both to the parents and to the school nurse or family doctor.

'Linctus' is just a strong syrup, whose high sugar content helps (like honey) to stimulate the bronchial flow of mucus, but do remember that if it is inhaled by mistake during a coughing bout, it can induce a serious broncho-constriction which could be extremely distressing to a small asthmatic child, whose lung tubes are very tiny in cross-section.

Two other specific medicines are often held in the nurse's room:

An adhesive plaster remover (such as 'Zoff'), which can be another great boon.

Athlete's foot powder (such as Tineafax). Skin fungus infections, generally between the toes, come on mostly after adolescence, so its use in a primary school is limited.

Besides these simple remedies, the clinic room will hold a carefully maintained first aid box, which is probably standardised for all schools in the district health authority's area.

Here is another demarcation which should be understood. Although a generally trained nurse will always help in an emergency, she does not, as defined in the Health and Safety (First Aid) Regulations 1981, necessarily have the responsibility to provide a first aid service to employees of another employer. This principle may extend to school children and students in their authority. Her job is in any case mainly to prevent ill-health and to monitor health.

Every health authority will, of course, formulate its own policy, but this may help to explain why a school nurse might decline to take on, for instance, the renewal (every three years) of a Certificate of First Aid for other school staff.

Head teachers are also frequently asked by parents to administer a child's medicine prescribed by a family doctor or from the hospital. This may be a simple antibiotic which kills or suppresses such bacteria as the occasionally very dangerous streptococcus, though sadly not the common viruses. Final doses may not have been given, yet the child may seem well. An incomplete administration of drugs may encourage antibiotic-resistant strains to grow, for instance inside the inner ear, and these can be passed on to others. If the child is clearly unfit to be in school, the parents should, of course, be asked to keep him or her at home and seek further medical advice.

Sometimes a medicine can in fact be given in slightly bigger doses before and after school and still maintain a reasonable concentration in the body, so it is worth suggesting that parents check with their family doctor whether an extra midday dose is really necessary.

But suppose the parents are out working all day? Here is another dilemma which might be solved quickly in a three-minute advisory 'phone call to a teacher's 'confidential health contact'.

Legally, it is the parents' responsibility to get the medicine to their child. If they ask for long-term maintenance medication to be given in school, in cases of asthma or epilepsy, then it is important, first, that they put this in writing, second, that the family doctor knows about the arrangement and ensures that the name of the medication is clearly typed on the label and, third, that the school nurse knows and has the matter properly recorded in the medical file.

In case of urgency when an unusual and dangerous condition is already known, such as the rare allergy to bee or wasp stings, or where the child has some other severe condition, such as status epilepticus (a series of non-stop seizures requiring that a tube of a potent anti-convulsant medication be squeezed into the child's rectum by any adult available, as a first aid measure), then any action taken in good faith on school premises to treat a life-threatening condition would be strongly upheld and supported from medical sources, especially if the teacher had sought prior medical briefing in anticipation. This support would, of course, be freely given. Should the 'confidential health contact' be a school or family doctor, the fact that the doctor's training and experience has included most varieties of emergency will then point up the usefulness of forging such links in advance.

Trained first aiders on the staff of a school, who would normally hold a certificate of an approved course (which lasts perhaps four days and leads, for instance, to the Harlow Industrial Health Service Certificate), would be likely to find themselves liable to criticism for any measure taken responsibly in an emergency and in good faith only if they had used non-approved materials.

If more of the rare welfare assistants are appointed, following the Warnock Committee's recommendation that most handicapped children have normal schooling, then both these tasks might usefully fall to them – of becoming a nominated first aider, and of giving in-school medications, especially in those health authorities who do not agree that these tasks should be in the school nurse's job description.

Although it is essential to have these matters clarified at the highest administrative level, this sensible precaution should never take the place of the good working practices with health colleagues, recommended above.

The samples given in this chapter of physical and emotional happenings among junior age children are not exhaustive, but are chosen to indicate how medical factors can overlie and interact with a child's psychological needs.

The examples of good practice are not, unfortunately, universal but may encourage expectation that they can be brought about, with a little work and some goodwill.

Some suggested headings for achieving this are appended in the form of a checklist of questions from teachers to their health colleagues.

Checklist (of not-too-subversive questions)

The district's screening examinations:

Which ones are selective or based on health interviews?
At what ages?   At entry/five years?   Seven years?   Eleven+/transfer?

Where can I find a copy of the district health authority's child health surveillance programme?

Do any local family doctors do child health surveillance?
Have any a special interest in child health care?
Who knows – our school doctor/the local medical committee?

Preventive health policies:

Does the district health authority's current annual plan have a specific health preventive policy for five to eleven year olds?
Is it funded for, (a) Year 1, (b) Year 2?

Does the local community health council regularly and specifically invite the opinions of teachers on this?

Is there a district health education or health promotion officer?
What are his or her contacts with junior schools?

School doctors and nurses:
Has our school MO a qualification in child health?
Has our nurse a certificate in child health experience?
Does her job-description vary much from the usual?

What are the arrangements for briefing teachers on a child's special health needs?

Liaison arrangements:

What are the communication links between our nurse and school doctor and the family doctors and health visitors?
Do they routinely receive copies of health information about a child, and vice versa?

What are the arrangements for continuity of health liaison from infants to juniors, and on to senior school?
Is it nurse-to-nurse, doctor-to-doctor?

Do our doctor and nurse regularly meet the educational psychologist for our school?

Who would help me to construct a realistic list of informally approachable 'health advisory contacts'?

First Aid and treatments:

Where is the list of first aid medications kept?

How do our nurse and doctor arrange other treatments?
If we are asked to administer these during school hours, do our nurse and doctor routinely know?

Arrangements for 'Special Needs' children:

Who are, (a), administratively and (b), medically, in charge of the school health service in this district health authority?

What are the advisory arrangements for educationalists to influence local school health policies and facilities?

'Disability lists' – what is the local definition?

Are there, frankly, any major deficiencies or difficulties in providing special facilities for handicapped children in our normal schools?
For special sense (vision and hearing) services?
Are there any therapist shortages? (speech, physio. etc)

Are there, (a) plans, (b) funding, to improve any such deficiencies and to provide for more welfare assistants?
Are the school's examination and treatment rooms adequate?

Do our school governors have a running (continued) Minute on
   (a) the special education building programme,
   (b) premises and facilities for examinations and treatments?

Where can I find a copy of the Education (Special Educational Needs) Regulations, 1983?

References

BAX, M. (1976) 'Assessment of the child at school entry', *Pediatrics*:58, 403–407.

BAX, M. and WHITMORE, K. (1981) *The Health Service Needs of Children in Primary Schools*, Report to the Kensington, Chelsea and Westminster Area Health Authority.

BURNS, D. D. (1980) *Feeling Good* (New York: William Morrow).

THE COMPASSIONATE FRIENDS (1985) *When a Child in Your School is Bereaved* (6 Denmark St., Bristol BS1 5DQ).

DES (1981) Education Act (London: HMSO).

DHSS (1976) *Fit For The Future*, Report of the Committee on Child Health Services (Chmn. Prof. D. Court) Cmnd 6684 (London: HMSO).

DHSS (1980) *Prevention in the Child Health Services* (London: HMSO).

DHSS (1985) *Children in School and Problems Related to AIDS* (London: HMSO).

GRAY, D. J. PERIERA (1982) *The Care of the Handicapped Child in General Practice*, Hunterian Gold Medal Essay, Royal College of General Practitioners: 'Healthier Children – Thinking Prevention', Report from General Practice No. 22.

HEALTH EDUCATION COUNCIL (1983) *Handbook for Sickle Cell Disease: A Guide for Families.*

LANSDOWN, R. (1980) *More Than Sympathy* (London: Tavistock Pubs.)

OFFICE OF POPULATION CENSUSES AND SURVEYS (1974a) *Morbidity Statistics from General Practice: Second National Survey*, 1970–71, Studies on Medical and Population Subjects, No. 26 (London: HMSO).

POLLOCK, T. (1985) Joint Committee on Vaccination an Immunisation in *The Times*, 25 Oct. p. 2.

RADAR (1986) *Educational Implications of Disability, a guide for teachers* (25 Mortimer St., London W1N 8AB).

RUSSELL, P. (1984) 'Changes and developments in policies for child health services', *Concern* No. 53: 11–12.

STEINBERG, D. (1981) *Using Child Psychiatry* (London: Hodder and Stoughton.

VALMAN, H. B. (1982) *ABC of 1 to 7* (London: British Medical Association).

WHITMORE, K. (1985) *Health Services in Schools – A New Look* (London: Spastics Pubs.).

Grateful thanks are due to Dr Jean Price, Senior Clinical Medical Officer, Southmead District Health Authority, Bristol, and Dr John Meadows, District Medical Officer, Bath.

Chapter 7
Counselling in Primary Schools

Tony Charlton
Lynne Hoye

The growth of counselling in schools has been closely linked with the emergence of vocational, educational and personal guidance. For this reason the need for counselling has been less apparent in primary than secondary schools where these forms of guidance, understandably, have assumed considerable prominence. Consequently, counselling skills have been slow in becoming established practices in the formal education of young children. While this has not prevented primary school teachers from assuming pastoral responsibilities on behalf of their pupils, their efforts have often been hampered by a lack of preparation during their initial teacher education in areas including Personal and Social Education and counselling. However, the current climate in society, and education in particular, indicates a need for teacher training establishments and primary schools to become more aware of the value of employing counselling skills and techniques in classrooms (Sisterton, 1983).

In an optimistic manner Burns (1982) suggested that as teachers become sensitive to their responsibility to oversee children's all-round (as opposed to a 'blinkered' preoccupation with their academic) development they become increasingly receptive to the notion that they require additional classroom management skills to augment those they have traditionally acquired and practised. Parallel to this awareness has been another which has realised that counselling skills and strategies are not the prerogative of specialist counsellors working individually with clients experiencing/presenting severe problems. They are also part and parcel of the considerable repertoire of skills which primary, and other, teachers require in order to help their children become 'fully functioning individuals' (Burns, *op cit*, p. 265).

The nature of counselling

In the primary school setting, counselling usually involves situations where teachers practise a variety of interpersonal skills to help individuals, or groups, reduce or resolve concerns/anxieties which they are either experiencing themselves, or their behaviour is generating within others. On other occasions teachers may use such skills to help pupils avoid problem events. The former is of a curative, and the latter a preventive, nature.

The range of personal problems teachers may encounter in primary school classrooms is infinite, and levels of severity may extend from the type which all of us encounter in our day-to-day activities to those sufficiently severe for referral to outside agencies. They include, for example, concerns or anxieties associated with:

onset of puberty;
isolation from peers/poor rapport with staff;
change in expected behaviour pattern/cries easily, loses temper, aggressive, mood swings, depressed;
change in standard of school work;
non-school attendance/lateness;
pending bereavement/death in the family;
long-term illness or disability in the family;
changed economic circumstances/unemployment/prison;
pending marital break-up/departure of one parent from family/arrival of step-parent, step siblings;
stealing;
parental alcoholism/pupil glue, gas, solvent abuse/self-inflicted wounds;
excessive attention seeking;
lack of school progress, i.e. achieving below potential;
no identity with home or school;
obvious loss of weight.

While Galloway (1981) highlighted problems which teachers, themselves, may be confronted with if they involve themselves with children's home-based problems, he acknowledged that:

> Using knowledge of difficulties at home to provide a more satisfactory education for the child at school is one of the most critical, but least developed, aspects of counselling and pastoral care. (p. 4)

Where children become burdened with problems and the troubled feelings often associated with them, it is important that teachers become alert to them and intervene (within the school or by referral to outside agencies) before those feelings become enmeshed in hardened feelings of helplessness, low self-esteem and unhappiness. It must be borne in mind, also, that these types of affective responses may be a consequence of, or precipitate, lowered levels of academic functioning (Lawrence, 1971, 1985; Charlton, 1985). It is, therefore, in children's best interests that problems are recognised as early as possible, or anticipated, in order that appropriate intervention can be organised.

Within this chapter we consider the relationship between primary school teachers' pedagogic and counselling roles in the classroom, and examine some of the basic counselling skills and strategies which teachers may need to practise to help meet the affective, and other needs of young children.

Teaching and counselling

There has been a tendency in past years for teachers to regard their classroom skills as being of a lesser import, or lower order, than those of a range of other professionals (e.g., educational psychologists, child psychiatrists, advisory and support staff) with whom they have contact in school. At times these beliefs have caused teachers to become hesitant about developing and utilising some of the skills with which these professionals have achieved much success. More recently, it has become apparent that improved initial and in-service training have helped teachers to reappraise their function in an increasingly realistic and healthier fashion.

The area of special education is one which typifies this change of attitude. More teachers (than was once the case), in addition to employing enhanced identification and needs' assessment skills, are now implementing and evaluating individual educational programmes which they have designed for their children. Consequently, in their relationships with educational psychologists and LEA advisory and support staff they have become less willing to see themselves only as referral agents, and more able and willing to perceive their role in terms of a partnership with these professionals in meeting the special needs of children with learning and/or behaviour problems. The removal of the mystique hitherto attached to the areas of needs' assessment and provisions has, for these teachers, facilitated their enhanced functioning in classrooms, at no cost to the outside professionals (who are usually confronted with burgeoning, and frequently unrealistic demands upon their time) and to the benefit of the children involved.

Counselling is another skills' area with which teachers, quite unjustifiably, have experienced some unease, yet when the term 'counselling' is demystified it is seen to include many of the activities and practices with which many class teachers have always been concerned. Marland (1980), for example, commented that, 'Good teachers have always talked over personal difficulties with individual pupils and helped them to make decisions; counselling in this sense is not new' (p. 22).

Galloway (1981) construed the counselling process as a response to a pupil's personal problems involving 'a teacher's careful assessment of the child's needs and the ways in which the school can meet those needs' (p. 2). Similarly, Sisterson (1983, p. 11) commented that it 'often focussed upon the intellectual and scholastic development of the individual when there is a problem or crisis' and warned that pupil concerns can be triggered by social or emotional factors. Within a broader context Hamblin (1978) suggested that the purpose of counselling:

> is to help a pupil find more effective ways of using what he has already got in terms of aptitudes, ability and personality in a truly satisfying way. (p. 5)

These definitions, either explicitly or implicitly, make reference to children's all-round educational development. Additionally, they imply that counselling is a 'conscious attempt to deal with the problem where it occurs – in the classroom or the playground' (Galloway, 1981, p. 2). They also suggest that problems are unlikely to emanate from, and remain rooted solely within, either the cognitive (thinking) or affective (feeling) domains; the nature of children's problems are often far more complex than this simplistic concept allows. In his study Lawrence (1971) contended that retarded readers frequently developed unhealthy affective responses to their reading failure and claimed that:

> Since reading is a skill which adults around him regard as important, failure in this area tends to invade the whole personality. The result is a child who has come to accept failure as inevitable and whose natural curiosity and enthusiasm for learning remain inhibited. (p. 119).

This thinking has been instrumental in alerting teachers to appreciate that, on some occasions, where academic failure occurs 'traditional remedial help' alone may be of little help to the children. Their needs may demand educational provisions on a broader front than has often been the case in the past. In addition to intervention designed to remedy their mechanical skills' and subskills' deficits they may require a therapeutic input to raise their affective functioning to a level where they are both able, and willing, to respond favourably to academic instruction. Investigations conducted by Lawrence (1972, 1985), Cant and Spackman (1985) and Charlton and Terrell (1987) have supported this reasoning. In their studies they demonstrated that school counselling interventions designed to promote children's affective well-being (e.g., raising self-esteem levels) effected improved reading performances as well as enhanced self-concepts (see case study p. 170). The nature of the counselling used in Lawrence's (1972) study was uncomplicated; adults were required to present themselves as responsible and sympathetic people who enjoyed children's company. They refrained from direct questioning and attempted to establish an uncritical and friendly atmosphere where children were encouraged to express their troubled feelings, or concerns. This type of counselling will not be unfamiliar to good primary school teachers. They will recognise the value of teachers presenting as responsible, trustworthy and sympathetic persons who enjoy children's company, as they will the need to build and sustain, with their children, relationships of a type which enables them to appear receptive to children's concerns. Teacher characteristics and skills of this kind are as crucial in teaching as they are in counselling.

It is understandable, therefore, if teachers encounter difficulties in attempts to differentiate between the teaching and counselling elements of their classroom endeavours. Counselling and teaching activities in classrooms are often so inextricably intertwined that no true separation is possible; they appear less as discrete skills and more as a well-integrated amalgam.

Two classroom incidents spring to mind which illustrate the interdependence of counselling and teaching. The first concerned a lonely, unhappy six-year-old whose aggressive behaviour frightened away his peers. Having noted this behaviour, the infant teacher, in a kindly, gentle and clear manner took the boy aside and counselled him, explaining how his unfriendly behaviour frightened the others away. Then, over a period of a few weeks she taught him (by modelling, cuing and praising) appropriate behaviours which successfully enabled him to build and sustain the type of relationships which he had always wanted, but not known how to accomplish. In the same class Amanda was becoming increasingly anxious about difficulties she was encountering in her attempts to grasp symbol/sound associations. Her father, concerned that she had begun wetting her bed, had contacted the school which was already aware of Amanda's learning problem. In a true partnership between school and home, efforts were made to resolve her problems. Each afternoon playtime the mother phoned school to hear about Amanda's accomplishments that day (e.g., in painting, games or other lessons; prosocial behaviour). Both at school and home she was praised for her accomplishments, and at school the teacher persisted in teaching the early reading skills. The combination of good instruction, school–home relationships, and a therapeutic programme designed to promote positive self-esteem proved effective.

On these two occasions, what did the counselling and teaching activities consist of, and how did they differ? Answers to both these questions are not easy to generate, and may prove to be rather more academic than useful.

One rather crude, though reasonably effective, way of discriminating between the two activities is to determine whether the teacher pro-acts, or reacts to, behaviour. In this way teaching can be thought of as behaviour initiated by the teacher to disseminate, for example, knowledge and skills. Similarly, counselling can be construed as a teacher response to problems evidenced or experienced by pupils. While these responses may also include a teaching element (e.g., where pupils need to learn new interpersonal skills) they are, foremost, a response consequent to the teacher's awareness (through observing or listening) of perceived, or anticipated, pupil problems.

Within the parameters of this definition counselling is a response by the teacher:

1. to help resolve or minimise problem behaviours which pupils present (disturbing behaviour) or experience (disturbed behaviour). It can also be a response to help prevent anticipated problems occurring;
2. conditional, on occasions, upon teacher vigilance (observing/listening) in identifying existing or potential problems;
3. which is likely to require a listening element in order to facilitate a thorough understanding of the problem;
4. which may require a teaching element in order to resolve or minimise the problem.

Levels of counselling

While there will be occasions when children's problems are so severe and/or complex that only counselling by specialists may be of help, teachers still have a crucial role to play. Because of their regular and protracted periods of contact with their pupils, teachers have unrivalled opportunities to detect signs and changes in children's behaviour which may be indicative of the need for counselling at the highest level. Equipped with proficient identification skills, and a sound knowledge of the location and function of other helping agencies (e.g., child guidance, educational psychologists, education welfare/social officers, school medical officers) teachers can refer the child to available help outside the school. The cruciality of referral has been highlighted in the media over the years. Tragically (and, perhaps, unfairly at times) publicity has usually been generated only when those charged with such duties (teachers, neighbours, NSPCC, social workers) have failed to discharge them competently. The misery, pain, suffering and even death which 'neglected' children have consequently suffered, provide salient reminders of the crucial importance of the teacher's role as referral agent.

There are, however, numerous occasions when children's problems are less severe and complex, and their needs can be satisfactorily met from the repertoire of skills teachers should possess. Concerns about school work, school in general, relationships with peers, family bereavements, onset of puberty, or pending secondary school transfer, represent but a few of a host of troubled feelings which primary school teachers may need to respond to.

For primary school children there are usually only two levels of counselling available. One involves the teacher in the classroom or elsewhere in the school, and the other the helping agencies usually working away from school. Additionally we argue, here, for a third level to bridge the divide between the other two.

Level one

All teachers should be equipped to contribute at this level. This does not imply that teachers should be fully trained counsellors, but it does imply that all teachers should possess an understanding of, and be proficient in using, basic counselling skills. The nature of these skills is discussed later in the chapter. One of the skills required at this level is teacher vigilance; the ability to be watchful over each child's behaviour and sensitive to changes that take place. It may also involve an understanding of behaviour in the way which Combs (1971) referred to when he commented that:

The kind of understanding we are talking about here is not a knowledge about, but a sensitivity to people. It is a kind of empathy, the ability to put oneself in another's shoes, to feel and see as he does. All of us have this ability to some extent, but good teachers have a lot of it. (p. 32)

During the last decade the promotion of teacher vigilance has been assisted by the emergence of a plethora of early screening inventories. While there is a danger that these schedules may result in the unhealthy labelling of an individual (and the generation of low expectations), their main value is that they encourage teachers to reflect upon, and become sensitive to, pupil behaviour and changes that take place.

Level two

At this level the severity of the problems presented may necessitate regular and protracted individual counselling sessions for which class teachers usually have neither the time nor competence. While the outside professionals mentioned earlier are the ones likely to provide this help, children (and their parents) may be more responsive to a counsellor who meets with them in the familiar school setting, rather than in a distant 'foreign' office or clinic. In secondary schools, teachers with pastoral care responsibilities, or school counsellors, usually have the facilities and expertise to cope successfully with this level of counselling. In some local education authorities (e.g., Wiltshire) peripatetic counsellors have been appointed whose work entails meeting secondary school pupils in their own schools. There is no reason to doubt that parallel initiatives in primary schools would enjoy similar successes to those experienced in the secondary sector.

A frequently invaluable source of help to primary schools and troubled or troublesome pupils are education welfare officers whose duties involve counselling pupils and their parents in their home, at school or at the education welfare offices. Increasingly, education social/welfare officers (see chapter 5 for information concerning this service) are becoming highly trained specialists holding Certificates of Qualification in Social Work (CQSW). These courses include counselling components which prepare the officers for working with pupils and families experiencing more serious problems. A good educational welfare officer is an invaluable asset to a school which practises an informed and caring concern for pupils, recognises the limitations of its own expertise and is willing to share its own concerns with other professionals.

Level three

Problems at this level will be serious enough for referral to outside agencies to be unavoidable and very necessary. They may also be of a kind, on occasion, where the local education authority makes a 'statement' of special educational needs. This action may, in extreme cases, necessitate the removal of a child from the parental home (e.g., to residential special schools, foster homes, children's homes), particularly where the child's parents are unable, or unwilling, to provide adequate parenting. Counselling at this level may be provided by child psychiatrists, educational psychologists, psychiatric social workers and a number of other professionals.

Basic counselling skills

While some skills are common to a number of counselling models (e.g., Rogerian, behavioural, psychoanalytical) others are peculiar to a single approach. A regard for this distinction is likely to be of less interest to the teacher than the specialist counsellor who may – though not always – operate from within the theoretical framework of a particular counselling model. We contend, however, that basic counselling skills are a characteristic not only of counselling but, also, of good teaching. Where teachers make appropriate and adequate use of them in their classrooms they are practising good teaching as well as engaging in on-going, informal counselling of a type likely to facilitate children's healthy all-round development. The application of listening, empathy and positive pupil-regard skills, for example, helps provide pupils with the security, warmth, sense of value and positive self-esteem that characterise (and arise from) healthy learning environments. However, even in the best classrooms pupils manifest problems; some are related to class- or school-related causes and others, outside-school factors. Many of these problems may respond to increased injections of informal counselling skills in the classroom, but others may require a more formal counselling session conducted either in the classroom, or elsewhere away from the noise and presence of peers.

The skills discussed below may be used in a variety of combinations at the informal counselling/teaching level, but where problems persist, or situations demand, teachers are likely to need a more structured approach and be selective in the skills they apply. Informal levels are concerned with preventive and curative counselling whereas the more formal approaches usually operate only in a curative manner.

Genuineness is a quality which people value and search for in their relationships with others. It implies a sense of honesty which attracts trust. In the counselling context it suggests that the teacher's interest in children and their worries reflects and communicates an honest, as opposed to a superficial, concern. Pupils, even very young ones, are very adept at assessing their teachers and it is to the 'honest' teacher to whom the troubled child is most likely to turn for help; to confide in, seek advice from, or confess to.

Burn's (1982) list of the behavioural characteristics of the genuine teacher indicate that:

1. His verbal and non-verbal behaviours are congruent (in accordance) with each other.
2. He is willing to be open about himself.
3. He does not draw attention to his status or role.
4. He is consistent in his behaviour when counselling and when he is not.
5. If challenged, he can tolerate it and explain his position without enlisting his 'authority' to put the pupil in his place. (p. 368)

An unconditional positive regard for pupils signifies they are accepted, valued and respected for what they are, without preconditions. It implies a liking and a concern for children (irrespective of the levels and ranges of their competencies and degrees of attractiveness) which are communicated through teachers expressing interest in the pupil and demonstrating a:

> concern for his welfare, involvement in his activities and development, support for him in his times of stress and an appreciation of what he is and what he can do. (Burns, 1982, p. 367)

In the reality of the classroom it is not always easy to sustain these types of communications to some children who, for one reason or another, do not intuitively attract or appear to merit it. Where they are sustained (particularly with children who have the least, but whose needs are the greatest), children are unlikely to detect disparities in the regard teachers distribute amongst pupils in the class and, therefore, unlikely to experience feelings of rejection. By preventing this rejection teachers keep open essential channels of pupil-teacher communication through which children can express their concerns or troubles. Where teachers, intentionally or otherwise, reject or neglect some of their pupils they may well be denying them access to them in their times of need.

Children sometimes feel that, compared to a majority of their peers, they are less favoured by teachers. While these feelings do not always accurately reflect a teacher's regard for individual pupils, teachers need to be aware that the type and degree of attention (non-verbal as well as verbal) they give to individuals in classrooms can be unfavourably misinterpreted by others. Unfortunately, there are also likely to be occasions when children quite correctly interpret the low regard teachers hold of them. Perceived rejections of this type, accurate or otherwise, often serve only to create barriers between teacher and pupil which are hardly conducive to the building of good relationships upon which effective teaching and counselling depend.

Desirable though it may be, it is not always easy, or practicable, to hold an unconditional positive regard for all children, particularly when their misbehaviour is frequent and, perhaps, offensive. In such circumstances a useful technique (and one which is often therapeutic in itself) is to divorce the child's behaviour from his/her 'self'. The teacher can then respond genuinely to a child's enquiry as to why no one likes him/her 'We do like *you*! It's your *behaviour* that we don't like.'

Empathy, according to Rogers (1969) is no less important to teachers than counsellors. It involves a sensing of other people's feelings, or their 'inner world', and conveying that understanding to them through verbalisations, gestures, posture and voice quality. The classrooms of teachers with high empathy have been associated with a range of desirable characteristics including low truancy rates, few behaviour problems, high academic performance and motivation levels (see Morgan, 1979). Burns (1982) suggests that the value of empathic contact is that it offers pupils the 'intensely reassuring experience of not being alone' (p. 367); it also enables teachers to experience the 'real' child and understand his/her behaviour (Morse, 1974).

Pupils with problems sometimes claim that teachers (and parents) don't understand (or empathise with) them. On at least some occasions this may well be true. Empathy is not an easy skill, or attribute, to develop; and not everyone develops it to the same level. However, where teachers are able to empathise with their pupils' feelings and concerns they open (or reopen if they were previously blocked) lines of communication which permit pupils opportunities to begin talking, listening, analysing and reasoning, as well as resolving.

Listening is another skill which is both difficult to acquire and make adequate time for in busy and crowded classrooms. Teachers sometimes delude themselves into thinking that they are listening, when they are not. The memory lingers, persistently, of the teacher who sat at her desk marking books while, on either side of her, a child stood reading aloud from a book. Even the most insensitive pupils would have been aware that the teacher wasn't really listening. How could she?

In counselling and teaching situations it is important that teachers listen to children. Bolger (1975) stresses that this means:

> we listen, not just with our ears but with our eyes, so that we perceive facial expression, gestures, eye-movements, posture ... Tiny changes in the eyelids are invaluable clues – a slight widening when he is frightened and a slight closing when hostile or thoughtful. (p. 166)

Simultaneously, teachers need to convince children that they are listening. This is often accomplished through responding by using appropriate facial gestures (e.g., looks of concern, surprise, excitement, pride) as well as pertinent questions and short confirmatory statements administered with the right tone (e.g., 'How did you feel?' 'Gosh, you must have been excited!' 'What happened then?').

Most of us have experienced situations where we are talking to someone (in a social setting, staffroom, classroom) who's quite obviously not listening. The facial, and monosyllabic vocal responses are 'out of tune' with the narration, and do little to enthuse us to continue; or maintain our self-esteem.

Where teachers successfully convince their children that they are listening, the likely outcomes are that the children will want to talk. It is most likely, too, that children with problems will confide in teachers whom they regard as good listeners.

On occasions a counsellor listens, and yet the counsellee also remains quiet – there is silence! While silence may occur for many reasons (breakdown in the counselling 'flow', emotional upset, attempts to persuade the counsellee to reveal more than intended), with young children it often occurs when they are trying to find words to express their feelings. This type of silence is natural and, correctly managed by the teacher (i.e., (s)he is given time to search for the right word), is helpful to the pupil.

At other times, the counsellor may make a judgement that the silence is appropriate because the youngster has left unsaid what needs to be said. Here the silence is used to urge the pupil to say more, perhaps to make that admission which finally throws 'light' upon the problem being discussed.

Restatements and clarifications. It is common practice in classrooms that children's verbal or written academic responses are questioned by teachers, for the best of reasons. By reflecting children's responses back to them for confirmation (e.g., 'So you think that the land belongs to the aborigines?') or by seeking further clarification (e.g., 'Do you think other people have a right to the land, too?'), teachers become aware whether or not children have understood the academic material. These reflecting techniques are as 'basic to counselling' (Lewis, 1970, p. 18) as they are to teaching. Used appropriately in the counselling process they reassure pupils they have a receptive audience and, perhaps more important, help clarify children's accounts and the teachers' understanding of them. At times they can also serve to help revive a flagging dialogue.

Robinson (1950) subdivided reflecting techniques to include restatement and clarification components. Restatements require teachers to rephrase and 'return' children's spoken thoughts and feelings in order to confirm they have been correctly understood. Where children have limited language skills or are too upset to vocalise coherently, teachers may also need to 'read' (and return) non-verbal messages (e.g., facial expressions, gestures, eye-movements, posture). Clarifications probe deeper into children's problem areas, and invite children to expand upon a previous statement. These probes are very necessary where teachers require additional insight into the 'inner and outer' limits of children's problems.

The apparent simplicity of these techniques belies both the high skills' levels required to employ them successfully, and the impact they can have upon the counselling. They require teachers to insert them carefully and appropriately – and with warmth and concern – into the dialogue. Inserted inappropriately, or bereft of the caring signals, they may confuse, misdirect or halt the child's train of thoughts, and so curtail the counselling flow.

The value of basic counselling skills

The techniques discussed so far, if practised skilfully can be termed facilitative in the sense that they provide for at least two essential happenings. First, they help foster the development of the good counsellor (teacher)/pupil relationships which are prerequisites for successful counselling (and teaching). Second – within those relationships – pupils sense feelings of security which encourage them to talk through their problems. In a manner similar to that in which Fontana (1981) stressed the importance of sympathy and trustworthiness, it seems to be the quality of counsellors' empathy, unconditional positive regard, genuineness and listening skills 'rather than any great familiarity with counselling skills that children appear to look for when deciding to whom they should turn for need' (p. 341). Kirby (1981) accepted the importance of these teacher attributes when he suggested that:

> the teacher has to have the sensitivity of the artist to understand children. Studies of child development are necessarily clinical and objective. Living with children deepens and humanises this knowledge and throws light on the importance of observing children within a closer relationship, listening to them and asking them questions with a real wish to hear their answers. (p. 54)

Types of counselling

From this stage teachers have a number of choices concerning the direction, and form, the counselling will take. One choice will be to continue within a client-centred framework (Rogers, 1951) which assumes that, given the good counsellor/client (pupil) relationships of the type just referred to, individuals are able to use their own inner resources to resolve problems (Noonan, 1983). Within this approach counsellors assume a non-directive, or non-leading role; their verbalisations are minimal; they neither make interpretations nor request clarifications, and refrain from suggesting ways in which clients can resolve their problems. Instead, counsellors continue to contribute the empathy, genuineness and unconditional positive regard which, hopefully, create and sustain a good counsellor/client rapport. Within this relationship they provide a 'kind of looking glass in which the pupil can for himself discover his own strengths and weaknesses, his aspirations and fears' (Hamblin, 1978, p. 35) by talking through his/her concern.

However, while older children in primary schools may derive benefit from non-directive approaches, younger children and others with limited language skills may not. Referring to disadvantaged children Biddlestone (1985) outlined difficulties they often experience 'thinking through logically the likely outcomes of their actions, and describing their feelings and explaining their needs' (p. 157). Those who cannot verbalise their inner thoughts and feelings, and have not yet fully developed powers of self-insight are unlikely to profit greatly from a counselling process which delegates to the counsellee the role of initiator and executor of self-adjustment or problem resolution.

An alternative approach, perhaps better (though not exclusively) suited to the needs of young children, is that of behavioural counselling where counsellors assume a more active and directive role, by employing a variety of strategies (e.g., reinforcement, modelling) to 'shape' pupils' behaviour in ways which help lead to a resolution of their problems. Within this approach it is recognised that the probability of a behaviour being learned is increased when it is reinforced (e.g., by teacher attention, praise) and decreased when it is not. The reinforcement concept is not, as many believe, a simplistic one and readers are referred to Harrop (1982) for a detailed account. Many problems children experience, or confront others with, are a consequence of this reinforcement concept having operated. Appropriate behaviours may not have been learned because they have not been reinforced. Alternatively, inappropriate behaviours may have been learned because they have been reinforced.

A classic instance of this happening is well illustrated in the case of Gary. His teacher complained that despite all her efforts she was unable to control his disruptive behaviour (shouting out, refusing to work). When the nature of the teacher's interactions with Gary were analysed it was discovered that while she attended to (i.e., reinforced) his disruptive behaviour, she, quite understandably, gave a sigh of relief and then ignored (non-reinforced) the few occasions when he behaved acceptably. Gary had no learning problems. He had learned well; but learned the wrong behaviours. The teacher would have been better employed ignoring the unacceptable behaviour and reinforcing him when he behaved well.

During a behavioural counselling encounter the counsellor, either independently or in collusion with other adults (e.g., colleagues, parents) or with the pupil, determines which existing behaviours appear to be causing the problems, and which alternative behaviours need to be acquired to resolve them. Pupils may then be taught target behaviours within the counselling intervention, and receive regular teacher reinforcements as they subsequently practise them. Eventually, pupils should function independently of teacher reinforcements as alternative reinforcements become forthcoming from successful outcomes (problem resolutions) derived from the practice of newly acquired coping behaviours.

On occasions modelling techniques can be put to good use in the counselling process. Children often learn 'chunks of behaviour' (Seefeldt, 1980, p. 153) through observing and copying (modelling) the behaviour around them. Indeed there is much evidence – which confirms common sense – that children tend to practise what they see rather than what they hear; although learning is perhaps best encouraged where children are advised what to do and then shown how to perform it. However, research by Bandura (1977) suggested that children are selective in terms of from whom they learn. There is a tendency for them to copy the behaviour of those who, in their eyes, have prestige or status (e.g., parents, teachers, sports and 'pop' stars, successful peers). Teachers will be well aware of the implications of this type of learning. Where classrooms include a number of good models, teachers' efforts are likely to be considerably more effective. They can highlight the behaviour and related successful outcomes of good models, knowing that many children will be encouraged to imitate such behaviour. In classrooms where good models are absent, teachers are denied this source of help and are likely to be hampered in their attempts to encourage children's healthy development.

Clearly, the development of children's prosocial behaviours (politeness, good manners, friendliness, helpfulness and a general positive regard for people's feelings and possessions) and others can be promoted where their attention is drawn to the behaviour of good teacher/pupil models. It follows, therefore, that counselling can benefit from the practice of modelling techniques. In the situation, for example, where Donna, a seven-year-old, is counselled because of her aggressive, and disruptive, behaviour she can have the negative consequences of her behaviour pointed out to her and, additionally, have her attention drawn to good models. The teacher can comment: 'Look at Alison and Gemma. They're not teasing or shouting at each other, are they? They're talking quietly, sharing the paints and helping each other. And they enjoy sitting together. Why don't you try to do that? Then let's see how many children will want to sit next to you.' This situation can be helped further if the teacher enlists the help of a cooperative, good model to sit next to Donna in order to prevent too much delay occurring before she experiences successful outcomes from her modelled behaviour.

The value of directive counselling of this type is that it can quickly help children to acquire 'chunks' of behaviour which were not previously part of their behavioural repertoire. Many children behave inappropriately, quite simply because they have not had opportunities to learn appropriate behaviours.

Summary

In this chapter it was suggested that if teachers are effectively to meet the needs of the whole child, they should be involved as much with children's affective, as they are their cognitive, functioning. The efficient use of basic counselling skills suggests one way in which this involvement can be arranged. Empathy, unconditional positive regard, genuineness and listening, appear to represent important teacher/counsellor characteristics which contribute towards the creation of healthy learning environments within which teachers become aware of, and both receptive and responsive to, children's needs. While teachers frequently employ such skills in their work, it is regrettable that they have not always received sufficient training to help them fully appreciate their value, and use them to best effect.

Counselling skills' practices in classrooms can be perceived usefully in three differing – though not necessarily exclusive – contexts. They may:

1. be used in a reactive sense where a response is made to problems which either teachers themselves have become vigilant to, or have brought to their attention by the pupil(s) concerned; or others. These problems, although they will be dealt with by the teachers, may be sufficiently complex, serious or sensitive to warrant a brief, or even extended counselling session conducted away from peers.
2. become so well-integrated within the day-to-day teaching activities that no true separation is discernible between teaching and counselling. Simultaneous to imparting, for example, knowledge, information and guidance, teachers remain vigilant and more-or-less immediately responsive to potential or prevailing problems evident within their class. Usually these types of problems will be relatively minor, perhaps transitory, and refer to difficulties children experience with material which is being taught, or facets of undesirable classroom behaviour.
3. be employed in both a planned proactive and reactive sense. Teachers may use counselling skills, in preference to more formal didactic methods, to promote some aspect of their children's personal and social well-being. This practice differs from that referred to in (1) in that it is likely to involve the whole class, either in groups or as an entire class. It may involve, for example, 'teaching' an explicit element of the personal and social curriculum. The proactive element refers to teachers' initial input. The reactive one refers to teachers' responses to (or consequent interaction with) pupils' analyses of, or other responses to the teachers' input.

Some examples of counselling practices in classrooms

1. SARAH: A NEED TO TALK WITH SOMEONE WHO WOULD LISTEN

Sarah, a very able intelligent six-year-old, was the older in a family of two. Her three-year-old brother had Downes Syndrome and Sarah was encouraged by her parents to take an active part in helping and understanding her brother's condition. She was an articulate, confident child, living in a loving stable family environment. During her fifth term at primary school, she and her mother went shopping, leaving her father and Simon, her brother, at home. In their absence, the house caught fire and was completely gutted: however, Simon and his father escaped. On returning from shopping, Sarah and her mother were faced with the sight of their home burnt to the ground.

The initial shock of the incident caused Sarah to cry a great deal both at home and at school. However, although previously articulate, she did not discuss the incident with either her mother or teacher. Daily, her tears persisted. Each playtime she would stand by the door, not wanting to leave the security of the classroom and the proximity of the teacher. This pattern continued for some three months. Her mother noted that the tears had stopped at home soon after the initial incident and that Sarah was enjoying the excitement of choosing new furniture for the home. Nevertheless, the tears persisted spasmodically in school, usually at playtime when there were fewer children in the class. Finally, during a rare 'quiet' moment in the day Sarah began to cry, and the tears turned into sobs and the sobs turned into a stammered account of how 'my hamster was burnt in the fire'. The teacher did nothing except offer Sarah a sympathetic ear. The initial trauma had been so great, that the parents had attempted to promote the 'positive' aspects of a 'new' home. Thus the unfinished business of Sarah's hamster had been overlooked – by everyone except Sarah. It took the security of the classroom, and the concern and genuineness of the teacher in wanting to listen, to unlock inner feelings.

Sarah was then able to confront her pain and fears concerning the death of a much cherished pet. She began to talk more openly about her 'hamster who died in the fire' and eventually a gerbil was acquired by her understanding parents. Playtime thus became a time for pleasure, and the clinging to the classroom and the tears subsided. Sarah had experienced a period of mourning for her lost pet. She had contained her pain and hidden it from her parents in an attempt to protect them from further dismay. She had 'played their game' of looking at the brighter aspects of the situation and brought her tears to her teacher.

Factors affecting the situation were:

(1) Understanding of the problem by the teacher involved.
(2) Close links with parents to monitor the situation at home and at school.
(3) Empathy and understanding on the part of the teacher.
(4) Time allowed for individual attention.
(5) Continuing communication between home and school to ensure the support was enhanced.

2. IMPROVING READING PERFORMANCES, THROUGH COUNSELLING

Lawrence (1971, 1972) examined the differential effects of three intervention strategies (two of which incorporated counselling techniques) upon reading achievements of retarded readers from primary schools. The author contended that as educational failure often induces feelings of low self-esteem in children which then present as a barrier to healthy learning, remediation should include help to promote positive levels of self-esteem as well as resolve children's mechanical skills' deficits.

Of the three interventions compared (i.e., remedial reading/counselling, remedial reading, counselling), counselling proved to be the most effective in terms of producing improvements in children's levels of reading performance over a six-month period. The individual counselling was non-directive (and non-interpretative) in nature, and required the adult to listen attentively, and with concern, to children, signal that they enjoy children's company, refrain from making judgemental statements, praise children's responses (not their achievements) wherever possible.

In the simplest of terms, the counsellor sought to establish a warm and caring relationship within which the child felt free to talk about him/herself, without fear of criticism or retribution, and able to release concerns and anxieties 'bottled' up within him/her. It seems likely it was the nature and quality of the counselling relationship, rather than the actual conversation content, which enabled the child to become unfettered from a handicapping low self-esteem and, so, respond more healthily to classroom instruction.

Of additional interest is that while Lawrence's (1971) study employed teachers as counsellors, a later enquiry (1972) used mothers. Even more startling was a further, unpublished, study where grandmothers assumed the role as counsellors; some of the retarded readers made twenty-two months reading gains in the six-month intervention period!

3. THE MISCREANTS: PROBLEM-RESOLUTION BY THE PUPILS

The perennial problem of fighting at playtime has been dealt with frequently through the use of behaviour modification and other techniques, with minimal effect at times. However, a group of five eight-year olds were frequent offenders and were constantly being referred to the head teacher.

A new strategy was considered. The Head, who had undergone a counselling course, decided to introduce a group counselling approach. She decided to adopt a supportive and non-directive stance. The five 'miscreants', as they had now been 'labelled', were sent to the head teacher yet again. However, this time the Head refused to accept responsibility for the incident, stating that it was up to those involved to 'sort it out' for themselves. It was the responsibility of the children involved to decide upon what behaviour was appropriate in the playground and how they were to ensure that this behaviour was maintained. The Head then stated that the next four playtimes would be spent in group discussion.

The first meeting of the group was spent in recrimination and accusation. The children seemed intent on blaming anyone for the misdeeds. This situation then altered to one of punitive justice, and such horrid measures were considered as 'Lock him up Miss'!

The second meeting proved much the same, in that the children were intent on punishment rather than considering possible alternatives or preventive measures.

The third encounter proved more creative in that the children suggested what sort of playtime they would enjoy. They devised a series of steps that would ensure that only acceptable behaviour would be tolerated by the group. For example, no one was to push or tease another person. The group said they would find it difficult to keep to all the rules, but decided that they would support each other.

The fourth meeting was more of a report-back session, with the children discussing their successes.

Playtime ceased to be a problem. The head teacher had placed the responsibility in the hands of the children concerned and they had taken the initiative and acted creatively.

4. COUNSELLING STRATEGIES TO PROMOTE LEARNING ASSOCIATIONS BETWEEN BEHAVIOUR AND CONSEQUENCES

Pearce (1984) suggested the four following statements could be used to underpin counselling in schools:

1. work hard and you will do well,
2. behave well and you will be rewarded,
3. if you are lazy you will receive negative feedback/punishment,
4. if you misbehave you will receive negative feedback/punishment.

In primary schools there will be many occasions when pupils' problems occur because they have been unable to learn the types of behaviour-outcome associations that Pearce referred to. There is ample evidence in the published literature showing that pupils who have not learned behaviour-outcomes associations tend to do less well academically and are less well adjusted than their peers who have (e.g., Charlton, 1985). Arguably, a crucial task in any form of counselling is to help pupils perceive how their behaviour can be instrumental in precipitating problems and, just as important, how behaviour change can effect more positive outcomes.

In Charlton's (1986) enquiry primary school teachers administered a classroom group counselling programme designed to help pupils become more aware of behaviour-outcome contingencies. The rationale of the study was that as pupils became more aware of this association they would increasingly accept responsibility for their behaviour-outcomes and be more receptive to the notion that they could avoid, or resolve, problems through selecting and practising appropriate behaviours.

The counselling programme comprised three components: listening, analysing and resolving. In the listening element pupils listened to the teacher relating problems that she had encountered in her school days. She was careful to pinpoint the role of her own behaviours in causing those problems. Pupils were then encouraged to talk about some of their own school-based problems (educational/social concerns) and then reflect upon likely causes indicating, where appropriate, the causal effects of their behaviour.

In the second component, pupils listened to three recorded audio plays depicting children in failure-climates (i.e., encountering problems) in the home, play and school settings. Pupils were then asked to analyse the failure-climates in order to identify children's behaviours which caused the problems.

Finally, in the third component, pupils formed small groups and wrote two short plays which were then performed in front of the class. Both plays were based on a similar setting. However, whereas the first was to incorporate a failure-climate, the second indicated a success-climate (i.e., problem-free). After the presentation of each play the audience were invited to account to the performers, for the failure/success outcomes with reference to the children's behaviour in the plays. The performers responded by confirming correct responses, and explaining the behaviour-outcome sequences where correct responses were not forthcoming.

At the end of the counselling sessions (one school period each week for eleven weeks) over 90 per cent of the pupils were found to have accepted greater responsibility for their behaviour-outcomes. Additional findings (Charlton and Terrell, 1987) also revealed that over a four-month period less competent readers registered more significant gains in their reading achievement scores than a matched sample of less competent readers who had not received the group counselling.

The success of the counselling seemed to derive from the teachers providing pupils with opportunities, with reference to Pearce's (*op cit*) four points, to understand how they can become masters of their own destiny. Arguably, an awareness of this type is crucial to classroom efforts to encourage independent functioning, particularly where problems are to be avoided, or become manifest and need to be resolved.

References

BANDURA, A. (1977) *Social Learning Theory* (Englewood Cliffs, N.J.: Prentice-Hall).
BIDDLESTONE, S. (1985) 'Parents as partners in a language enrichment programme for young children', *Remedial Education* 20, 4 154–8.
BOLGER, A. W. (1975) *Child Study and Guidance in Schools* (London: Constable).
BURNS, R. (1982) *Self-Concept Development and Education* (New York: Holt, Rinehart and Winston).
CANT, R. and SPACKMAN, P. (1985) 'Self-esteem, counselling and educational achievement', *Educational Research*, 27, 1, 68–70.
CHARLTON, T. (1985) 'Locus of control as a Therapeutic Strategy for Helping Children with Learning and Behaviour Problems', *Maladjustment and Therapeutic Education*, 3 (1), 26–32.
CHARLTON, T. (1986) 'Differential effects of operant conditioning and counselling intervention upon children's locus of control beliefs', *Psychological Reports*, 59, 137–138.

CHARLTON, T. and TERRELL, C. (1987) 'Enhancing internal locus of control beliefs through group counselling: Effects upon children's reading performance', *Psychological Reports*, 60, 928–30.
COMBS, A. W., AVILA, D. L. and PURKEY, W. W. (1971) *Helping Relationships* (Boston: Allyn and Bacon).
FONTANA, D. (1981) *Psychology For Teachers* (London: Macmillan).
GALLOWAY, D. (1981) *Teaching and Counselling* (London: Longman).
GOOD, T. L. and BROPHY, J. E. (1980) *Educational Psychology* (New York: Holt, Rinehart and Winston).
HAMBLIN, D. H. (1978) *The Teacher and Counselling* (Oxford: Basil Blackwell).
HANKO, G. (1985) *Special Needs in Ordinary Classrooms* (Oxford: Basil Blackwell).
HARROP, A. (1982) *Behaviour Modification in the Classroom* (London: Hodder and Stoughton).
KIRBY, N. (1981) *Personal Values in Primary Education* (London: Harper and Row).
LAWRENCE, D. (1971) 'The effects of counselling on retarded readers', *Educational Research*, 13, 119–124.
LAWRENCE, D. (1972) 'Counselling of retarded readers by non-professionals', *Educational Research*, 15, 48–51.
LAWRENCE, D. (1985) 'Improving self-esteem and reading', *Educational Research*, 27, 3, 194–200.
LEWIS, E. C. (1970) *The Psychology of Counselling* (New York: Holt, Rinehart and Winston).
MARLAND, M. (1980) *Pastoral Care* (London: Heinemann).
MORGAN, S. R. (1979) 'A model of the empathic process for teachers of emotionally disturbed children', *American Journal of Orthopsychiatry*, 49 (3), 446–453.
MORSE, W. (1974) Personal Communication (Michigan: Ann Arbor).
NOONAN, E. (1983) *Counselling Young People* (London: Methuen).
PEARCE, J. (1984) 'Attitude Modification and Evaluating the Pastoral Curriculum', *Pastoral Care in Education*, 2, 1, 53–61.
PRING, R. (1984) *Personal and Social Education in The Curriculum* (London: Hodder and Stoughton).
ROBINSON, F. P. (1950) *Principles and Procedures in Student Counselling* (London: Harper and Row).
ROGERS, C. (1951) *Client-Centred Therapy* (Boston: Houghton Mifflin).
ROGERS, C. (1969) *Freedom to Learn* (Colombus, Ohio: Merrill).
SEEFELDT, C. (1980) *Teaching Young Children* (Englewood Cliffs, N.J.: Prentice-Hall).

SISTERTON, D. (1983) 'Counselling in The Primary School', *Division of Educational Child Psychology Education Section Review*, 7, 2, 10–15.

Chapter 8

Teachers, Parents and Other Professionals

David Galloway

Introduction

This chapter considers how relationships between teachers and parents and between teachers and other professionals contribute to children's general welfare at school, and more specifically, to their personal and social education. As in many other areas, the difficulties experienced by children with special educational needs help us to identify issues which affect the welfare of all pupils. Hence, some of the illustrations in this chapter are provided by children with special needs, though the underlying issues apply throughout the school. The aims of Personal and Social Education may be defined as providing learning activities which help each pupil to establish a personal identity as a contributing member of the school with a developing sense of her or his own rights and responsibilities, not only in school but also in the family and in society. That primary schools have a responsibility for Personal and Social Education is not controversial. There is, however, legitimate cause for concern in the ways some schools set about providing it.

Provision of learning activities implies the need for conscious planning, which in turn implies the need for a curriculum. The fact that Personal and Social Education should permeate all the school's activities does not negate the need for planning. The theme of this chapter is that planning a Personal and Social Education curriculum includes the relationships that the school develops with its pupils' parents and with other professionals. These relationships cannot, however, be considered separately from all the other, perhaps more obvious, learning experiences that the school provides for its pupils. To put this a different way, attempts to develop constructive relationships with parents and with the support services are unlikely to succeed unless the school has a very clear idea what it is trying to achieve for its pupils.

Identifying and meeting children's needs is a long-standing piece of education rhetoric. We cannot, however, need something without in some sense also wanting it. As teachers, when we talk about children's needs we are generally referring to the opportunities we want them to have, or the knowledge, attitudes, skills or concepts we want them to acquire. This seems straightforward enough, but unfortunately there is a snag. A teacher's first priority, rightly, is the welfare of the majority of pupils in the class. Discussion about children with special needs, either with parents or with other professionals, is often motivated by concern about their effect on other children. This is entirely reasonable. Problems can arise, though, when the real reason for referral is not openly acknowledged. To take an extreme example, research on children with moderate learning difficulties is virtually unanimous in concluding that they make better educational progress in ordinary classes than in special schools or classes. Yet they continue to be placed in the latter (Swann, 1985; Galloway and Goodwin, 1987). Ostensibly, the aim is to benefit the children concerned. The real reason is much more likely to ease the burden on the teacher and pupils in the class from which they were removed. Unfortunately, other examples of teachers and parents 'talking past each other' are much closer to hand, and affect a much larger number of children.

Conflicting messages to parents

Background

The Warnock Report (DES, 1978) emphasised the importance of parents as partners with teachers in their children's education. Subsequently the 1981 Education Act gave parents both rights and responsibilities in the process of assessing their children's special needs, and in reviewing their progress. The 1980 Education Act had extended parents' rights to choose their child's school and greatly increased the information which schools are required to provide about the curriculum and general organisation. More recently the government's proposals on school managing and governing bodies intend to encourage greater parental participation (Education Act, 1986).

These developments may be seen as yet another example of government interference in education. Alternatively they can be seen as an exciting opportunity to develop a fuller partnership with parents. They cannot be ignored; the law is specific about the information that parents must be given. Nevertheless, they can be subverted. This can occur intentionally. For example, reports provided for the formal assessment of special educational needs are given to parents, and a policy of providing the minimum amount of information is not unknown. More often, though, the process is more subtle.

Parent or problem?

In two of the first three primary schools I visited on returning to Britain from New Zealand a notice about procedures for reporting non-accidental injury to children occupied a prominent place on the wall in the head teacher's office. It is, of course, important that teachers should be aware of the possibility of non-accidental injury and of the procedures to follow. One wonders, though, whether ensuring that all parents visiting the school see this notice is the best way to establish a relationship of trust and confidence, especially with those parents who are worried about their own relationships with their children. In fact, the parents most likely to be deterred from seeking advice by seeing the notice are precisely those whose cooperation teachers claim to need most.

The hidden, non-verbal messages that parents receive when they visit their children's school, or simply collect their children from school, are often far more powerful than the verbal messages. Notices saying 'no parents beyond this point' may have gone, but the underlying message is evident in the total absence in many schools of parents in the classroom after their child's first week or two. When teachers visit their pupils' homes they are generally offered a cup of tea or coffee. Some schools make a point of welcoming parents in the same way, but they are in a minority. In any case, there are other, easier ways to welcome parents and put them at ease. It is surprising, for example, how many head teachers decorate their offices with administrative notices and glazed prints of old masters. The corridors and classrooms may be full of children's work, but the non-verbal message to parents is that the Head has no time for such trivia.

Towards a partnership

Partnership implies sharing. Thus partnership with parents implies that parents have something valuable to offer their child's education at school. Thinking about most of their pupils, teachers can generally accept this at an emotional and at an intellectual level. In the case of children with learning or adjustment difficulties, especially when they come from homes which teachers, perhaps with good reason, consider grossly disadvantaging, it is more difficult but no less important. To put it bluntly, seeking a partnership with parents implies that teachers have something to learn from the people they may consider to be the source of the child's problems.

Children are quick to sense what their parents think of their teachers and vice versa. Children are just as sensitive as parents to the hidden curriculum which makes parents feel welcome or unwelcome at school. The reason is simply that their own sense of identity and self-worth is established as a member of the family group. If they sense that their parents are held in low esteem they also will feel held in low esteem. This is the danger behind remarks, made with disturbing frequency to educational psychologists and school doctors, such as, 'We're social workers here as much as teachers' or 'Parents undo all the good we do in school'.

Schools which seek an active partnership with parents demonstrate a respect for children's experience at home, and a willingness to build on this experience. Children who start school with social confidence and a sense of self-worth generally cope quite easily with a school regime totally unlike anything they have experienced before. It is disconcerting, though, to read Moore's (1966) conclusion that 80 per cent of children experienced difficulty in adjusting to their infant schools. Children whose family life is disturbing are more likely to lack a sense of self-worth, but will have a correspondingly greater need to know that teachers acknowledge and build on such strengths as do exist within their families. This is why children from the most disturbing backgrounds frequently have the greatest difficulty in adjusting to the needs and demands of the school. How then, have teachers moved towards a partnership with parents?

Parents as coteachers of reading

Learning to read has probably attracted more attention than any other topic in educational research. Yet the most important research of recent years was striking for its simplicity. Hewison and Tizard (1980) and Tizard *et al* (1982) found that children's progress in reading was facilitated by their parents listening to them read at home. In a subsequent, carefully controlled, study parental collaboration was found to be more effective than extra help from a specially appointed teacher at school. This extra help was greater than would normally be provided in 'remedial' or special needs classes in ordinary schools. The message was simply that cooperation with parents was more effective in facilitating children's progress than specialist teaching at school. Two aspects of these studies are of particular importance. First, parents were not given elaborate training or guidance in how to listen to their children reading. Second, the studies were conducted in Haringey, a socially disadvantaged and multi-ethnic part of London. In other words, the parents whose cooperation proved so beneficial were precisely the parents who, according to a lot of conventional staffroom wisdom, would be least competent and least willing to provide it. This tendency to underestimate the capacity of working-class children and of their parents has also been emphasised in a study of pre-school children's language development (Tizard and Hughes, 1983).

The Haringey research has been confirmed elsewhere. The Coventry Community Education Programme, for example, has confirmed 'a clear linear relationship . . . between the amount of parental support for their children's reading and the reading scores obtained' (Widlake and Macleod, 1984, p. 49). Nor are the advantages confined to 'ordinary' children. Young and Tyre (1983) found broadly similar results with children with specific reading difficulties, who are generally thought to require highly specialised forms of help.

Even when parents could not read English, or even could not read at all, the Haringey research suggested that children still benefited from reading to them. It is instructive to consider how parental cooperation in the teaching and learning process may exert its beneficial effects. Four possibilities come to mind.

1. It is well known that skills learned in one context do not necessarily transfer to another. By listening to their children reading from books they bring home from school, parents help to overcome problems of learning transfer.
2. By listening to their children read, parents demonstrate the importance they attach to their progress at school and thus increase their motivation to succeed at school.
3. Arising from the last point, parents who are themselves illiterate often value literacy extremely highly. Friendly encouragement to cooperate with the school is welcomed and leads parents and children to view school attendance in a different light. (In this connection, as an educational psychologist I once 'cured' a six-year-old boy of soiling by demonstrating to the father that his son was making excellent

progress in reading. The father was illiterate. The child's soiling appeared to be associated with the pressure resulting from his father's extreme anxiety that his son, too, might grow up illiterate.)
4. Establishing cooperative contact with parents and observing the beneficial results on children's progress is likely to change teachers' perceptions of their pupils' parents. As noted earlier, children are sensitive to their teacher's attitudes. A sense that their parents and teachers are working together seems likely to contribute to a climate of security favourable to successful learning.

A partnership for problem solving

An obvious aim in recent education legislation is to make teachers more accountable to their pupils' parents. The 'secret garden' of the curriculum may not yet be open to the public, but the public does have a legal right to a free copy of a prospectus. Accountability does not necessarily imply partnership, but in practice the teachers' responsibilities to their pupils' parents are matched by those of parents to their children's teachers. To take a simple example, the law still upholds the school's right to insist on children conforming to fairly strict rules of dress. The partnership implicit in teachers' and parents' legal obligations is, nevertheless, limited.

Children with learning or adjustment difficulties constitute a majority of the 20 per cent regarded by the Warnock Report as having special educational needs. These children illustrate the direction in which a partnership with parents must logically lead us. Paired reading techniques can explicitly enlist the parents' involvement in the process of learning to read. When the initiative comes from schools, as is almost invariably the case in the reported literature, the implicit question is, 'Can you help us?' In the case of children with learning or adjustment difficulties the same question can underlie the school's approach to parents. Asking parents if they can make any suggestions that might help teachers to solve a problem is a far cry from merely drawing their attention to it and seeking their agreement to enlist expert professional help.

There are, however, two major obstacles to overcome if we are to enlist the help of parents as partners in their children's education. The first is that partnership, paradoxically, implies that we as teachers are retaining responsibility for teaching the child. The second is that if we seek a partnership with parents, their comments and suggestions may require changes in our teaching methods and classroom management procedures. It is worth considering each of these separately.

As a university teacher, when I ask my students for feedback on a course I have taught or on the comments I have written on their essays I am involving them in the teaching and learning process. In this sense I am seeking a partnership with them. Yet in seeking this partnership I am underlining my own responsibility for my teaching. If I receive no feedback this will be both disappointing and disturbing, yet the fact of receiving or not receiving feedback from my students does not, on its own, have any implications for my responsibility as a teacher. Exactly the same applies in schools when teachers seek help from parents in solving some problem their child is experiencing. This point becomes clearer when we consider the alternatives. I could attribute my students' poor performance in course work assignments or exams to their own laziness or lack of intelligence. In this case I am denying my own responsibility for their work. If I ask them for feedback I am accepting responsibility. In the same way, teachers can base earnest discussions with parents on the 'crude, naive and lazy simplicity'* of terms such as 'hyperactive', 'disturbed' or even 'has learning difficulties'. Responsibility for the problem is thus located in the child, absolving the teacher. In asking parents for help our responsibility is retained, and with it the possibility of tackling the problem.

Partnership also implies the possibility of critical feedback and hence the need for evaluation and modification of existing methods. If my students tell me that my favourite lecture is unintelligible and that the helpful, detailed suggestions I write on their essays are obscure to the point of being meaningless, I have to review my materials, my presentation, and possibly the whole balance of the course. Partnership with parents in primary schools has similarly far-reaching implications. We have already mentioned Moore's (1966) evidence that up to 80 per cent of children were said by their parents to experience difficulty in adjusting to infant school. The greatest obstacle to partnership may well be fear of the implications.

---

*This phrase was used by Dr Kingsley Whitmore in a lecture to the Association of Child Psychology and Psychiatry in 1972, referring to the terms ESN and maladjusted.

Other professionals: Dogsbodies, experts or partners?

Reasons for referral

Ostensibly the reason for referral to members of the LEA support services is straightforward. The aim is to help the child or, less obviously, to help the teacher to help the child. The distinction is often blurred but is none the less important. The unstated reasons for referral illustrate this.

Teachers often refer to a child as being 'under the educational psychologist' or doctor. Implicitly they are thereby shifting responsibility for the child's future progress or behaviour on to the individual concerned. At one level this is quite reasonable. A teacher's main responsibility must be to the majority of children in her class. In addition, children's poor behaviour or progress is known to be one of the major sources of stress in teaching (e.g., Pratt, 1978; Galloway *et al*, 1984). Teachers can legitimately demand support in teaching these children. Demanding support, though, implies continued acceptance of responsibility. Sometimes the real, but unstated, reason for referral is to initiate transfer to a special school or class. In such cases the child is likely to be said to be 'under' the psychologist, even though the psychologist may see her role as helping the present teacher to teach the child successfully.

Someone else's responsibility?

Referring a child to a specialist agency such as child guidance or the school psychological service is one way of devolving responsibility. The way in which some schools use their educational welfare office illustrates another. Historically the educational welfare service has had responsibility for school attendance. Cases of truancy or suspected parent-condoned absence are referred to the EWO who is expected to get the child back to school. In most schools teachers welcome information from the EWO about problems the child may be having at home, and occasionally the EWO is asked to arrange for parents to visit the school for a meeting with teachers. This, however, happens relatively seldom, even in cases when the LEA is considering legal action over a child's poor attendance (Galloway, 1985a).

All these uses of EWOs require them to work essentially as messengers. At best their task is to explain the school's position to parents and to give teachers relevant information about the home. This implicitly negates any attempt at partnership either with EWOs themselves or with parents. EWOs who come back to the school after a home visit with criticisms of teachers are unlikely to be well received. They find themselves under powerful pressure to work within a model which sees poor school attendance as the result of the family's problem, not as a result of the school's failure to establish a relationship which enlists the family's confidence and cooperation. The educational welfare service is the lowest paid and professionally the least qualified of all the LEA support services. While they may disagree privately, EWOs seldom feel able to challenge publicly the teacher's perception of the situation. Far from establishing a partnership between teachers and parents, moreover, their very existence can sometimes constitute an obstacle to partnership.

If a service exists to investigate and deal with cases of poor attendance, teachers are likely to feel that this is not their own responsibility. Because EWOs often act as 'go-betweens', passing messages from teachers to parents and vice versa, any incentive for teachers to establish a direct dialogue with parents is reduced. This is not an argument for the abolition of the service, but rather for a radical shift of emphasis to enable EWOs to act as catalysts in establishing cooperative relationships between teachers and parents. That, however, requires acceptance from teachers that the EWO's investigations may reveal tensions in the school's organisation or social relationships which require attention. A cooperative relationship implies willingness to change on both sides.

Working together

I have argued that when teachers refer a child to a specialist agency they may implicitly be reducing their own responsibility for finding solutions. Moreover, by accepting the referral, specialists put themselves in an 'expert' role which has two unfortunate side effects. First, it gives them responsibility for a problem they almost certainly cannot solve. Second, because the problem is seen as the child, the expert's responsibility is to the child rather than to the referring teacher.

The alternative model implies a partnership between teachers and members of specialist agencies in which each have clearly defined responsibilities. In seeking help the teacher's question is, 'What can you suggest that may enable me to meet this child's needs more effectively?' Here, the teacher accepts his responsibility for the pupil. The educational psychologist (or other specialist) also has a responsibility, but to the teacher rather than directly to the child or family. Having a responsibility to the teacher also means that the psychologist is accountable to the teacher. Indeed, accountability is reciprocal, as in any working partnership. The psychologist may suggest activities, materials or classroom management techniques to help the teacher tackle the problem. The critical word here, though, is 'suggest'. The teacher will consider these in the light of her present work with the class, and may suggest modifications. If the agreed programme proves unsuccessful, the teacher and the psychologist will together analyse the reasons, and the psychologist's accountability to the teacher will require him to propose either a realistic alternative or some modification to the original programme.

The argument, then, is that a partnership between teachers and other professionals implies acceptance on both sides of a teacher's responsibility for the pupil's progress and behaviour. In this respect the same relationship applies as when parents seek advice from an educational psychologist. The parents retain full responsibility for their child, but expect the psychologist to provide information and suggestions that will be of practical benefit. There will, of course, be occasions when teachers refer a child or family who needs help in their own right, independent of anything that happens in school. In such cases professionals are accountable immediately to parents in providing the necessary support or treatment. This does not, however, invalidate their accountability to teachers in helping them to explore more effective ways to work with the child at school.

Whose responsibility?

School organisation and management

Responsibility for the 'all-round' development of their pupils has long been accepted as an integral part of the primary school teacher's job. Although pastoral care is attracting an enormous amount of attention in secondary schools, the same is not true in primaries. The probable reason is simply that pupil's general welfare and their personal and social education are considered so pervasive in all primary school activities as to be entirely unproblematic. Yet observation suggests that this rosy picture is not entirely justified. Elsewhere I have drawn attention to four ways in which the class teacher's work with individual pupils can be limited in primary schools:

1. The head centres pastoral care on herself and/or the deputy, insisting on holding all discussions with educational welfare

officers, educational psychologists, social workers and other "outsiders" herself. Some headteachers rationalise this as 'protecting' their colleagues. The effect is to devalue class teachers' knowledge of the pupils and to reduce its potential usefulness by filtering it through a third party.
2. Assembly involving the whole school is held daily, with class teachers being encouraged to deal with administrative chores such as registration in the first five minutes of the morning and afternoon. As a result the class has little or no time allocated for activities which are not seen as part of the formal curriculum. Thus, teachers who in theory pride themselves on teaching the whole child – "children not subjects" – in practice define educational activities in unnecessarily limited terms.
3. The head insists on class teachers not approaching parents direct to discuss their children's progress. Again, this is rationalised as "protecting" class teachers. Yet in practice, this too devalues the class teacher's knowledge. Occasionally heads who are happy to allow class teachers to discuss their children's progress with parents draw the line at discussion of behaviour problems, except at a superficial level on the annual open evening. Again the spurious distinction implicitly conveyed to class teachers is that their responsibility lies in the area of educational development rather than social/emotional development.
4. The head encourages teachers to "play down" concern about a pupil's behaviour, either on the grounds that "we can cope with him for the time being", or that "it's not really too much of a problem yet", or that "he'll grow out of it", or that "we mustn't expect too much: just look at the home background" (from Galloway, 1985b, pp. 107–108).

The teacher's needs

Interviewing parents about their children's progress or behaviour was seen as a major source of stress by primary school teachers in New Zealand (Galloway *et al*, 1982). The implication, though, is not that this should be devolved to the Head, but that senior teachers should aim to equip their less experienced colleagues with the necessary skills. All head teachers would see their colleagues' professional development as an essential part of their job, at least in theory. Relatively few systematically incorporate interviews with parents into a programme of school-based in-service education and training. From the individual class teacher's perspective, meetings with parents contain a distinct element of trial and error – a notoriously inefficient form of learning.

Children's self-esteem depends at least in part on feeling that they are learning new skills, that they can participate in and contribute to their own learning, and that their effort and achievement is recognised. The same applies to the self-esteem of teachers. In attributing the cause of children's learning or adjustment difficulties to personal or family problems, teachers devalue their own skills. In accepting responsibility for individual pupils, other professionals de-skill teachers by implicitly accepting that the classroom problem is beyond the teacher's ability to solve. In such cases the teacher is unable to learn from the professional's experience, nor is the professional able to learn from that of the teacher. Partnership involves both parties in a willingness to learn from each other.

Conclusions

The Head of a large multi-ethnic school in New Zealand once told me he would know he was running a good school when parents drank as much coffee in the staffroom as teachers. He did not claim to be near this target, but at his school and at some other schools in New Zealand there was nothing unusual about parents' presence in the staffroom. His argument was that a partnership based on mutual learning and cooperation could not be confined to formal interviews, and that making part of the school a no-go area for parents would inhibit them from contributing.

Children's attitudes to school are inevitably influenced by those of their parents. Yet the extent to which parents work with or against the school depends to a large extent on the school's teachers. A recent study in Wales showed enormous variations between secondary schools in the amount and nature of links they established with parents (Woods, 1984). The school that stood out for the high quality of its contacts with parents served a predominantly working-class area. There is every reason to think that primary schools have at least as much influence. Converting the rhetoric of partnership with parents and other professionals into practice requires leadership and support from head teachers and their senior colleagues. In the short term this could be stressful. In the long term, though, the benefits will be felt as much by head teachers and class teachers as by pupils and their parents.

References

DES (1983) *Better Schools* Cmnd. No. 9469 (London: HMSO).
GALLOWAY, D. (1985a) *Schools and Persistent Absentees* (Oxford: Pergamon).
GALLOWAY, D. (1985b) *Schools, Pupils and Special Educational Needs* (London: Croom Helm).
GALLOWAY, D. and GOODWIN, C. (1987) *The Education of Disturbing Children: Pupils with Learning and Adjustment Difficulties* (London: Longman).
GALLOWAY, D., PANCKHURST, F., BOSWELL, K., BOSWELL, C. and GREEN, K. (1982) 'Sources of Stress for Class Teachers', *National Education* (NZ), 64, 164–169.
GALLOWAY, D., PANCKHURST, F., BOSWELL, K., BOSWELL, C. and GREEN, K. (1984) 'Mental Health, Absences from Work, Stress and Satisfaction in a Sample of New Zealand Primary School Teachers', *Australia and New Zealand Journal of Psychiatry*, 18, 359–63.
HEWISON, J. and TIZARD, J. (1980) Parental Involvement and Reading Attainment, *British Journal of Educational Psychology*, 50, 209–215.
MOORE, T. (1966) Difficulties of the Ordinary Child in Adjusting to Primary School, *Journal of Child Psychology and Psychiatry*, 7, 17–38.
PRATT, J. (1978) 'Perceived Stress Among Teachers: The Effects of Age and Background of Children Taught', *Educational Review*, 30, 3–14.
SWANN, W. (1985) 'Is the Integration of Children with Special Needs Happening? An Analysis of Recent Statistics of Pupils in Special Schools', *Oxford Review of Education*, 11, 3–18.
TIZARD, B. and HUGHES, M. (1983) *Young Children Learning* (London: Fontana).
TIZARD, J., SCHOFIELD, W. N. and HEWISON, J. (1982) 'Collaboration Between Teachers and Parents in Assisting Children's Reading', *British Journal of Educational Psychology*, 52, 1–15.
WIDLAKE, P. and MACLEOD, F. (1984) *Raising Standards: Parental Involvement Programmes and the Language Performance of Children* (Coventry: Community Education Development Centre).
WOODS, P. (1984) *Parents and School: A Report for Discussion on Liaison between Parents and Secondary Schools in Wales* (London: Schools Council Publications).
YOUNG, P. and TYRE, C. (1983) *Dyslexia or Illiteracy? Realising the Right to Read* (Milton Keynes: Open University).

PART III

One chapter reflects on the difficult issue of the values that underlie teachers' work, and the concluding presentation again emphasises the purpose of the book by offering material for discussion and possible action.

Chapter 9: Values in Primary Education

Norman Kirby MA, AKC, lecturer and writer, formerly Head of Middle School Education Department of Goldsmith's College, University of London, attempts the difficult task of reviewing the values that underlie a teacher's work in developing children's values and attitudes. As we occasionally agonise over children's searching questions on today's confusion of values, we can at least start from the hope that their primary school has set foundations of caring, listening, discussing, sharing and assessing. We can perhaps offer the basis for their own future rational decisions.

Chapter 10: An Agenda for Discussion and Possible Action

The Editors consider how, in this book, a number of differing viewpoints on children's development in primary schools begin to make a picture of the teacher and school that can best help children of today to live in their new world of the twenty-first century. The conclusion is put in the form of a series of opinions and questions for discussion in initial and in-service training.

Chapter 9
Values in Primary Education

Norman Kirby

Teachers' tasks

It would be interesting to consider how many teachers think of themselves as transmitters of values along with their other duties. But what values? There are so many to choose from, and not all the daily commitments of teaching appear as aspirations but rather as jobs to be done. There are diagnoses of each child's learning abilities and difficulties to be attempted, a firm grounding in the basic skills of reading, writing and Mathematics to be given, groups to be organised, Physical Education and aesthetic experiences in Art and Craft to be provided, scientific investigations to be carried out, interests in the home and school environment to be extended through visits and displays, assemblies to be arranged, school journeys to be planned, music and dramatic performances to be undertaken, not to mention the prospect of having to keep abreast of the computer revolution as well as wrestling with the problem of presenting Religious Education to a class of mixed cultural origins. They will be mixed in every other way as well, in ability, intelligence, interests, temperament and behaviour. Is it possible to do all this, to be loyal to the profession, straightforward with employers, charming and diplomatic yet honest with parents, and all in obedience to a consistent moral philosophy?

Differing settings

Times change. People and values change with them. Those who were involved in primary education in the 1960s remember them as times of optimism, of adequate provision, stimulating experiment and growth. They were sometimes referred to as a golden age. There was 'the bulge', the promise of an expanding school population, and the undisputed need felt by all parties in Parliament to provide resources for educational improvement. New schools were built according to attractive designs which reflected the most recent knowledge of children's development and concern for their needs.

In the 1980s the scene has changed. Economic recession has created problems unsuspected twenty years earlier, the worst of these being unemployment on a large scale. In many industries the rate of technological development has made human beings replaceable. New concepts of work and leisure have brought about changes in social mores and in the expectations of the young. A society which, through its mass means of communication and advertising, gives prominence to material rewards yet cannot promise a working future for its young members, manufactures discontent and increases the pressures of competition.

Searching for guidelines

The purposes of education with its traditional values of human respect and cooperation are called into question. The teacher is required to be an encourager in a discouraging society. New attitudes compete with the older values. To consider one of the most traditional of institutions: family life and what it was supposed to contribute to the physical and mental health of children is being challenged, not only on the sociological front, but also in chemical laboratories with sperm banks, test tube births and other inventions of genetic engineering. In this brave new world the young teacher may look to philosophy for some guiding principle in the quest for values. A general atmosphere of enquiry and uncertainty is more stimulating to the student than a world of dogmatic certainties, yet when thought has to be translated into action it is reasonable to seek some justification for the line chosen, especially where the education of the young is concerned. The young teacher remembers his course at college, but how could his philosophical studies there be other than scant, with sociology, psychology, child development, professional studies and school practice to be encompassed as well? With only a nodding acquaintance with Plato's vision of absolutes – Goodness, Truth and Beauty – perhaps a deeper involvement with Christianity's doctrine of love, a few lectures referring briefly to Hume's scepticism, the self-orientated theories of Hobbes, the utilitarianism of Jeremy Bentham, a closer look at Darwin's revolutionary findings which altered the whole concept of man and the economic determinism of Karl Marx which did the same for society, a glance at Nietzsche's will to power, and a rather longer consideration of Dewey's pragmatism because of his influence on primary education, the novice in the classroom feels confused rather than guided. This is too much name-dropping, but only to emphasise that help in the search for values must come from elsewhere and nearer home.

Added to the complexity and contradictions presented by different philosophies is the plurality of society itself into which different ethnic groups have imported values from their own cultures.

Rationality and common sense

In the world of values we are faced with a multiplicity of choices and the choices need to be justified (L. A. Reid, 1962; Bridges and Scrimshaw, 1975). One first choice is clear and finds support from most philosophies, ancient and modern: the over-riding value of rationality. It is reason itself which supplies the impulse to search for value. Fundamental, too, to this search is a sense of right and wrong, more culturally determined than rationality, yet in the commonsense world of the classroom a value without which education and the teaching profession make no sense. To talk of common sense is not to turn one's back on philosophy but to examine the values which a teacher can reasonably hold while busy with the demands of everyday reality.

Primary education and the needs of children

In the interests of sanity one solution is to look at the children themselves, the very *raison d'être* of the teacher, the school and the entire edifice of the educational system. There are distinguished precedents for this line of approach and among them a number of renowned philosophers. Primary Education has an honourable tradition of its own originating from the Primary School Report (Hadow) of 1931, though the seeds were sown in earlier times. The dynamic for this movement was provided by observation of children and the conditions in which learning took place. The list of pioneers stretches back over the centuries but in the early decades of the twentieth century the application in practice of their ways of thinking about children led to one of the greatest revolutions in educational history, culminating in what we know as the English primary school.

The place of dialogue in learning is conspicuous in the teaching of Socrates who gave his name to the Socratic method. Plato emphasised the importance of the learner's environment, the beauty of which engendered beauty in the soul. Jesus, in his dealings with children, exemplified respect for their own particular nature from which adults would do well to learn. Rousseau believed in childhood as a period of life to be valued for its own sake. Pestalozzi upheld the value of activity and responsibility for productive work. Froebel gave encouragement to children's investigating, experimenting and finding out for themselves. The essence of his system was to make 'the inner outer and the outer inner', thus legitimising the child's contribution to his education from his own experience, a foretaste of Piaget's research with its insight into learning experienced as well as observed. Dewey applied the idea of democracy to education. Maria Montessori maintained that children could be encouraged to work hard by being given freedom to use their own initiative.

It was not until the 1931 Report of the Board of Education Consultative Committee on the Primary School (Hadow) that educational ideas derived from observation of children gained governmental support, and little by little filtered into official policy. It is encouraging to know that this report, with its practical concern for the needs of children and its confidence in their resourcefulness, was published at a time of economic hardship. This was a watershed in the history of education, but it was not until the years after the Second World War that the educational atmosphere became congenial enough for the more widespread growth of child-centred education, learning from experience and the sometimes partially understood 'activity methods'.

More fundamental than methods were the values inherent in the new primary schools and in what the Plowden Report of 1967 describes as 'the best of primary education'. It is these values, derived from ethical principles and inspired by an attentive attitude towards child nature that are a most reliable guide for practising teachers, because they are undeniably observable on a factual level and are not subject to contradiction through the vagaries of social change. They are simple ideas but have an eternal quality about them.

Respect for children

The first is respect for children and their work. To give allegiance to this value presupposes that intellectual development depends upon treating the child as a rational being and encouraging freedom of thought and expression. Moral education, too, depends upon the autonomy of the individual and not upon indoctrination (Piaget, 1950; Kohlberg, 1966). Freedom to express ideas implies ease of communication which is itself dependent upon positive relationships between teachers and learners and between the learners themselves, a social atmosphere created in the first place by the head teacher and the staff. In a school where human relationships are central to its life, and in a climate of work where each person is valued and receives unconditional acceptance, individuals come to accept each other and appreciate each other's work (Downey, 1977). In such a school children can develop standards from within which may be far higher than any externally imposed standards.

Respect for the opinions of children entails the encouragement of discussion and debate. This does not rule out positive criticism or even correction of children's views and behaviour, for the role of the teacher as guide is consistent both with the idea of democracy founded upon mutual respect and with the notion of children as people who are learning self-respect along with the acceptance of responsibility for their own actions (Hirst and Peters, 1970). An intellectual investigation in partnership with an educated adult can surely be an invaluable educative experience for any child. Teachers in this situation ask real questions with a genuine desire to know the answer, because they are not only interested in the answer given by a child, but are interested also in the mental functioning of the child. Every piece of child behaviour is of significance to them. As Barnes (1976) and Stubbs (1976) point out, much time is spent by inexperienced teachers asking closed questions, to which they already know the answers, resulting in what Stubbs calls 'pseudo-dialogue'.

Individual differences

The second simple idea which has had a far-reaching effect on educational practice is the idea that human beings are different from each other. Consideration for individual differences has meant more freedom for the child to learn in his own way (Piaget, 1950, 1952), while the close observation of children's differing interests has led to the provision of varied materials for work, a greater variety of books, more attractive library corners, and the exercise of choice and appropriate space in which to work. It has meant the dethronement of conformity as a special learner's virtue and a greater interest in the diversity of individual talents and aptitudes.

Because children learn at different speeds the use of time also demands greater adaptability. Allowances have to be made for deeper involvement in an interest and time to pursue it without interruption. Adjustment to individual differences has had far-reaching effects upon the architecture and furniture of schools, has brought about greater flexibility in teaching methods and the abolition of rigid timetables. Greater demands are made upon a teacher's skill in exploring many different kinds of learning: for multiple choices on the part of the learners, for projects undertaken by small groups, or for the varied ways in which individuals can respond to the same experience whether it be a visit, a story, a play, a film or a mathematical problem. There is room for the pursuit of an idiosyncratic interest and for sharing in the work of others, for individuals are also social beings and they are of value not only in their uniqueness but in their human attributes and relationships. Both aspects must be catered for in their education. Not all independent work is based on choice and interest, for some basic skills are circumscribed by a child's ability, but children of all abilities can share in group work.

Experiential learning

A third finding which dates back at least as far as the eighteenth century, to the empirical philosophy of John Locke, is that experience, and particularly sensation, is at the root of learning. Since then this theory has been given support by psychological research, by investigations into human perception and concept formation, and by studies in child development. Psychologists have demonstrated that before learning can take place its subject matter must make an organic connection with what a child has already experienced, or, in Piaget's terms (Piaget, 1950, 1952), there must be assimilation of the new and accommodation by the old (the existing mental structures). Again, individual differences are implicated. Experience varies from one child to another, so learning has to be assimilated in a variety of patterns. Flexibility is again required from a teacher who must not only extend, but provide, experience.

Research has shown that cognitive development is influenced by emotional experience and by the attention given to the affective aspects of education. Schools should therefore be places where positive personal relationships encourage healthy emotional growth and where the arts provide varying opportunities for the expression of feeling (Sinclair de Zwart, 1969; Jones, 1972).

Where social experience is concerned, arrangements must be made for children to learn from each other, for teachers to use each other's skills and knowledge, and for the school to be accepted as part of the community, with parents as participators. Where communication with parents leads to mutual understanding and to appreciation of the school's philosophy and aims, not only does the school receive support for its values, but children are more likely to make progress in their education. (Plowden, 1967; Shipman, 1975).

It is important, too, for teachers to realise that it is probably at school that many children receive the first glimmerings of their membership of the human race, their political education in its widest sense. It is here that the attack can be made, and sustained, in positive ways through the encouragement of mutual help and cooperation, through teachers' views and example, through Religious Education, visitors to school, environmental and historical studies, upon all forms of prejudice, including racism and sexism. Where else but here can the foundations of peace, international understanding, and practical sympathy for the poor and the disadvantaged be laid? When otherwise than in the earliest years of a person's education?

Environmental influences

A fourth idea of importance to education is linked with the preceding one. Children's environment is inseparable from their experience, so modern education in its endeavour to understand children and employ them as agents in their own learning makes use of many individual and group experiences originating from the local geography, history and sociology of home, family and school. Teachers create deliberate links with the neighbourhood of people and things. The neighbourhood, in the form of libraries, museums, town halls, police, post office and fire services, reciprocates by placing local resources at their disposal.

In Bruner's (1966) view cognitive growth is directly linked with the child's interaction with the environment, a process most profitably fostered by the intervention of a teacher who arouses his pupils to action and to speech as the means to acquire concepts. The child is not left to the mercy of the environment, in a hit or miss fashion. This applies equally to technological extensions of the environment in the forms of film, television, radio and teaching-machine, because the teacher is there to provide the opportunities for questioning, discussion and activity, and to structure the experiences upon which conceptual development depends.

A positive teaching role

Recent research has tended to restore the confidence of teachers in a more positive role because of, rather than in spite of, the advances made in the understanding of children (Flanders and Simon, 1969; Rosenshine, 1971; Gage, 1972; Dunkin and Biddle, 1974). It is acknowledged that children need teachers, and teachers, according to McNamara and Desforges, need an applied knowledge of teaching centred in the classroom and based on research (McNamara and Desforges, 1978). The experienced teacher shows a proper respect for educational theory by ministering to needs as they are observed, rather than by taking up some established or fashionable position. The purposes and interests of children take no account of dogma. Children are what they are and have an annoying habit of confounding educational doctrines, especially those which are too tidy but which to adult minds are logical and consistent. With the new approaches to primary education and the change from didactic methods to more 'active' learning some of the older generation of teachers (but not all) felt that what they had imagined to be their own particular gifts – for example, of exposition, instruction and demonstration – had become devalued. There were others who went overboard in a superficial acceptance of letting children do as they liked, inducing one headmaster in a newspaper article to express his disapproval of the idea that 'learning is fun' and to explain his reasons why he was applying for early retirement. Both extremes, the didactic and the *laissez-faire* are distortions of educational theory because they ignore both the complex nature of children and the demands of learning.

Achievement

Children enjoy a challenge. One of their basic motivations is the desire for achievement. Some characteristics of middle-school pupils are more in harmony with the goals of teachers than some teachers themselves realise. Workers with very young children and babies affirm from their observations the repeated efforts of infants to gain mastery over their environment. Dr Montessori, in a lecture delivered in London in 1946, talked of the child's need to engage in 'maximum effort' to conquer the environment, and of the importance, for both physical and psychic development, of providing for him opportunities to carry heavy objects and to practise difficult movements.

Children in the primary school often draw attention to their ability in feats of daring. It is possible that in these self-imposed tests of skill and courage a child depends for his self-esteem as much upon being acceptable to himself, according to his own standards, as upon the good opinion of others. Emulation of other enterprising children seems to be one way in which a child proves his potentialities to himself as well as to onlookers. Thus J. McV. Hunt (1971) refers to complexity or competence models who may be adults, or older or more skilful children, whose behaviour spurs on those less competent to match them in skills and achievements. My own observation of children during playtimes showed that the harder the feat was the greater its attraction, and satisfaction in the accomplishment of a difficult task did not necessarily wait upon the presence and the approval of others. Neither were marks, prizes and team points an essential part of this satisfaction. The reward for having built a bridge was having built a bridge, not to mention the bonus of enjoying involvement with others in a joint enterprise. Teachers are also aware that achievement and involvement can also be motivating factors in schoolwork as well. To give children 'harder' sums at the appropriate time *is* to be child-centred. They are proud to be able to swim an extra length of the baths and to drive a nail in straight 'first time', but also to read a more 'difficult' book. Boredom is an ever-present threat when children sense that they are not being 'stretched', when their burgeoning impulses towards self-reliance, autonomy and adulthood are ignored. An interest in railways may be ephemeral, but the interest in achievement is lasting, and the wise teacher exploits it.

The teacher as authority and model

A teacher, though no longer authoritarian, is still an authority and in authority, professionally employed to be an initiator and instigator of learning. Consider, for example, learning by discovery. Children are motivated by curiosity, but this is sometimes easily satisfied, often partially and sometimes by incorrect information. Motivation needed for permanent grasp and thorough understanding needs to be sustained over a long period of time by an experienced teacher. Learning by discovery, if there is no guidance, can be unstructured and confusing.

In practice there are few real dichotomies in education. A close acquaintance with children on a practical level will disclose many truths about the nature of learning. In the world of children there are no false antitheses, no contradictions in having a teacher as a central figure who nevertheless allows freedom for personal discovery, who teaches and also lets you explore, who tells a story and treats listening as a worthwhile educational activity, who considers that language as communication involves both receiving and giving, speaking and being spoken to on a personal level.

The importance of observing children does not imply that the teacher is neutral or passive where educational values are concerned. Because the ultimate responsibility for the quality of education rests with the teacher it is essential that members of the profession should trust their own judgement and have confidence in themselves and in their work. If children are learning in a free atmosphere of individual investigation and expressive activity, the teacher has created that atmosphere. If there is a warm climate of personal relationships, the teacher has created or contributed to the warmth. If situations are open ended and flexible and allow full rein to a child's curiosity and creativity, it is the teacher who has arranged that it should be so. The classroom already has a sense of purpose before the children have burst in upon it with their own purposes which the teacher will be careful to use.

Children come into school knowing that someone has been there before them, planning and providing. The environment is not only attractive but intentionally thought provoking as well. The greatest responsibilities and initiatives belong to the head teacher. A visitor to a 'good' school can sense immediately a positive atmosphere of warmth and welcome, whether it be the well-watered plants, the artefacts in the entrance hall or the spoken greeting from a child at the door.

Seeking significance

Though the good teacher may be the inconspicuous one, the educator who recognises the great potential of children themselves, nevertheless he cannot avoid serving as a model for those values which he is seeking to promote. Children desire to achieve significance for themselves and to be identifiable not only as individuals but as contributors to the life of the group. A child's feeling of worthwhileness and belonging can be conveyed by the teacher who has a listening ear, who can share the child's enthusiasms and who finds time, even in a class of 30 children for some positive talk to each individual on a personal level. It is a matter of great importance for a teacher to note that John is keen on history, that Mary is a good swimmer, to enquire after Peter's mother who has just been admitted to hospital, to congratulate Malcolm on scoring the winning goal last Saturday and to wish Susan a happy birthday. The central conveyor of values has to be seen by the critical eyes of children to be an embodiment of those values. (Have pity on the writer of this chapter who does not pretend to be such an embodiment, but a recorder and admirer of what he has seen of teachers at work. It is always invidious to talk of values as if one possessed them oneself.)

Practical values as a foundation

At primary school level values come across to children not as abstract virtues but in direct practical ways: taking your place in the queue, keeping promises, sharing materials and possessions with others, showing respect for the opinions of others in discussion, giving help where it is needed, owning up to one's mistakes, making strangers feel at home, opening doors for visitors. These are the small beginnings of integrity, maturity and democracy, and of such virtues as justice, honesty, kindness, truthfulness, courtesy and consideration. How else can the seeds of tolerance be sown than in practice and in the mutual understanding thus fostered between one child and another?

Endemic values in the work of the school

At a later age the heroes of youth tend to be people of their own age and generation, but in the primary school the teacher is never far from parents in occupying the limelight. Television personalities have their share, too, but a teacher is with children for the greater part of their working day and is, moreover, professionally equipped to influence them. Some teachers may protest that they deliberately shun the preaching role, which they assume to be that of the traditional authoritarian, but values are endemic in the curriculum itself. The basic skills are vital for all forms of human communication. Mathematics and Science, properly taught, are aspects of the truth, of the way things are in the universe. History is full of examples of the evil effects of human blindness and error. The appeal of stories is in the empathy one human being feels for another.

This is to talk in terms of subjects, anathema to the primary teacher, but, leaving aside the curriculum, even the methods and organisation of primary school work imply the existence of a world of values: situations created for the encouragement of learning, positive relationships, sharing in the use of materials between children and between classes, groupings of children for maximum use of their potential, the teacher's use of time and availability to give help where it is needed, the various ways in which children's own experience is discussed and extended, enjoyment of the natural environment, and the reverence for living creatures – education seen in terms of significant activity, with the teacher endlessly seeking worthwhile things for children to do.

Caring is a value

In spite of these requirements to live up to a seemingly impossible ideal, primary school teachers have, up to the present, been fortunate in being able to focus their energies on education in its own right, on the personal development of the child without having the additional preoccupations with external examinations, career problems and other derivatives of education. However unnoticeably, they do act as upholders of positive values in a society notable for its utilitarian concerns, for its rivalries, and for the impersonal attitudes prevailing in a mechanistic age. They work on the assumption that the daily, pragmatic care for children in the present is the best guarantee for their future. With all their difficulties and responsibilities teachers need to feel fulfilled because of the time they spend with children, trying to help them to live and learn most effectively and happily, and because education itself is based upon optimism. However daunting the obstacles, the business of education is with the improvement of the human condition, a thought which should give the young apprentice to the profession confidence in himself and in the importance of the teacher's role.

Values and decisions

We all have to choose our own values eventually, for we cannot easily have them imposed upon us, and the primary school task is to lay the foundations of the ability to make decisions on values while offering a framework of thoughtful care.

References and recommended reading

BARNES, D. (1976) *From Communication to Curriculum* (Harmondsworth: Penguin).

BRIDGES, D. and SCRIMSHAW, P. (eds.) (1975) *Values and Authority in Schools* (London: Hodder and Stoughton).
BRUNER, J. (1966) *Studies in Cognitive Growth* (Chichester: Wiley).
CENTRAL ADVISORY COUNCIL FOR EDUCATION (1967) *Children and their Primary Schools* (Plowden Report) (London: HMSO).
CONSULTATIVE COMMITTEE ON THE PRIMARY SCHOOL (1931) *Report of the Consultative Committee on the Primary School* (Hadow) (London: HMSO).
DOWNEY, M. E. (1977) *Interpersonal Judgements in Education* (London: Harper and Row).
DUNKIN, M. J. and BIDDLE, B. J. (1974) *The Study of Teaching* (New York: Holt, Rinehart and Winston).
FLANDERS, N. A. and SIMON, A. (1969) 'Teacher effectiveness', in Ebel, A. L. (ed.) *Encyclopedia of Educational Research*.
FROEBEL, F. (1887) *The Education of Man* (translated from the German and annotated by W. N. Hailmann) (New York: D. Appleton and Co.).
GAGE, N. L. (1972) *Teacher Effectiveness and Teacher Education* (Pacific Palo Alto).
HIRST, P. H. and PETERS, R. S. (1970) *The Logic of Education* (London: Routledge and Kegan Paul).
HUNT, J. McV. (1971) 'Using intrinsic motivation to teach young children' reprinted in Cashdan, A. and Whitehead, D. (eds.) *Personality Theory and Learning* (London: Routledge and Kegan Paul).
JONES, R. M. (1972) *Fantasy and Feeling in Education* (Harmondsworth: Penguin).
KIRBY, N. (1981) *Personal Values in Primary Education* (London: Harper and Row).
KOHLBERG, L. (1966) *Moral Education in the Schools* (Chicago: School Review).
McNAMARA, D. and DESFORGES, C. (1978) 'The social sciences, teacher education and the objectification of craft knowledge', in Bennett, N. and McNamara (eds.) *Focus on Teaching – Readings in the observation and conceptualisation of teaching* (London: Longman).
PIAGET, J. (1950) *The Psychology of Intelligence* (New York: Harcourt Brace).
PIAGET, J. (1952) *The Origins of Intelligence in Children* (International Universities Press).
REID, L. A. (1962) *Philosophy and Education* (London: Heinemann).
ROSENSHINE, B. (1971) *Teaching Behaviours and Student Achievement* (London: National Foundation for Educational Research).

ROUSSEAU, J. J. (1762) *Emile*.
SHIPMAN, M. D. (1975) *The Sociology of the School* (London: Longman).
SINCLAIR DE ZWART, H. (1969) 'Developmental psycholinguistics', in Elkind, D. and Flavell, J. (eds.) *Studies in Cognitive Development* (Oxford: Oxford University Press).
STUBBS, M. (1976) *Language, Schools and Classrooms* (London: Methuen).

Chapter 10
An Agenda for Discussion and Possible Action

Kenneth David
Tony Charlton

In considering the issues raised by contributors in this book we offer now some opinions and questions as an agenda for discussion and possible action in the staffrooms of schools, in colleges, in in-service groups, curriculum working parties and similar groups. We find ourselves constantly debating and reflecting on these themes, and we presume that many others are also puzzling away trying to find the right answers in differing situations. Many questions one can be positive about in giving opinions, others cannot have clear answers. All the time we are attempting to distinguish between our own feelings and wishes and the needs of primary children whose future we are seeking to support.

1. The primacy of relationships

(a) All teaching has to depend on relationships: to imagine that the careful providing of information alone creates learning is clearly nonsense, for feelings are involved as well. Numerous recent enquiries (Lawrence, 1985; Cant and Spackman, 1985; Charlton and Terrell, in press) support this contention. These findings, amongst others, indicate that personal and social well-being is inextricably linked to children's ability to profit from learning, academic learning in particular. As long ago as 1967 Hargreaves wrote on parallel themes.

(b) Teachers are still influential. The competent and concerned teacher helps to translate information and skills into understanding, and often then into attitudes and even values. However modest the teacher, whatever reluctance there may be to accept responsibility, however much there may be arguments about not daring to challenge differing values, the teacher does influence the personal lives of children, for better or worse, and frequently influences their future ways of living.

(c) Can we attempt to pick out some essential skills and information, constantly varying, depending on differing situations, which children must consider: a checklist of personal and social education?

Are all teachers to be involved in this?

Can weaker and less competent members of the profession do harm rather than good?

How can such work be evaluated?

2. Preparation for life

(a) Media reports frequently highlight the dissatisfaction, unhappiness and crises which many people experience. Their inability to manage their lives successfully may indicate that their education, as well as their family life, has failed them.

(b) '... there is a growing consensus that we have more disruption, more truancy, less academic competence, and less adequate preparation for the world of work and adulthood than is desirable. We have taught for 10 years the baby batterer, the football hooligan, the vandal, the alcoholic, the suicidal, and the wife beater but with little apparent effect.' (McGuiness, 1982)

(c) Much of the present public debate about education seems wrong in emphasis when it concentrates so much on traditional academic standards. The nurturing of pupils' emotions and attitudes may eventually loom larger in their everyday lives than scholastic achievements.

(d) How many adults could successfully resit past examinations without very long notice, and at which times in our lives did we really find ourselves motivated to learn?

Does children's emotional well-being underpin intellectual standards?

Can a 'clever' person be an unhappy and unsuccessful person? So?

(e) Does the initial training of teachers need to be changed in emphasis?

How can in-service training of teachers best help teachers in pastoral matters?

How can higher education institutions best be influenced in these matters?

Are we asking too much of teachers?

3. The effective school

(a) The effective primary school can usually be recognised when we attempt assessment. The attitudes of teachers, including their relationships with each other and with their children, and the ways in which the children themselves interact, provide important indicators.

(b) The effective school is a place of warm enthusiasms, of smiling as well as stern endeavours, of pleasure as well as purpose, of industry as well as enjoyment. It depends on teachers who know that learning is based on their skill in relating to, and motivating, pupils, and who accept that pupils' social and emotional development is an integral part of pupils' intellectual growth, and therefore within the parameters of the teacher's responsibility.

(c) The children of Barbiana wrote: 'People who get no criticism do not age well. They lose touch with life and the progression of events. They turn into poor creatures like yourselves.' (School of Barbiana, 1969, p. 29).

(d) What is meant by 'effective'?

Would the views of teachers, parents, and pupils be similar?

What opportunities should exist for constructive criticism of a school?

How can appraisal of the work of teachers be helpful and not threatening?

Who can help to revive a less effective school?

4. Accommodating change

(a) 'Almost every child, on the first day he sets foot in a school building, is smarter, more curious, less afraid of what he doesn't know, better at finding and figuring things out, more confident, resourceful, persistent and independent, than he will ever again be in his schooling or, unless he is very unusual and lucky, for the rest of his life.' (Holt, 1971)

(b) We have always sought flexibility of mind in educating pupils for a changing society, but what this means in detail is often obscure. Intelligence probably provides the basis of flexibility, but attitudes underpin it. Probably we mean minds that are quick to make associations and inferences, and are willing and able to adapt; minds that *enjoy* challenge and change and alternative views, and minds that can assess both what people are saying and what they are not saying.

(c) A school ethos develops in many ways. It is a mixture of leadership, enthusiasm, commitment and humour in teachers; it is a reputation for skilled and lively teaching; it includes rituals and practices, the hidden curriculum, which have been recognised and discussed; it includes the expectations, reactions and initiatives of parents and pupils.

(d) Is John Holt correct? If he is, what happens to children *en route* through the education system?
Are pupils more sophisticated and mature than we sometimes wish to acknowledge, and do we challenge their thinking enough?
What other meanings can there be for 'flexibility of mind'.
Does a school ethos just evolve, or can it be constructed?

5. Adding to intuition

(a) Primary teachers usually pride themselves on an intuitive and child-centred approach to their work, following children's interests and enthusiasms, and thus maintaining motivation and learning. With careful monitoring of the progress of children this can be very successful. Not all teachers, however, do keep careful records of general progression to agreed aims, and intuition can be a careless guardian of steady progress; there can be a benign neglect of pupils' all-round development.

(b) What systems can best ensure careful recording of progress?
How insistent should teachers be that children's enthusiasms are not the only parameter in learning?
What actually happens in the classroom to ensure that a progress chart is kept up to date in various subjects, including personal and social education topics?

6. Choosing knowledge

(a) 'Renaissance man' can no longer exist, for the storehouse of knowledge is too great for anyone to have even a tenuous grasp of all areas. The polymath is dead, and the computer user is king.

(b) Should we be attempting to develop the skills of processing knowledge, of learning the keys of knowledge banks more?
Which skills and what basic knowledge is essential for primary children in preparing them for a computerised society in which relevance of, and means of access to, knowledge changes rapidly?
What must still be memorised, and how do we improve memories?
How do we define an 'educated' person nowadays?

(c) Some evidence (Sandow and Stafford, 1986) suggests that parents may not wish to become partners in our work in primary schools. Cunningham and Davis (1985) make use of a Professional Assumption Grid for schools to measure the extent to which they involve parents in their children's schooling.

(d) If we attempt to assess what we mean by essential or basic knowledge, and what we mean by the skills of processing knowledge, can we expect all parents to become involved in such an exercise? Is it likely that we can really enlist parents as partners? While individually and collectively parents constitute a major source of support to schools, has the maximising of such help been a major success story in schools?

7. Health education

(a) In considering the part that health education plays in the umbrella term Personal and Social Education we can consider the following selected aims from the Health Education Council Primary Schools Project.

To discover what the consumers see as important health education topics at different ages and stages.

To provide a simple, coherent and flexible framework within which every primary teacher feels confident to work and which:

- sees Health Education as a dynamic, active area of the curriculum, changing and being changed by new knowledge, new perspectives and social demands,
- starts 'where children are' and is committed to on-going consultation with all those in the community of the school who are concerned with children's health and happiness,
- is not prescriptive but provides the teacher with a structure to clarify appropriate pace and direction,
- offers a range of cross-curricular models for planning and practice for every school, whatever its size, geographic location, form of organisation, ethnic grouping, special needs or opportunities,
- is concerned to develop the growth of skills essential to health education, e.g. skills of active learning, information seeking and using,
- takes account of the children's growing mastery of – or struggle with – spoken language, reading and writing,
- takes account of the many opportunities which the curriculum affords to health education.

(b) Should each school have a teacher qualified or experienced in health education, and equal in status to teachers who specialise in Mathematics and language?

8. Pastoral care

(a) One school circulated the following causes for concern among its pupils.
1. Isolation from peers/poor rapport with staff.
2. Change in expected behaviour pattern/cries easily, loses temper, aggressive, mood swings, depressed.
3. Change in standard of school work.
4. Non-school attendance/lateness.
5. Pending bereavement/death in the family.
6. Long term illness or disability in the family.
7. Changed economic circumstances/unemployment/prison.
8. Pending marital break-up/departure of one parent from family/arrival of step-parent, step siblings.
9. Stealing.
10. Parental alcoholism/pupil glue, gas, solvent abuse/self-inflicted wounds.

11. Excessive attention seeking.
12. Lack of school progress, i.e. achieving below potential.
13. No identity with home or school.
14. Obvious loss of weight.
(b) Might there be additions to this list, or are there any causes for concern which could not arise in some schools? With which statutory and voluntary workers should schools develop clear liaison links, perhaps better than exist at present?

9. Counselling

(a) There are reasonably clear distinctions between interviewing children and counselling children, and there is a continuing debate as to how much personal counselling is feasible with younger children. Research referred to in chapter 7 suggests that counselling is invaluable. Teachers also realise, however, that its practice, even at the informal and lowest level is very demanding of time. Additionally, teachers themselves do not always appreciate the value of counselling or possess the necessary skills. Teachers certainly do have to comfort and offer supportive relationships to many troubled children who are unfairly burdened with family and other problems. Often we counsel parents as well.

(b) Is there a need for an extension of counselling skills among primary teachers, and how should this best be done?
Is there a case for some kind of team approach, involving other professionals?
Are we to have at least one member of staff with developed counselling skills?

10. Values

(a) Following Professor Pring's suggestions in the excerpt in chapter 3 (Pring, 1984), could the following eight points form the basis for an examination of the moral atmosphere of the school or classroom?
How can the classroom teacher:
1. encourage greater mutual respect between teacher and pupil and between pupil and pupil;

2. create a climate of caring and fairness;
3. ensure a sense of achievement, rather than of failure, and of personal worth;
4. develop a habit of deliberation and reflective learning;
5. introduce systematic discussion of significant socio-moral issues;
7. approach learning cooperatively rather than competitively;
7. foster care for the group and eventually the wider community rather than for self-interest; and
8. increase group responsibility for decisions taken.

(b) What step-by-step plan of action could introduce such an examination of values? Would such a plan include parents, governors and children? What additional issues should be included?

(c) Who could advise the school on what outsiders think of the school, and particularly its 'hidden curriculum'?

(d) What values are still in fact commonly accepted in our society?

11. Future relevance

(a) The great creaking educational edifice in this country shifts direction slightly at times with many grumbles, but true change is minimal. School organisation, curriculum content, teaching methods, teacher training, staffroom attitudes and habits do not change much. There is, of course, value in stability and steadfastness – the words themselves are ennobled – but the same words can also be excuses for inaction and lack of imagination in a period of our history when tradition and experience are being stood upon their heads. We are a very safe profession on the whole, caring and worthy but safe, more inclined to follow than to lead, disinclined to guess at the future.

(b) Are we to lumber along patiently behind society, or can we lead society more?
Are we continuing to be supporters of the 'sabre toothed' curriculum?
What exactly are the features of modern society which we personally fear or deplore? Might it be worthwhile listing them and comparing them with parents and children?
What are the exciting and encouraging features of life today?

What are the changes we wish to initiate in preparing children for their future?
Do primary schools now have to accept a greater responsibility for the personal and social development of children?
Does such greater responsibility weaken family responsibility?
May we be accused of radicalism and be misunderstood if we are clumsy in commending change to parents?
(c) Does the world need to foster greater caring abilities, greater skills in relationships, more community and environmental awareness, more ability to listen to opposing views?
Where does change begin?

References

CANT, R. and SPACKMAN, P. (1985) 'Self-esteem, counselling and educational achievement', *Educational Research*, 27, 1, 68–70.

CUNNINGHAM, C. and DAVIS, H. (1985) *Working with Parents: Framework for Collaboration* (Oxford: Oxford University Press).

CHARLTON, T. and TERRELL, C. (1987) 'Enhancing internal locus of control beliefs through group counselling: effects upon children's reading performance, *Psychological Reports*, 60, 928–30.

HARGREAVES, D. H. (1967) *Social Relations in the Secondary School* (London: Routledge and Kegan Paul).

HOLT, J. (1971) *The Underachieving School* (Harmondsworth: Penguin).

LAWRENCE, D. (1985) 'Improving self-esteem and reading', *Educational Research*, 27, 3, 194–200.

McGUINESS, J. B. (1982) *Planned Pastoral Care* (Maidenhead: McGraw-Hill).

SANDOW, S. A. and STAFFORD, P. (1986) 'Parental Perceptions and the 1981 Education Act', *British Journal of Special Education*, 13, 1, 19–21.

SCHOOL OF BARBIANA (1969) *Letter to a Teacher* (Harmondsworth: Penguin).

Index

PSE – Personal and social education
EWO – Education welfare officer
HMI – Her Majesty's Inspectors

abuse (*see* child abuse)
academic learning, 3, 12–13, 154, 155–6
   and HMI papers, 15
   balanced with PSE, 17–18
accidents, 138
accommodating change, 207–8
accountability, 6, 181
achievement, 198–9
adding to intuition, 208
admission to school, 111
advisory health contact (*see* health contact)
affective education, 3
affluence, 4, 67
aggression, 6, 62, 167
AIDS, 143
ailments, 99
alcoholism, 6, 68–9, 153
alienation, 5
allergies, 142, 147
ambitions, 4
anaemia, 141
analgesics, 145–6
ancillary help, 19
anonymity, 6
anxiety, 7, 70, 99
appraisal, of curricula, 3
   of teachers, 14–15, 112–3
asthmatic children, 146–7
athlete's foot, 146
attendance orders, 111
attitudes of teachers, 27–8
audiometricians, 125.
authority, 5–6, 58, 66–7, 199–200
autonomy, of pupils, 49–50
   and needs, 4–5, 10
   of competent persons, 17
   and Warnock Report, 20
   fully functioning individuals, 152
   impulse towards, 199

basic study skills, 30–6
bed wetting, 130
behavioural counselling, 166
behavioural problems, 10, 153 (*see also* counselling)
bereavement, 62, 127, 133, 153

care orders, 114–5
career prospects, 13
caring as a value, 202
catarrhal deafness, 36–7
checks (*see* health checks)
child abuse, 6, 10, 70, 130, 139
   liaison between agencies, 100, 113
child and family guidance service, 105–6, 183–5
Children's Act (1975), 6
Children's Society, The, 9
Children and Young Persons' Act (1969), 103, 108, 121
choosing knowledge, 209
Citizens' Advice Bureaux, 5
classroom organisation, 48 ff
   academic aims, 48
   social aims, 49
   emotional aims, 49
   display, 50
   work areas, 50–1
   storage, 51–2
   children's work time, 52
   teacher's time, 53
   interaction, 53–4
cognition, 42
cognition therapy, 127
cognitive education, 5, 15, 96, 168, 196–7
collaboration in language, 42
colour blindness, 130
communication, 6, 39
community handicap team, 144
comprehension skills, 31–2

computers for monitoring progress, 83–9
confidentiality, 61, 129
control systems, 89
coordinated approach to PSE, 56 ff (*see also* management of PSE)
corporal punishment, 112
cough suppressants, 146
counselling, 3, 18, 24, 102, 152 ff, 211
  skills and techniques, 152, 154
  nature of, 153–4
  teaching and counselling, 154–7
  personal problems, 153
  mystique, 154
  and reading, 155–6
  proaction and reaction, 157
  definition, 157
  levels of, 157–60
  empathy, 159
  vigilance, 158–9
  and EWOs, 159
  basic skills, 160–4
  value of skills, 164–5
  types of, 165–7
  behaviour and consequences, 172–3
crime, 5
criticism, 5
curriculum, vii, viii, 3
  modification, 13
  and PSE, 15, 18–20
  hidden, 27, 179
  coordination, 56 ff
  planning, 176

DARTS (directed activities related to text), 35–6
decision making, 4, 69
delinquency, 6, 67
Department of Education and Science, 13, 16, 18, 21, 40
Department of Health and Social Security, 108, 132
diabetes, 138
dialysis, 141
differences in progress and development, 36–8
directive counselling, 167
disease, 68
disfigurations, 142
divorce, 7, 65, 153
doctors (*see* family doctors, school doctors)
drugs, 6, 62, 69

eczema, 142
Education Acts, 122
educational psychology service, 104–5, 134, 149, 183–4
  and counselling, 154, 158 (*see also* psychologists)
education welfare service, 100–103, 158–9, 183–4
effective school, the, 207
empathy, 159–60, 162
employers, 13
employment, 6, 13, 101–2, 110, 122
entertainment certificates, 102, 110
environment, 5, 8–9, 67–8, 197
epilepsy, 138–41, 147
ethos of school, 27, 178, 208
evaluation by children, 34–5, 182
exclusion from school, 101, 112
experiential learning, 196–7

family doctor, 126–8
family life, 5 ff, 65
  democratic family, 10
  shaping children's development, 11, 57
  strengths and values, 59
  routines, 73
feelings, 5
fibrocystic disease, 141
first aid, 62, 69, 145–8, 149
freedom, 67
friendship, 64, 70

general practitioners (*see* family doctors)
group teaching, 30
growth and development, 59
groups, 64–5, 172

handicapped children, 62, 125–6, 129–30, 132, 138 ff
Head's Legal Guide, 73–5
Head's responsibilities, 73–6
headaches, 138
health, 4, 69, 123 ff
health advisory contacts, 137, 142–3
health checks, 123 ff
health education, 63–4, 69–70, 209–10
health problems, 138
health service, schools, 24, 149
hearing therapists, 125
HMI, 14–15, 45
helplessness, 6
Hillfields scheme, 134
home tuition, 101
hyperactivity, 182

Index

immigrants, 124
individual teaching, 29–30
individuals, 10–11, 14, 195–6
infections, 130
influence, teachers', 27–8
initial teacher training, 16–17, 21
in-service training, 16, 19
intolerance, 65
intuitive approach, vii, 57
isolation, 153

juvenile court, 102, 114

kidney failure, 141
knowledge explosion, 6

language, 39–40
law and order, 70
law and parents, 109
leadership, 18
learning, 27 ff
learning strategies, 40–1, 72
legal obligations, 73–6
leisure, 66, 192
leukaemia, 132
liaison, 98–121, 124, 136, 149
  with doctors, 126–7
  with local education authority, 183–5
listening, 5, 162–3
local education authorities, policies, 13–14
  guidance, 18
  guidelines, 21
  welfare service, 104
  appeals, 109
  new patterns, 144
  staff, 154
  support services, 183–4
local health authority, 106–7
loneliness, 5

magistrates' court, 102
management, Head's task, 96
management of PSE coordination, division of work, 60
  materials, 60
  visitors, 60
  recording, 60
  size of groups, 60–1
  confidentiality, 61
marriage, 7, 65
media power, 5, 70
medication of children in school, 146–7
meningitis, 124

mental health services, child, 135–7
mental illness, 8, 62, 69
modelling techniques, 166–7
monitoring pupils' progress, 24, 76 ff, 208
moral and social awareness, 15
morality and human behaviour, 68
multi-cultural society, 5, 65–6, 69, 124, 180
muscular dystrophy, 145

National Association for Pastoral Care in Education, 16, 19
National Marriage Guidance Council, 7, 68
National Society for Prevention of Cruelty to Children, 68, 100, 103, 113, 158
  authorised agency, 108
National Youth Bureau, 120
noise, 7, 69
needs, 177, 193–4
  human and individual, 4
  physiological, 4
  Maslow's hierarchy, 4
  educational, 11–12
  orientation, 20
  teachers', 186–7
non-accidental injury, 178 (*see also* child abuse)
non-directive counselling, 165

obesity, 62, 130, 138
offences against Education Act, 112
one parent families, 8
oral language, 40–3

paediatricians, 125–6, 144–5
painkillers, 145–6
parents,
  and pastoral care, 12
  as partners, 24–5, 178–82
  and child's attitude to school, 37
  pre-school profile, 77–83
  child's progress, 86
  truancy and absence, 99
  and EWO, 100–104
  medical treatment of child, 106–7
  and law, 109–110
  special educational needs, 111
  offences against Education Act, 112
  as governors, 112
  and children's health, 130
  and school doctors, 132
  and psychiatrists, 136

child's medication, 147
and counselling of pupils, 157 ff
communication with school, 170
and teachers, 176 ff
1981 Education Act, 177
liaison with Head and school, 186–7
(*see also* family life)
partnership with parents, 178 ff
with other agencies, 183–5
(*see also* liaison)
pastoral attitudes, viii
pastoral care, vii, 3, 12, 98
teacher's role, 14
lack of preparation for, 17
link with homes, 153
lack of attention in primary schools, 185–6
causes of concern, 210–11
pastoral curriculum, viii, 23
personal data recording, 129
personal and social development, 11, 17, 63
personal and social education (PSE), vii, 12, 15, 152, 176
initial training of teachers, 16–17
rival to academic work, 18
training for, 18–19
coordination of, 56 ff
objectives, 62–3
general aim, 62
personal fulfilment (*see* autonomy)
philosophy of education, 192–3
phobia, school, 101, 119
phonics, 32–3
physiotherapy, 130, 141, 144
place of safety order, 113–4
police, 100, 101, 103
poliomyelitis, 124, 131
preparation for life, 206–7
pre-school profile, 77–83
prejudice, 62, 65, 197
privacy, 4
Probation and After-Care Service, 100, 107
profiling, 24, 76 ff
psoriasis, 142
psychiatric social workers, 134
psychiatrists, 135–7
psychologists, 137, 144–5
puberty, 153
purpose of education, 17–21, 56–7, 192

qualifications, 4

racial tension, 7
rate of learning, 36–8
rationality, 193
reading, 43–5, 170–1, 179–81
record keeping, 76 ff
referral support, 19, 136, 154, 160
registration, 73–4, 99, 110, 122
rejection, 5
relationships, 5, 65, 205–6
religion, 5, 68–9
renal failure, 141
respect for children, 194–5
responsibility for others, 59
responsibilities, civic and societal, 5, 69
routines and rituals, 72–3
Royal Association for Disability and Rehabilitation (RADAR), 145
rubella, 131–2

safety, 59, 62, 68
school as an institution, 58
school health service, 123 ff
school doctors, 131–2, 149, 158
school nurses, 129–30, 146–9
school routines and administration, 72 ff
scoliosis, 130
screening, 148
seeking significance, 200–1
self actualisation (*see* autonomy)
selfishness, 6
sessions, school, 109, 112
sex education, 62–3, 65
sexual abuse (*see* child abuse)
sexual identity, 9
skills and personal development, 33–4
skills, counselling, 154–5
skin disease, 130, 143, 146
smoking, 69
social and affective domains, 15
Social Services, 100, 103, 104, 106, 137
socialisation, viii, 10, 19, 57–8
society and changes, 3, 5–6, 11, 17, 192
special educational needs, 20, 101, 150, 177, 181
and Education Act, 111–12
special school, 106, 111–12
speech therapy, 125, 144
stereotyping, 65
study skills (*see* basic study skills)
stress, 7, 14
supervision orders, 112, 114
suspension, 101

talk in classrooms, 38 ff
teacher as authority and model, 199–200
teachers' influence, 27–8
teaching strategies, viii
teaching styles, 23, 28–30, 39
technology, 4, 23, 192
television, 57–8, 67, 123
therapists, 137
topic work and study skills, 34–5
topics of PSE, 59, 61 ff
training of teachers, 16–17, 18–19
transport to school, 101–2, 109
treatments, 145–8
truancy, 99–101
tuberculosis, 124

unemployment, 6, 153, 192

values, 4, 5, 59, 191 ff, 211–12
   teachers' tasks, 191
   different settings, 191–2
   guidelines, 192–3
   rationality, 193
   needs of children, 193–4
   respect for children, 194–5
   individual differences, 195–6
   experiential learning, 196–7
   environmental influences, 197–8
   achievement, 198–9
   teacher as model, 199–200
   significance, 200–1
   practical values, 201
   endemic values, 201–2
   caring as a value, 202
vandalism, 6, 7
violence, 5, 6
virus illness, 138
vision testing, 115–6, 130
voluntary societies, 108

Warnock Report, 20
welfare, 3, 24, 98 ff, 185
welfare assistants, 148
wheelchairs, children in, 143
whole class tuition, 29
Womens' Royal Voluntary Service (WRVS), 108
work, 66, 192
working class parents, 14
worthwhileness, 200
writing, 45–8